CW01497360

Financing the World

SPINK

LONDON
1666

Rare uncancelled example of a 1923 bond for the South Manchurian Railway Co. Ltd.
The line repeatedly changed hands between Russia (the original constructors), Japan and China.

Financing the World

Keith Hollender

SPINK

LONDON
1666

Typeset by
Cavalier Creative
Unit 6 Sarum Complex
Salisbury Road, Uxbridge UB8 2RZ
www.cavaliercreative.co.uk

Printed and bound in Malta
by Gutenberg Press Ltd.

for the publishers
Spink & Son Ltd.
69 Southampton Row
Bloomsbury
London, WC1B 4ET
www.spink.com

ISBN 978-1-907427-74-9

Contents

Introduction

Over 4,000 years have passed since the beginning of bond and share trading by the merchants of ancient Assyria. But apart from some dramatic incidents in the eighteenth century, not least of which was the South Sea Bubble and, of course, the Industrial Revolution, we mostly link early activity to the great infrastructure and mining projects of the 1800s'. All this was encouraged by those organisations, banks, governments and stockbrokers, who either needed the money or benefited from raising it.

It might be fairly said that investment was always a two-part process linked by time. Those wishing to raise money were unwilling to wait for the successful outcome of their schemes, or alternatively, without the funds, were unable to develop the schemes in the first place. Whereas, those prepared to fund ideas simply saw short term profits as their principal objective and the underlying reason for the investment as secondary. Today this has become the norm with investors, usually institutions rather than individuals, having little feeling for the investment itself, which may no longer be tangible, such as a railway, a mine or indeed a cemetery, but instead merely a financial vehicle managed by others which *appears* to offer the promise of high returns. Thus, the key reason for investment has slightly shifted in emphasis to one of potential financial gain rather than the greater good, a situation encouraged by the increased obsession with index tracking. Today shares are often only bought because they are components of an index not necessarily for of any specific merit.

It has only been in the last few years that share trading has largely become an electronic activity but in the early days well before the internet, exchange traded funds ("ETFs'"), high frequency trading and computer codes, the whole process was dependent on paper. It is that paper which has spawned the collecting hobby we know as 'scripophily'.

This book focuses on paper. Paper, in the form of bonds and shares (and numerous other financial instruments) which tell their own stories…. stories which affect us all and often condition our way of life. The book is, to a large extent, a brief history of finance from the seventeenth to the twentieth century. As such, it contains nothing new but draws attention to the surprising frequency of major events, many of which were considered catastrophic at the time, and, when they re-occur are considered catastrophic again.

It would be difficult and lengthy to cover the detailed development of financial trading from the outset, so reader, you will have to forgive the gap between the Assyrians and the rise of the European stock exchanges in the early seventeenth century. It might come as a surprise to a trader of today to learn that his craft has been actively practised relatively unchanged for well over 500 years despite the number and size of transactions having rocketed over the last few years. The number of trades in shares alone has increased by over 700% since the year 2000 and over the same period, the total worldwide value of share trading has increased by over 60%.

Can we contemplate a life without investments? Could the world have progressed without the natural human desire to invent and devise new ways of doing things?

In writing this book I have drawn on a library of material both in printed and web form. Inevitably, stories have been shortened, even omitted! But the aim is to provide an indication of the scope of financial investment over the years and its impact on our lives of today. Often pilloried (and sometimes imprisoned), entrepreneurs are the ones who have taken risks, not only for their own benefit but also for the benefit of economic progress.

I am indebted to those authors and raconteurs, most of whom (I hope) are listed in the bibliography section. Additionally, I thank the many individuals who have given their time and expertise to check my facts and provide photographs; in particular, John Herzog, Mario Boone, Michael Veissid, Scott Winslow, George Labarre, Michael Weingarten, Mathias Schmidt and, of course, Spink.

After all,

"There is nothing new in the world except the history you do not know."

Harry S Truman

Part 1

SOME BACKGROUND

Not everyone is familiar with international finance, so it might be helpful to provide some background to bonds and shares and explain how they fit in to today's world. Companies and governments periodically, indeed frequently, need to raise money; companies, when they start and when they expand, and Governments in order to achieve a balance between their country's financial inflows and outflows…and, to fund the unusual. The 'unusual' might be war or major financial collapse, as we saw in 2008.

Whereas stamp collecting began shortly after the issue of the first Penny Black in 1840, the collecting of bonds and shares (known as 'scripophily') did not really begin until the mid 1970s' despite their existence for many hundreds of years. Why was this? There were 3 reasons:

1. From their inception stamps were readily available, and indeed essential. Bonds and shares, on the other hand, were not readily available to the general public and were a mystery to most;

2. Bonds and shares had a value which went beyond a single transaction, often well into the future; and,

3. Bonds and shares were rarely discarded but often retained by individuals, banks or the companies that originally issued them for reasons of hope or regulation.

It might also be worth pointing out that these documents are relatively scarce when compared with stamps and, indeed, banknotes (there were, after all, some 55 million Penny Blacks issued).

There are three reasons why collecting bonds and shares may be considered unusual – rarity, availability and the need for specialist understanding. This book sets out to address the latter and remove their mystery demonstrating how, amongst other things, they help us trace and understand economic history.

Since publication of the first catalogues in 1976, the hobby has grown both in numbers of collectors and variety of material. Bonds and shares (or stocks) are a convenient way of initiating and transferring debt and investments. They are not complicated. Their fundamental purpose is to enable companies or governments to raise money from institutions or individuals to enable an enterprise or country to flourish.

Before going further lets just clarify what we are talking about.

Bonds

A bond is simply evidence of debt owed to an investor by a company or country. In the case of corporate bonds, the bondholder has no ownership rights over the underlying company, although it is not unusual today for bondholders to be able to make use of their power to gain such rights where a company falls on hard times and requires restructuring. There are three elements to a bond, its face (or nominal) value, the interest rate (or coupon) payable to the holder and its term, that is to say the period of the debt. Bonds are not always called bonds, of course, a frequent problem of semantics which permeates finance; for example a debenture is simply a type of bond. If the United States Government wants to raise funds, it does so through the issue of 'Treasury Bills', similarly the British Government issues 'Gilts'; such investments provide a regular

flow of interest and give the investor a defined maturity date – all are bonds with different names.

An interesting feature of many early bonds related to their repayment dates, which in some cases were determined by chance. In the case of Chinese bonds, for example, redemption was drawn by lot so it was not always possible to predict the actual end date of a particular bond.

But, not all government bonds have a repayment date, indeed many British gilts fall into this category, examples being the 4% Consols of 1926 and later issues of 'War Loan'. An unexpected announcement by the Chancellor of the Exchequer in 2014 advised its repayment in 2015.

Bond Redemptions

It might be useful to clarify some terms frequently used to describe certain bonds, in particular "redeemed" and "outstanding".

Bonds represent a debt and as such must be repaid over a specified number of years. The benefit to collectors of knowing how many bonds of a particular issue have been redeemed is an immediate guide to rarity of those remaining but calculating that number poses certain problems. There are two methods adopted by borrowers to determine redemption:

1. The first is that adopted by the Chinese – the simplest but least common approach. In this case, a constant percentage of bonds is repaid each year, so if the loan was for a term of 50 years and 25 years had elapsed, then it is correct to assume that half of the original issue will have been repaid.

2. The more usual approach is rather more complex. Here the total monetary value of the loan including interest is divided by the number of repaying years (this may differ from the 'term' as there may be a grace period before redemptions commence). The resulting figure represents the amount of money which the borrower needs to put aside annually in order to meet interest payments and the gradual redemption of the bonds (known as the 'sinking fund'). Unfortunately this is not as simple as it sounds, as in early years most of the fund goes towards interest and very few bonds are redeemed (similar to a real estate mortgage). In due course, however, an increasing amount of the principal is repaid.

Accurately determining the number of outstanding bonds of a particular issue can be complex and collectors might find it easier to check the relevant Stock Exchange Yearbook.

One final point on this issue relates to the determination of which bonds (defined by serial number) are selected for redemption. This may be decided by lot and the chosen serial numbers published in the press. Redeemed bonds are described as "drawn" and this handwritten or stamped word often appears on repaid bonds.

Shares

The term 'shares' is used throughout this book. But in several countries, notably the United States, 'stocks' is more common, although nowadays the generic term 'equities' is most frequently used. Once again we are up against the basic financial premise – if it can be made more complicated, lets do it. This can be confusing and made more so by the fact that 'stocks' can also mean 'bonds' in the UK and as mentioned earlier, bonds can be described as gilts or bills! However, lets focus on shares (otherwise known as equities….). A shareholder is a part owner in the business and his or her investment has no guarantees. If the business fails, the shareholders lose their money. If it does well they may benefit from regular payments known as dividends. Shares may be "ordinary" or "preference", the former have no 'guaranteed' return whereas the latter, will pay a fixed percentage each year. Shareholders may also profit from appreciation of the value of their shares due to on-going success, fashion or perhaps a takeover of the company. Shares are generally traded on a stock exchange but not necessarily so, particularly in the case of small companies. Not all shares have voting rights and preference shares usually fall into this category.

Registered v Bearer

Just to add another layer of complexity, bonds or shares may be 'registered' or 'bearer'. If the former, each certificate is made out to the owner and on its sale, the certificate is returned to the company registrar and a replacement issued to the new owner. If the investment is 'bearer', however, there is no need to re-issue a certificate on sale or purchase. This latter approach has certain advantages:

1. The company/government has no need to keep a register of holders;
2. The owner is secret, and therefore unknown to the tax man; and
3. The number of bonds or shares issued as bearer is known at the outset and fixed, thus helping the collector determine rarity.

Many international bonds are traditionally bearer and the number of bonds issued is printed on each one along with its unique serial number. However, because of the dangers of fire, theft and fraud, bearer items are nowadays issued less frequently and indeed the US Tax Equity and Fiscal Responsibility Act of 1982 removed the tax preferences from such bonds. However, Eurobonds are still issued in bearer form and many US corporations and the US Treasury are able to issue bearer bonds in Europe. Apart from the European market the trend of issue has been downwards, thus, whereas in 1991 the Depository Trust Company, one of the worlds largest 'custodians' (a holder of certificates on behalf of the owners) handled 21 million such

bonds and employed 600 people to do it. The number of bearer bonds held by 'DTC' has now fallen to below 700,000.

The most obvious differentiator of registered v's bearer is the presence of interest coupons, usually attached to the side or bottom of the certificate. Physical submission of these coupons enabled the bond or shareholder to receive annual or bi-annual payments or dividends until the bond ran its term (achieved 'maturity') or, in the case of shares, the company failed. By definition, owners of registered material are known to the issuer and dividends or interest tend to be paid by cheque or bank transfer.

The Markets – An Historical Snapshot

The Assyrians

Mention has already been made of the earliest known shares, those issued in Ancient Assyria (now northern Iraq) around 2000 BC. Indeed, the development of writing by the Sumerians in around 3000 BC was largely caused by the need to monitor business transactions. By 2000 BC, corporate trading ventures began to be organised whereby investors received a share of the profits. These trading activities were supplemented by 'temple days' such that a 'shareholder' bought the opportunity to share in the profits of a commercial activity organised by a temple. Taking the form of clay tablets, the 'share' gave the holder rights to one day's income of the temple (temples then tended to be rather more commercial than they are today). What is remarkable about these 'shares' was that they were transferable by sale, gift or inheritance.

Europe

The concept of share trading largely ground to a halt in ancient Greece, where trade was regarded as something for the lower classes. It was not until about 1100 AD that bond trading became active in the (now Italian) City States of Genoa, Venice, Amalfi, Pisa and Florence. These bonds were known as "Monti" and proved invaluable in financing military adventures. By the end of the 15th century, the bonds were negotiable and traded in city exchanges. Similar bonds were issued with the involvement of the church known as Monti di Pieta. But the countries of northern Europe felt their issue contravened Christian law and a further 500 years elapsed before bonds became acceptable.

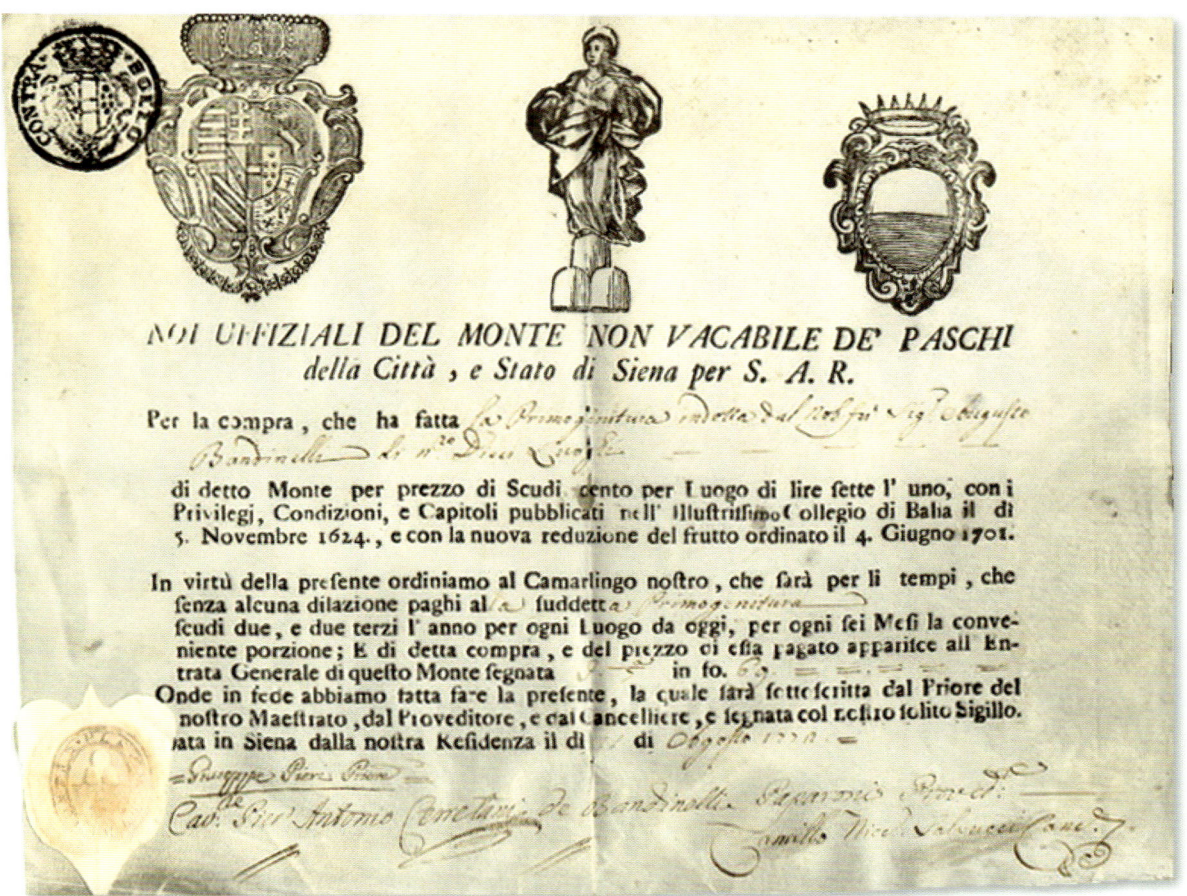

The Monte dei Pascha di Siena was founded in 1472 and is still the world's oldest surviving bank. Reforms in 1624 by the Medici Grand Duke granted depositors security from the state-held pasture lands of the Maremma (the "Paschi"). Recently flagged as Europe's weakest lender. Despite a rights issue the Bank has had to be bailed out by the Italian government and its shares have been suspended.

By 1530, Antwerp had become the financial centre for the merchants of Europe. Its ruler, the Duke of Brabant (who was also King of Spain) built a new bourse and encouraged trading in all kinds of financial instruments through low taxes and minimal regulation. Bonds issued by the Court of the Netherlands, the English Crown and the City of London, amongst others, were actively traded. However, its reign as financial capital of the world ended in 1566 with the outbreak of civil war and it was replaced by Amsterdam, which dominated share trading in joint-stock companies throughout the seventeenth century. The Amsterdam Stock Exchange was formed in 1611 and initially focussed on shares of the Dutch East India Company (abbreviated to "VOC"), founded in 1602, and the Dutch West India Company (1621). Alongside the stock exchange, the Amsterdam Exchange Bank was established. The Frankfurt exchange was formed in 1685.

London

Following the demise of Antwerp, London began to raise its head. Sir Thomas Gresham, who had been Britain's 'Crown Agent' in Antwerp resolved to create a major rival financial centre. By 1567 he had built the Royal Exchange with the financial backing of the senior Livery Companies. Despite a hiccup when the building burnt down in the Great Fire of London of 1666, share dealing was in full swing, sometimes not always to the liking of the establishment. In 1698 the brokers were expelled from

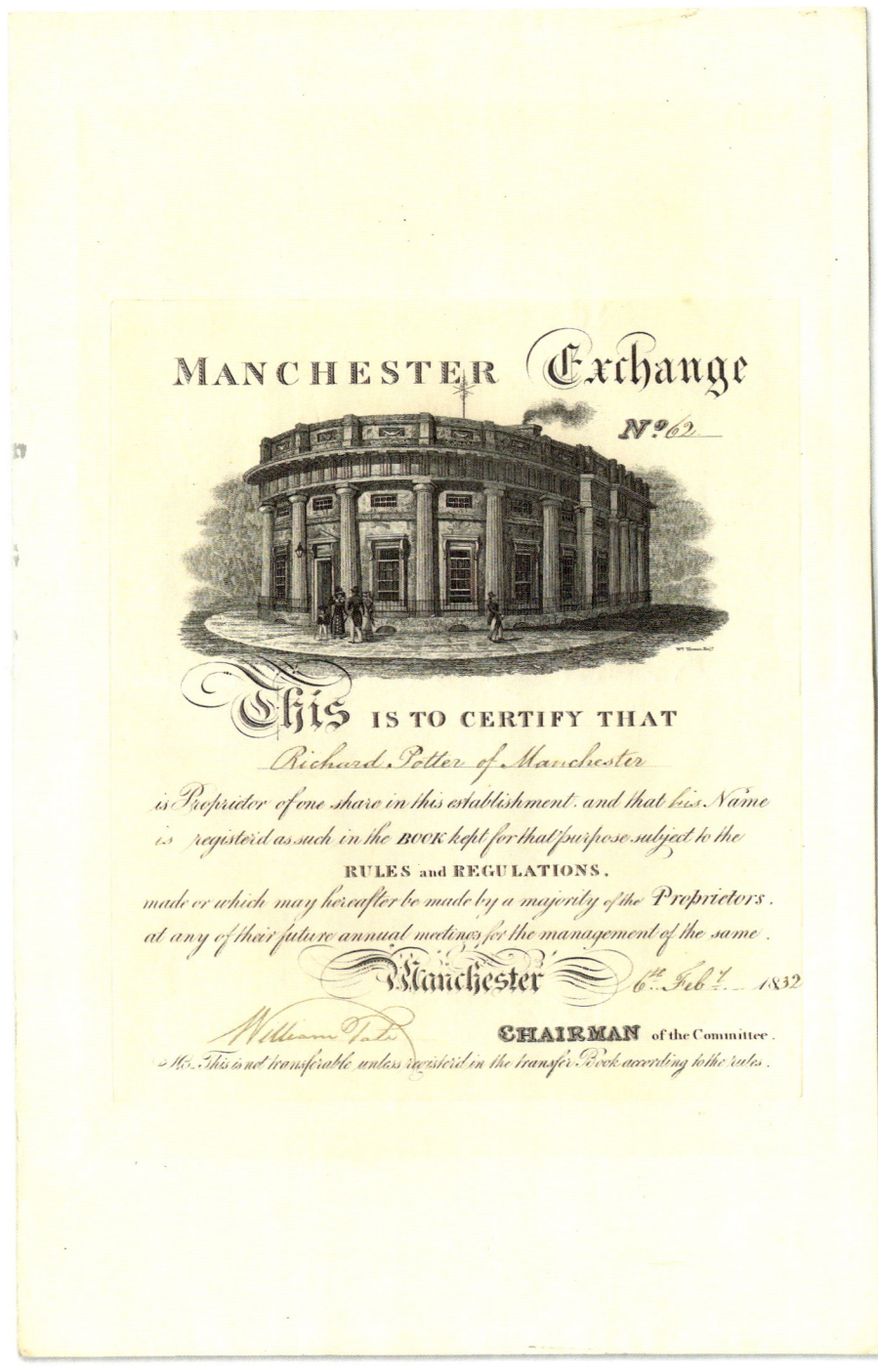

The Manchester Exchange was built by Sir Oswald Mosely* and first opened in 1729 to support the cotton trade. It was replaced in 1806 by the building portrayed on the certificate and later re-modelled. Despite being bombed during the Second World War it continues to this day in its revised form as a theatre and shopping centre.

*The Mosely family history is complicated by the inclusion of three baronetcies. Sir Oswald, referred to here, was the 3rd cousin of the earlier second Baronetcy. A third Baronetcy yielded the notorious and similarly named, Sir Oswald Mosely, leader of the British Union of Fascists whose second wife was Diana Mitford. Their son, Max, headed F1.

the newly reconstructed Royal Exchange for rowdiness and began to operate in the streets and coffee houses nearby, in particular, Jonathan's Coffee House in Change Alley round the corner.

Plaque indicating site of Jonathan's Coffee House, City of London. The original location of the "Stock Exchange".

In 1698 John Castaing began to issue "at this Office in Jonathan's Coffee-house" a list of stock and commodity prices called "The Course of the Exchange and other things". But in 1748 the coffee houses, were also destroyed by fire. Once rebuilt the stockbrokers formed a club at Jonathan's to buy and sell shares, but it was not until 1773 that they erected their own building in Sweeting's Alley, with a dealing room on the ground floor and a coffee room above. Briefly known as "New Jonathan's", members soon changed its name to "The Stock Exchange". In 1802 the Exchange moved to a new building in Capel Court when its members established its constitution.

During the nineteenth century some 20-30 regional stock exchanges operated in the United Kingdom, the two most important being Manchester and Liverpool serving the canal and railway industries of the North.

The United States

Share trading in America prior to the Revolution was very limited and largely controlled by the British. Activity in financial markets really only began with the issue of bonds to finance the Revolutionary troops in the 1770s'. Philadelphia was the country's financial centre immediately after the Revolution but by 1790, New York had taken over. 1792 saw one of the great financial crashes of all time unfold on the American stage following the emergence of the (first) Bank of the United States. Alexander Hamilton, the first Treasury Secretary of the United States, did much to resolve the crisis. The banning of futures trading and the introduction of tough regulation was supported and implemented at a meeting of twenty four brokers under a Buttonwood tree and the New York Stock Exchange was born. The traders signed the 'Buttonwood Agreement' agreeing to trade securities on a commission basis. However, it was not until 1817 that a formal constitution was adopted establishing the New York Stock Exchange & Exchange Board, but by 1820, only 30 different securities were traded. Even by this date, the country only had five banks despite the efforts of Hamilton, (in contrast; by 1907 the country had 22,000 banks, one for every 4,000 people). In 1863 the Exchange changed its name to the New York Stock Exchange ("NYSE") and relocated to Broad Street.

During the nineteenth century approximately 250 different stock exchanges were opened (and mostly closed) across the country.

Around the World

Today there are stock markets in over 110 different countries with many countries having more than one. The United States has long dominated in both bonds and equities with Japan, second and the United Kingdom third. Founding dates of some of the world's major stock markets, taken from Goetzmann and Jorion (1999) are shown on the timeline below:

Over the last decade, the need for a physical presence has declined. No longer is 'open outcry' the norm. Transactions are effected electronically, often in less than a second.

In 1900 the British stock exchange was the largest in the world listing some 783 companies (six times as many as were quoted on the NYSE). Today it ranks third. But trading is no longer a simple matter of buying and selling specific securities. Financiers have created new investment products designed to shield the investor from sharp fluctuations in individual stock prices. These products and the markets on which they are traded have become 'internationalised' and are far removed from the simple shares of old. This is an area of passing interest to the collector but nevertheless is a trend which has contributed to a declining knowledge amongst professionals in their own history.

TIME LINE

● **Founding Dates of the major stock Markets.**
Source: Goetzmann and Jorion (1999), based on the founding dates of exchanges now within the borders of the identified countries with some minor additions/modifications

● **The Great Stock Exchange crashes**

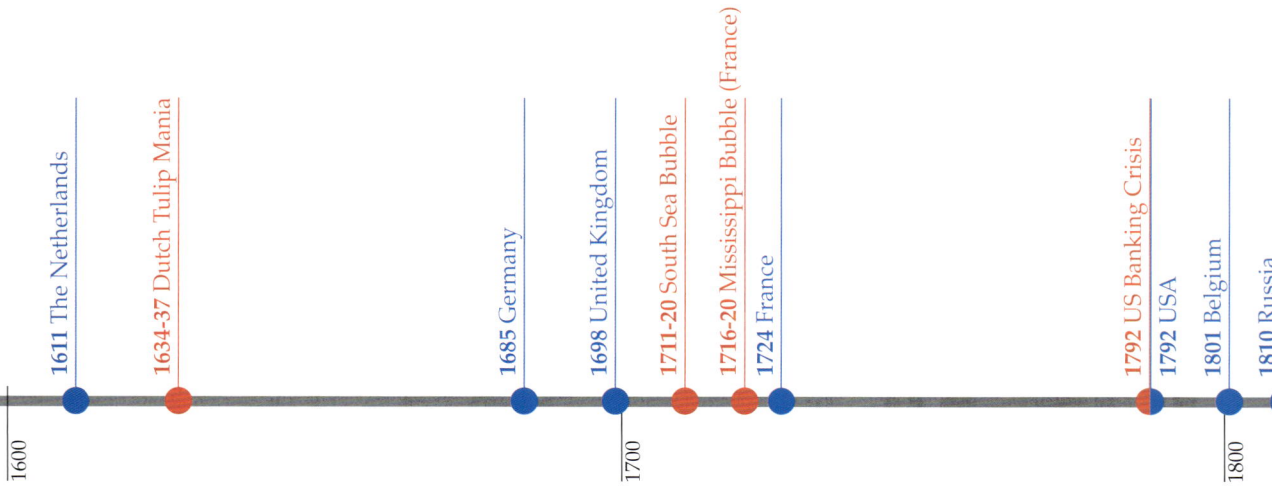

The Great Crashes

Growth is rarely possible without the occasional set-back. It might be argued that such set-backs add strength but looking at the financial crashes that have slowed the progress of investment, one can only surmise that history has not been a valuable lesson, or those who should have been listening were not. Sadly, but inevitably, money encourages greed and it is greed which over

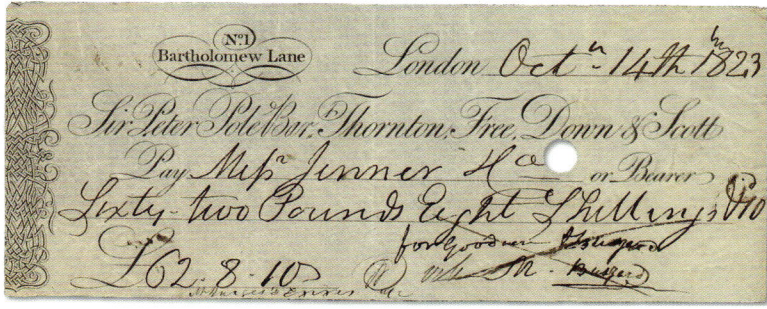

At the heart of the 1825 crash, Pole & Co. (later becoming Thornton, Free, Down & Scott) failed, bringing down 38 country banks. This cheque is dated 1823, two years prior to the great crash.

history, and no doubt over the future, will fuel an endless supply of financial crashes, each one larger than the last. Of course, for the collector of financial history, this provides a wonderful opportunity to acquire fascinating material. See the time line at foot of these pages which takes us to our latest crash, that of 2008, triggered by the failure of the US sub-prime mortgage market and undoubtedly the largest to date.

One of the earliest crashes in England was that which occurred in December 1825 when some 60 banks failed, mostly as a result of the collapse of the London bank, Pole & Co and the Yorkshire

bank, Wentworth & Co.. The result reverberated throughout the City involving both the Bank of England and the Government. Financial disaster was eventually averted by Rothchild's decision to deposit £300,000 in gold coin with the Bank.

The result of repeated crashes has been a steady increase in regulation and a growth in numbers of those employed in corporate governance. Regulation is often regarded as a bug-bear by financiers but is an inevitable result of the reckless activities they have persisted in following over the last 400 years.

1825 UK Banking Crisis
1837 US Banking Crisis
1840's Railway Mania
1857 International Crisis
1861 Canada
1866 Overend & Gurney (UK)
1871 Australia
1877 Brazil
1887 South Africa
1890 Barings / Argentina
1890 Hong Kong
1920's Florida Real Estate Collapse
1929 'The Great Crash'
1987 'Black Monday'
1998 'Dot Com' bubble bursts
2008 USA

1900

2000

More than Bonds & Shares

It would be wrong to think that bonds and shares are the only documents of interest to collectors. Not only are there different names for the same thing (shares=equities or stocks; bonds=gilts, etc), but, there are also many financial instruments, which might also drop into the collectors box. Here are just a few:

Instrument	Description and Collector Appeal
Debentures	Similar to bonds but limited to corporates. Known number issued. Usually issued for a specific funding purpose with a stated repayment date or date on which they might be converted into equity. Once popular with British companies for tax reasons. Often as decorative as bonds and similarly engraved.
Scrip Certificates	Various meanings for this one! Sometimes a document indicating entitlement of a 'free' issue of shares, other times a document representing a fraction of a bond or share usually to make up value of an investment. Owners of Confederate State bonds held by Coutts of London following default were issued with "Scrip Certificates" proving ownership whilst group actions to recover the debt were initiated.
Receipts	Proof of shareholdings in early companies may be limited to a receipt showing the holding as being registered in the company's share register. Good early examples are those issued to represent holdings in South Sea Stock or early government gilts.
Share Warrants	Usually bearer these are similar to shares in appearance and may provide the holder with an option to convert to equity at a later date.
Transfer Certificates	Historically, whenever a registered share was sold, a transfer certificate had to be issued identifying buyer and seller. Some early examples can look as good as the shares themselves and it is easy to confuse the two.

You will find many illustrated examples in the following pages.

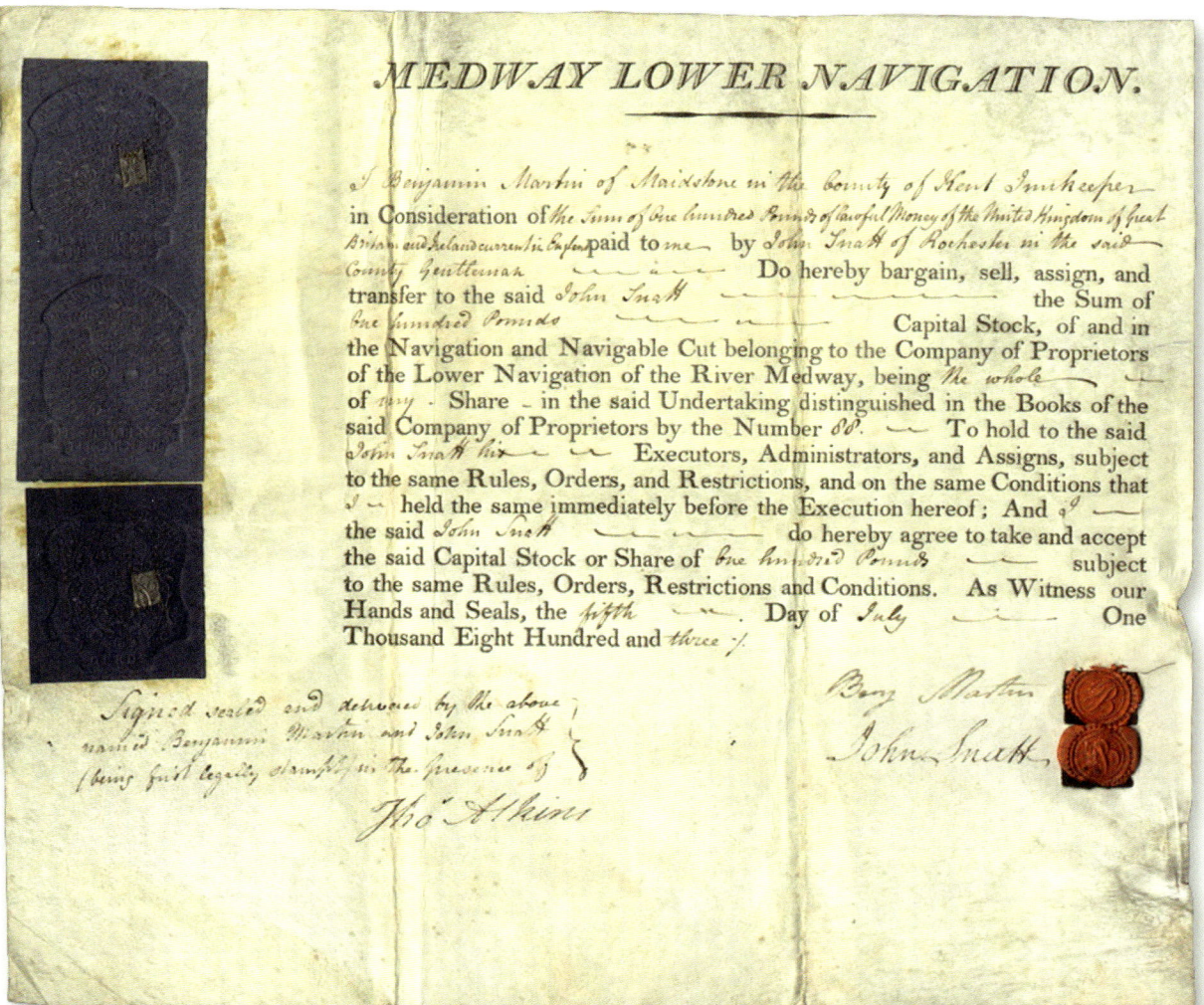

Example of early 'transfer certificate' dated 1803 in the Medway Lower Navigation Company.

Sometimes things go wrong — The Great Defaults!

Most bonds and shares collected today were, at one time or another, quoted on a stock market somewhere in the world. In the normal course of their life, bonds would ultimately be redeemed (i.e. paid) and cancelled. Some companies, US railroads for example, may have been taken over or merged with other companies, but others will have failed ('defaulted'). A bond default occurs when the borrower, which may be a government or company, fails to meet interest payments and ceases redemptions. The act of default may not necessarily result in the removal of a stock exchange quotation as it is always hoped that the position will be corrected in the future, however, historically default prevents the defaulter from issuing new bonds on a stock exchange until the default has been rectified. Over time several countries or states, legal or otherwise, defaulted on their bonds, thus creating much of the material for today's collectors.

In some cases these defaults have been resolved or avoided, possibly by a settlement but more often by amendment (for example, a changed interest rate or term) as we have seen recently with many examples from the weaker European Union countries.

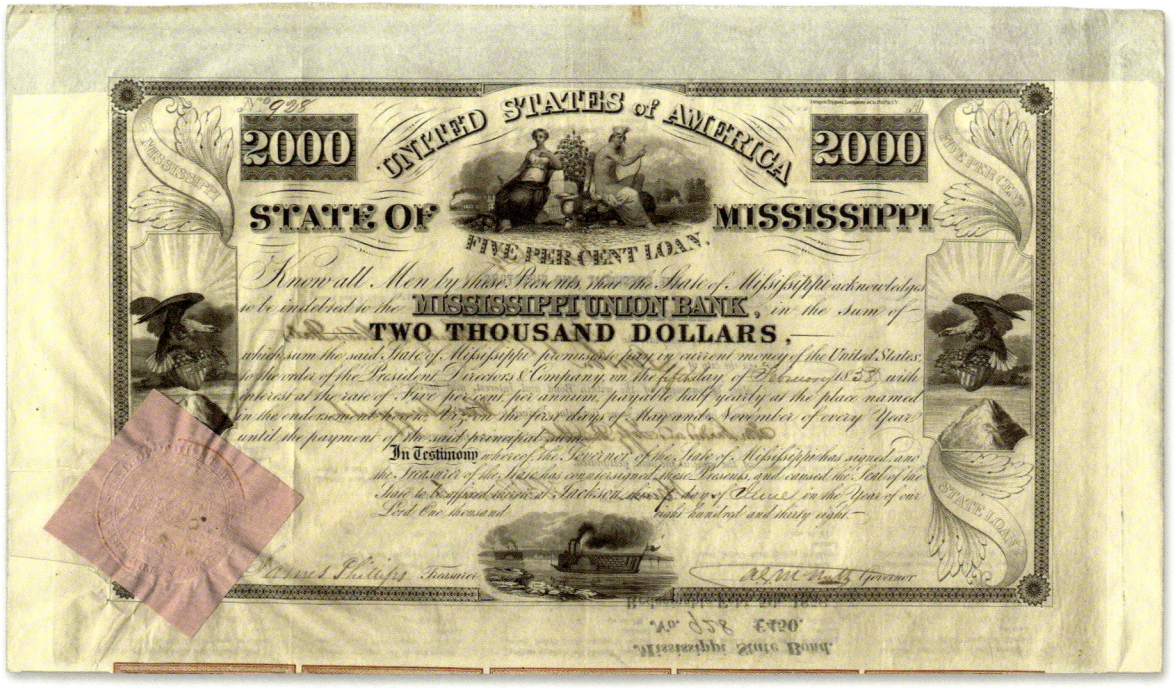

$2000 bond issued by the Mississippi Union Bank in 1838. Despite repeated attempts to gain a settlement the issue remains in default

Major country defaults were:

Country/State	Date	Approximate size of default
China	1938	£60 million (c.$90 million)
Russia	1917	>£1 bn ($>1.5 bn)
Confederate States of America	1865	$712 million
Mexico	1914	$12 million
State of Mississippi	1841	$7 million

These are far from being the only defaults but certainly ones which have been of most interest to the collector, particularly if rectified later, notably in the cases of Russia and China.

However, South America led the way in defaulting on its international debt in the early 19th century and several countries particularly Argentina have retained the habit. Since 1820 there have been 80 major sovereign defaults by South American countries:

Country	No. of defaults
Argentina	8
Ecuador	10
Venezuela	10
Uruguay	9
Costa Rica	9
Peru	8
Brazil	9
Chile	9
Mexico	8

Sources: Carmen Reinhardt and Kenneth Rogoff; Moody's

Missing from this list is Colombia, which was the first sovereign defaulter when it failed to pay coupons in 1820, 1822 and 1824, all resulting in the default of 1826. In fact, loans to Guatemala, Peru, Nicaragua, Mexico and Greece all repeatedly defaulted between 1826 and 1879.

Closer to home, many weaker members of the European Union have suspended bond payments or negotiated extended borrowing terms but all have eventually returned to normality. It might also be worth mentioning Turkey, which since 1880, has defaulted eight times.

Two of the biggest defaulters by value, China (in 1938) and pre-revolutionary Russia (in 1918) have restored their financial credibility by agreeing settlements in selected countries. Details of these settlements are covered later in the book but it might be worth mentioning that despite settlements in some countries and for some bondholders, this has not always stopped speculation. Chinese bonds, in particular, have frequently attracted attention, not least because many of the bonds were described as "Gold Loans" with values linked accordingly. Similar situations have arisen with Mexican and other state bonds. Interestingly, despite the Confederate States of America not being an accepted legal entity, there have been repeated attempts to claim settlement from later governments of the United States.

A positive effect of this somewhat nefarious market in 'hope', apart from high prices, has been a continuing interest in the paper at large and its retention, not only by collectors but also by those intent on speculation.

Of course, government defaults are not the only source of material for the collector. Corporate failures are far more numerous and account for most of the material available today.

Shares of History

Nowhere can art, history and money come together as succinctly as they do in the world of scripophily. Just as finance has played its part since the beginnings of trade, so the certificates themselves provide opportunities to plot progress through the ages. Economic development may be grouped into five stages:

1. Early and primitive commodity trading by the Assyrians and others;
2. Government/country financing;
3. Establishment of trading companies in the 16th and 17th centuries;
4. The Industrial Revolution of the late 18th century;
5. Railway construction from the 1830s'; and,
6. The marketing and technological age of the late 20th and early 21st centuries.

This book has touched on the first but will more thoroughly examine the second, third, fourth and fifth. The last has little to offer the collector. Most of the corporate material collected today post-dates the 'Industrial Revolution' which may be regarded as the starting point for the formation of so many major industries which we now take for granted.

Whereas most collectable material originated from the formation of commercial enterprises, some had other objectives such as funding of the Red Cross, the American Civil War and even the beginning of Israel. Some are a lasting reminder of countries which no longer exist. In the chapters that follow, some of the fascinating stories and themes are described.

Collecting

Readers wanting to learn more about the beginnings of finance may find the idea of building a collection of bonds and shares an attractive way of doing just that. Like any type of collecting, the first step is to decide on a theme. There are many and in the following pages several are touched on.

The principal split tends to be between countries and subjects. Countries tend to raise money for non- specific purposes, whereas corporates are focused on their own business and ultimate profits. Inevitably there is overlap and perhaps the most obvious arises with China where many bonds were issued to finance railways. In most other countries such funds were raised by private companies rather than the state.

There are many subjects, such as mining, railways, shipbuilding, oil and banking, which cross borders and time periods. But collecting is not limited to industries. There are several sectors which can satisfy the most determined collector. For example, famous signatures, such as John D Rockefeller, J Paul Getty, Nathan Rothschild or Thomas A Edison. Or major events such as the South Sea Bubble, the Panama Canal or the formation of the East Indies Companies. But before looking at entrepreneurial activity, lets first consider funding by governments in Part 2.

Part 2

GOVERNMENTS ALWAYS NEED MONEY!

Big players on the world stage

One of the major collecting themes relates to those bonds issued by governments and states. Most are either defaulted, repaid (and thus 'cancelled') or in specimen form. This section briefly looks at the economic history of some key countries, not only the government issued bonds but also major financial ventures affecting the development of infrastructure and industry:

- China
- France
- Germany
- Great Britain
- USA
- Russia

Today Governments usually issue bonds for general purposes, the most common being to balance the books between imports and exports (known as balance of payment loans) but historically, countries tended to define the purpose of their bond issues, for example, infrastructure projects. These purposes are usually stated on the back of the bonds.

China

Historical context

Throughout the nineteenth century Britain, Russia and France sought permanent bases in China. Whereas Russia was keen to establish an eastern seaboard, the other major powers were intent on preserving their profitable trading outposts based largely on tea, silk and opium. Several land licences were granted over the years, the main ones being Hong Kong to the British, Amur Province to the Russians and Indo-China (now Vietnam) to France.

In the 1830s' William Jardine and James Matheson were, amongst other things, importing opium to China from India. The Chinese wanted to abolish this trade and in 1839 the Emperor ordered a total crackdown and the destruction of all opium held in their warehouses. Jardine cried foul to the British Government and persuaded Palmerston to send a naval force to blockade Guangzhou (now known as *Canton*) and reintroduce the trade – an ultimately 'successful' operation.

Although in later years, the continued presence of foreign governments led to some major uprisings, there were considerable benefits to China in respect of industrialization and infrastructure. The 1870s' (a hundred years later than Europe), saw the first stirrings of the country's industrial revolution and several government supervised companies were formed, but perhaps the most significant event was the opening of the first steam railway in 1876 – a line from Shanghai to Woosung (an area of Shanghai, now known as Woosong). The line was viewed with huge local suspicion and eventually dug up and buried following the death of a local.

Railway construction is covered in more detail later, but it is interesting to note its political significance and impact on major events in Chinese history.

The Russians, for example, sought to pressurize the country by building the Trans-Siberia Railway as close to the northern borders of China as possible with a view to ultimately annexing Mongolia, Manchuria and Korea.

Endless land-grabbing by foreign governments resulted in the formation of a nationalist society popularly known as the "Boxers", although, more correctly, 'The Society of Righteous Harmonious Fists'. Their uprising culminated in a siege of foreign embassies in Peking (now 'Bejing') in 1900, which was not only put down by an international force but encouraged the western powers to intervene even more intensively. The incident was exotically portrayed in the 1963 film, "55 Days at Peking" starring David Niven and Ava Gardner.

Continuing dissatisfaction with the Manchu Government's failure to curb 'foreign land grabbing' resulted in the formation of a new revolutionary movement led by Dr Sun Yat-sen. In 1911 the Manchu dynasty was overthrown and Sun Yat-sen was elected "President of the United Provinces of China". The change was noted on the bonds themselves, which, prior to 1912 were issued by 'Imperial Edict' but thereafter carried the words 'Republic of China'. One of the first issues under the new regime was the *5% Gold Loan of 1912*, the so called "Crisp" Loan.

However, Sun Yat-sen did not control the military and his days were numbered. He moved south and formed the Nationalist Party, known as the "Kuomintang" but died from cancer in 1925 (the Kuomintang Party is still a major player in the politics of Taiwan). Repeated uprisings were put down by the new government fearing civil war but it was Yuan Shih-K'ai, as Prime Minister, who came to the fore in March 1912. Yuan became the first president of the Chinese republic and negotiated a £25 million loan from the major powers in 1913 to finance military preparations and 'reorganise

Bonds to finance the Hukuang Railway were the last to be issued by Imperial China's Manchu Dynasty. Four countries participated in the loan, Britain, France, Germany and the USA

government finances'. Known as the *Reorganisation* Loan, and today the subject of frequent repayment speculation.

It is interesting to see where the money went (see opposite).

Yuan endeavored to lead a new dynasty but the move was met with hostility. He died in 1916 and 12 years of civil war and revolution followed during which time Chiang Kai-shek, once head of the military academy set up to train Kuomintang officers, became leader and opposed the communists led by Mao Tse-tung. Chiang lost the tussle and also the war with Japan. In 1937 he was expelled to Taiwan and the cessation of payments on China's foreign bonds followed. That default was reaffirmed in 1949 when Mao proclaimed the formation of the People's Republic of China. A default, which lasted until 1987.

External Bonds

Between 1865 and 1937 China issued more than 57 "external"

Known as the 'Crisp' loan after London stockbrokers, C Birch Crisp & Co., this was the first foreign issue under the Chinese National Government

bond issues, of which 23 were used to finance the railways. Many were repaid in the normal course of events but by the time of the 1937 default around £60 million of such bonds were still outstanding. They had been issued in hard currencies (sterling, francs, yen, marks and roubles) for the very simple reason that they were destined to be traded on foreign exchanges. In today's world such a position would be considered a frightening exchange risk but in days of fixed rates (most of the time tied to gold) that was not such an issue.

Making funds available was seen as a means of exerting continuous control over China by the major powers. The conditions of repayment were often onerous, imposing difficult obligations on the population, a factor which contributed to the anti-foreign feelings of the Boxers and ultimately the Communists.

One of the largest issues was the 1913 *Reorganisation* Loan referred to earlier and instigated by Yuan Shih-K'ai. As this is one of the most common government bonds it might be worth taking a closer look.

The 5% Reorganisation Loan of 1913

The total loan amounted to £25 million, which in today's money, taking account of inflation, is equivalent to £1 billion – a sizeable figure at the best of times. The bonds were issued at 90% of face and out of the proceeds, the issuing banks received 6%. This left the Chinese with £21 million, of which £10 million was used to settle other maturing debt, £5.5 million to cover "current and extraordinary expenses of administration" (i.e. bribes…), £3 million to meet army back pay and disbandment of troops, leaving only £1.5 million for the reorganization of the 'Salt Gabelle' (salt tax) - the stated prime purpose of the loan. This was one of the largest Chinese bond issues assembled by the major powers and incorporated stringent conditions of repayment. The issue was four times oversubscribed in Britain, which accounted for 30% of the total issue, and five times in

Germany. The bonds, engraved by Waterlow are some of the most attractive of all issues.

The story does not end there; recent speculation in Chinese bonds has tended to focus on the Reorganisation Loan in view of its link to gold. Speculators have frequently and recently paid up to £350 for a £20 bond in the hope of settlement. Interestingly the price of gold has increased by around 60 times since 1913 which would make

Example of the 1913 Reorganisation Loan, a £20 bond issued by the Russian Asiatic Bank. The issue was described as a 'Gold Loan' and as such has been in great demand by those seeking repayment in gold. That aside, a fine example of Waterlow engraving.

each £20 bond "worth" £1,200 today – if you are very, very optimistic!

Internal Bonds

Foreign (external) bonds were not the only source of government money. From 1912, funds were regularly sought from the local population through a series of internal public issues. In fact, this process began as early as 1894 when the war with Japan required substantial funds, initially to fight and then to pay reparations following its loss. The first 'internal' loan (the 'Patriotic Loan of 1894') was secured on opium taxes and receipts of the Imperial Household but it failed to arouse the public's interest and the country was forced to turn to 'foreign' bonds such that between 1894-1898, six such loans were concluded. However, the costs of external borrowing irritated the government and it went ahead with another internal issue ('The Trust Loan') in 1898; but once again money raised fell well short of the target (in fact, barely 4% of the authorized total issue).

The failure of early internal issues has been put down to a lack of stock exchanges and a coordinated banking system. But whatever the reason, the government largely put the subject on hold until the end of the Manchu dynasty and the formation of the Republic (10th October 1911).

The first Republican Loan was unsuccessful but despite this, a subsequent '8% Military Loan' was sanctioned in Nanking in January 1912; subscriptions were poor and repayment was erratic. This issue was followed by the 6% Consolidated Loan and a series of others followed, usually defined according to the number of years since formation of the Republic. Because the number of bonds sold invariably fell short of the total required there was a constant need to issue more paper simply to repay the old. In the early years the Government secured repayment

on several private companies, such as China Merchants' Steam Navigation Company, Hanyang Iron & Steel Works and the Pinghsiang Collieries Company. The whole process was somewhat chaotic and by 1920 the financial position of China had become untenable with $300,000,000 (silver dollars) of internal bonds outstanding. Failure to agree on a solution led to further deterioration. The many civil wars which raged across the country in the mid 1920s' exacerbated the problem by diverting funds allocated for bond settlements to the military. Repeated consolidations and revaluations (in particular the 6% and 7% Consolidated Loans of 1921) attempted to resolve the problem but corruption and politics (in particular the attempt by Yuan Shih-kai to claim the throne) drained state resources. Despite these crises, internal bonds continued to be issued even into the 1930s' but by 1932 the terms of all outstanding issues were scaled back reducing both the interest rates payable and the redemption dates; at the same time, those issues secured on the tobacco tax were instead secured on the less specific 'customs revenue of the country'. Despite these efforts, the loans continued to grow and the problems of short terms and high interest coupons belaboured the government.

By 1932, a total of 52 loans had been issued under the auspices of the Ministry of Finance totaling $1,639,109,588 (silver dollars) of which 57% remained outstanding. The position was simply untenable and a programme of resolution had to be implemented which was completed in January 1932 despite the war with Japan. Once the Shanghai Bond Exchange had reopened, the internal issues resumed their quotes, albeit on revised terms, and no new loans were issued in 1932/33. Some later issues took place but these were better controlled and relatively small in size. What is perhaps surprising is that despite all this chaos the country was able to raise huge funds on the international markets in the form of its external bonds.

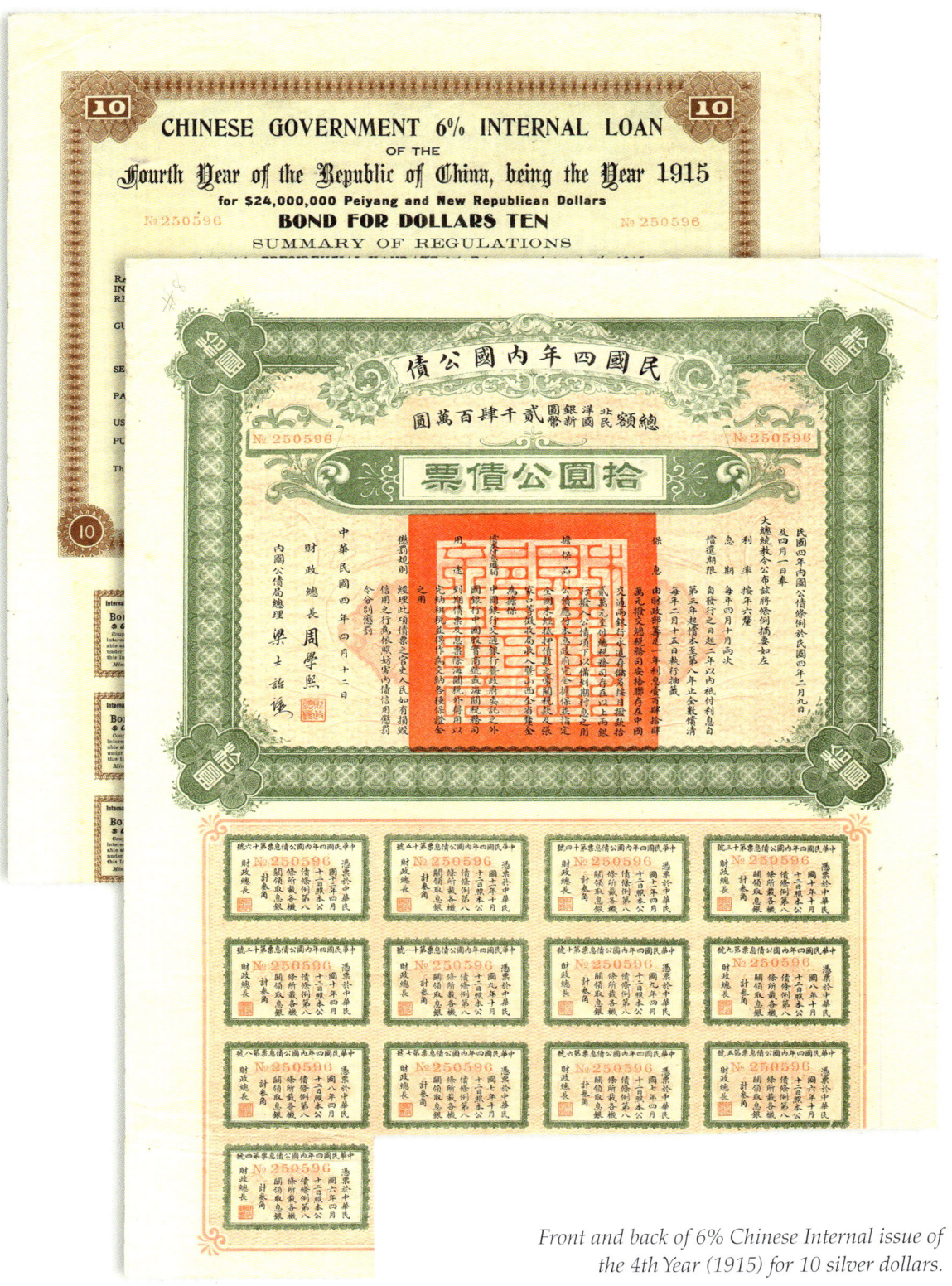

Front and back of 6% Chinese Internal issue of the 4th Year (1915) for 10 silver dollars.

There is a growing collector interest in this sector, particularly in China itself. The bonds are usually of smaller format than the foreign loans and often written in English on the reverse.

The 1987 Settlement

Quite unexpectedly but following considerable diplomatic pressure by the British Government, the Peoples Republic of China ("PRC") was prevailed upon to settle outstanding claims by British holders of external Chinese bonds and those whose assets had been confiscated following their expulsion from China in 1948.

Chinese bonds arrive for setttlement in 1987

Under the terms of the compensation agreement signed 5th June 1987, £23,468,008 was made available by the PRC to settle all outstanding claims and thus allow the country to seek future finance through the London markets (a default automatically bans a borrower from access). At the time of the announcement it was felt that outstanding bonds and other claims would receive no more than 5-8% of their face value, indeed the advertisement from the Foreign Compensation Commission stated: "It is likely that the total amount of claims will greatly exceed the amount available for compensation and that distributions will be only a small percentage of the amounts claimed". This was based on an assumption that 30-40% of outstanding bonds would be submitted. In fact, that figure turned out to be a gross over estimate, as less than 10% of outstanding bonds were submitted, thus resulting in a final payout of 62.25% of face value.

So far as collectors today are concerned this means there are still around 2 million foreign bonds available. Although a large number, it is a little misleading as over 50% are accounted for by only two issues, the 1913 Reorganisation and the 1925 Boxer issues.

So why were so few submitted? There are several reasons:

1. Despite several advertisements, many holders were unaware of the offer;
2. More bonds than thought were held outside the UK and therefore did not qualify under the terms;
3. Many bonds had been destroyed over time; and
4. Holders were unduly influenced by the predicted low payout and felt those bonds not submitted would command a greater premium in the growing collectors market.

France

It is easier, when considering French economic history, to divide into pre- and post- Revolution (1789). This book is mostly concerned with the latter period but in the case of France, the former is so fundamental that it cannot be ignored. The Royal Loans of 1689-1789 represent a classical period involving intrigue, war, corruption and waste; essential ingredients for financial disaster.

Early Sources of Funds

Money was typically raised by the King through the issue of 'rentes'. These were, in effect, annuities usually issued and administered by the Provost of the Merchants and Aldermen of the City of Paris. The amount of the annuity was paid over to the Keeper of the Royal Treasury who issued a receipt on vellum. Against this receipt a notary prepared contracts on printed forms. The receipt was tied to the contract and having been registered was issued to the annuitant. There were three types of rentes:

1. *Viagere;* meaning for the lifetime of the person nominated:
2. *Perpetuelle*; payable indefinitely; or,
3. *Hereditaire;* which is similar to perpetuelle but allows for repayment of principal over a set period.

Viageres were overstamped "to the profit of His Majesty" on the death of the annuitant and earned a higher rate of interest. Many such issues were divided into age classes. Prior to 1758 all viageres were issued on a single life but from then on more beneficiaries could be added. Perpetuelles were payable until repurchased by the State, although they were more likely to be cancelled. Hereditaires gradually replaced perpetuelles.

The whole procedure was subject to frequent change and reductions in principal and income were commonplace. The continuous issue of rentes combined with the costs of wars and the royal household brought the country to its economic knees. Thus, the Revolution.

The Revolution

Prior to the 'Revolution', there was minimal public banking in France. The Seven Years War with the resultant vast increase in expenditure exacerbated the country's financial problems. Loans were raised from all quarters. The King continued to spend, building new palaces yet at the same time requiring that candles at Versailles be allowed to burn to their end rather than just half way down. By the time of the Revolution in 1789, the country was almost bankrupt. Inflation was running well ahead of earnings and the unemployed gravitated towards the cities fermenting the general feeling of discontentment. Revolution was inevitable.

Assignats (paper bills used as currency from 1789-1796) were issued to finance the huge debts of King and State. These were eventually broken down into small sums in order to act as banknotes but general mistrust by the population did not encourage their use.

By 1799, Napoleon's armies had not been paid for ten months relying on indemnities from vanquished foes and the unpopular assignats. Napoleon was not a lover of central banks nor finance for that matter but needs must and in 1803 he and his generals (under his compulsion) subscribed equity to the newly formed Banque de France lead by Frederic Perregaux. Perregaux was a revolutionist and a known womanizer (no connection). After his death (1808) one of his partners, Jacques Laffitte, took over from him

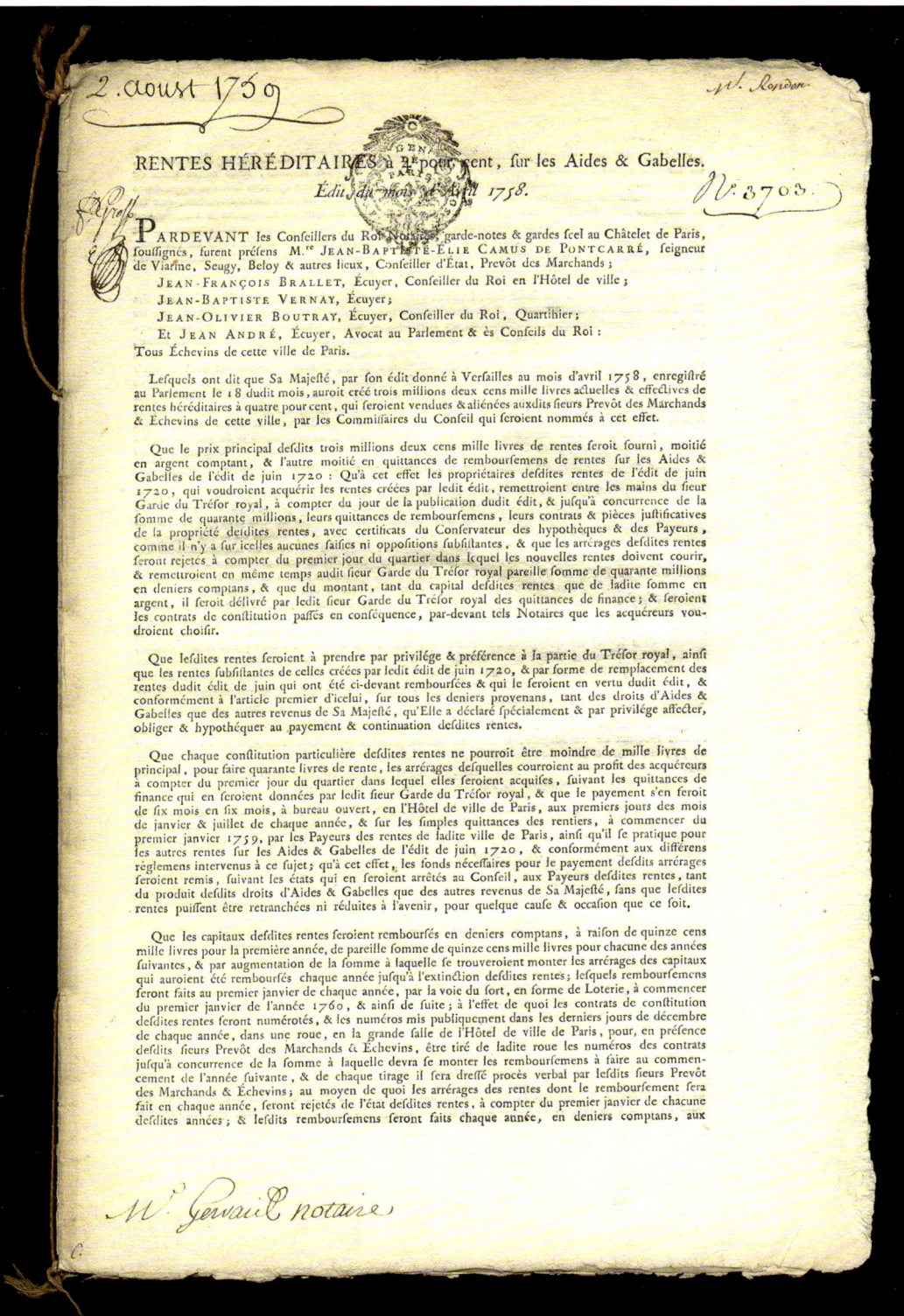

Typical Rentes Hereditaire dated 1758

French Assignat dated 1792 for Livres 50

as President of the bank and ran it from 1814 to 1819. Lafitte tried to start a private Bank of Commerce and Industry but was blocked by the Conseil d'Etat. Eventually, after a change of government he succeeded and formed the *Caisse General du Commerce et de l'Industrie* making loans to industry. Lafitte did much to open up finance and commerce over the next 20 years and after Napoleon's defeat at Waterloo stopped France slipping back towards bankruptcy. He was instrumental in the overthrow of Charles X and placing Louis-Philippe, Duc d'Orleans on the throne, in return for which he was made Prime Minister. Meanwhile Charles X, after 6 years on the throne, fled to England.

The period after the Revolution was dotted with yet more revolutions (1830, 1848 etc.) and extreme government instability.

The 'blue plaque' in London's West End identifying the home of Charles X after moving to England

*The home of Charles X in London's South Audley Street.
He lived here for the last 9 years of his life.*

Industrial Progress

In 1808 three types of company were created; *the joint company* (owner managed and financed), *the limited company* (externally financed) and *the joint-stock company.* Of these, the most common was the first and the most unusual, the last. Regulations restricting joint-stock companies were so rigid, at least until 1867 (largely thanks to the John Law episode – see page 78) that between 1815 and 1848 only 342 such companies were formed. This explains the dearth of early share certificates available today. The joint-stock companies formed were generally in the areas of coal mining, metallurgy, chemicals and textiles. One of the largest company's of the time, *Creusot,* however, was a limited company.

Road transport was good, even during the eighteenth century, and this was eventually supported by an efficient canal system which was developed during the early part of the next. Railways were only used to carry coal and it was not until 1837 that the first passenger service was opened between *Paris and St. Germain.* By 1848, France had 1,800 kilometres of track as compared to Britain and Belgium, each of which had in excess of 10,000 km. But once building was underway, progress was fast with railway construction naturally leading to industrial development.

Early French railway company from Paris to Lille serving Calais

Germany

With most of Europe largely decimated by the conquests of Napoleon, individual countries (and their monarchies) only began to establish themselves after 1815. 'Germany' and 'Italy' did not exist as single countries but had instead been an assortment of Kingdoms, Principalities and Dukedoms. It was not until 1871 that Germany may be regarded as one country. At that time, the country standardized its currency moving away from its seven different silver currencies based on Talers or Gulden, and on adoption of the gold standard all were replaced by the 'Gold Mark'. These currency changes are apparent from the wording on bonds and shares of the period.

In the 200 years between 1750 and 1950 the population of Europe increased almost fourfold with the greatest increase of 51% between 1850

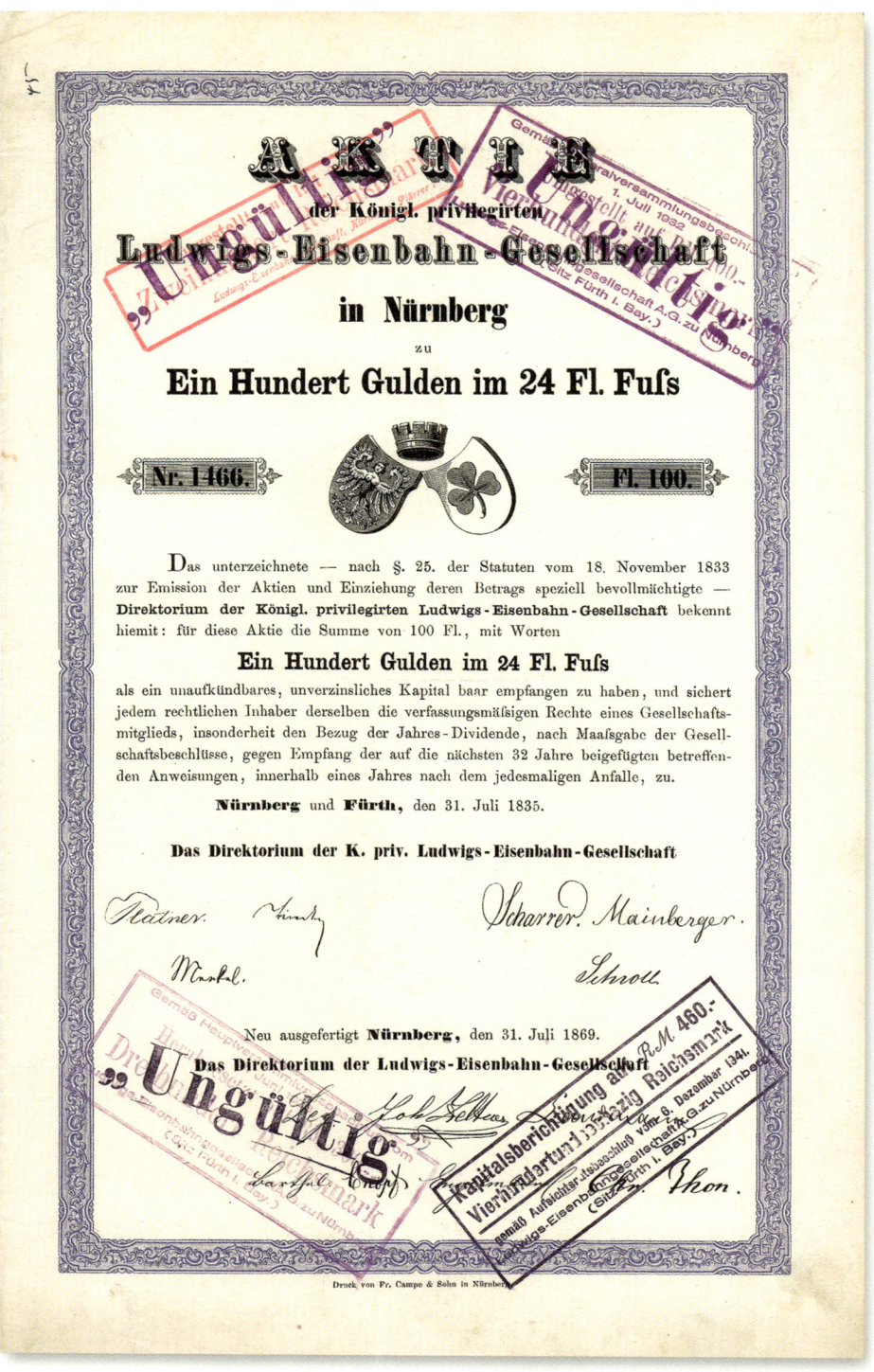

The Bayerische Ludwigseisenbahn, subsequently named the Ludwigs-Eisenbahn-Gesellschaft, was the first railway to be constructed in Bavaria. The line ran between Nuremberg and Furth connecting two of the key commercial centres of the State. The line was originally founded in 1833 and built in 1835. It generated a significant financial return to its shareholders. Illustrated is a share certificate dated 1869. The line eventually closed in 1922 and the station building at Furth was demolished to make space for a Nazi parade ground.

and 1900. Largely due to a decrease in death rates rather than an increase in birth rates, the dramatic improvement can be better attributed to a reduction in the number of wars. Another change was taking place – the move from rural to urban domicile encouraged by the industrial revolution.

It was only following unification in 1871 that Germany, as a single country, really began to catch up with the industrialization of Britain and France. However, the arrival of steam traction a little earlier helped change the position. By 1848, there were 2,500 kilometres of track on Prussian territory and during the next two years that figure doubled, significantly exceeding that of France. Indeed, railways played an important part in shaping the country and paving the way for unification.

The Railways

The first railway from *Nuremberg to Fürth* (6.25 km) in Bavaria was built in 1835 with its train, the 'Adler', supplied by George Stephenson's company in Newcastle. This was followed by the longer *Leipzig-Dresden Railway* in 1839. During the 1840s' over 100 million Thalers were invested via shares and debentures in the upcoming railway companies. Among the many lines constructed, the major ones were:

Munich - Augsburg	1840
Cologne - Aachen	1843
Berlin - Hamburg	1846
Cologne - Minden	1847

Railway construction fell back in the 1850s' but by 1875, 8,000 km of track had been built. During this period almost a quarter of the country's net investment was devoted to the building of railways. From 1874 with railways as the base and reunification romping along, industrial investment followed. This period also saw a major growth in urban population encouraging a housing boom and expansion of the associated industries of glass, gas, water and electricity.

Although railways were privately financed and controlled, between 1850 and 1875 most railway companies were purchased by the State for economic or strategic reasons. Infrastructure development was not limited to railways but was extended to canals and roads, many of which were privately owned and paid for by means of a toll system (much like the American 'turnpikes') an example was the *Mecklenburg-Strelitz* road which continued to charge users until 1915.

A key player in the construction of German railways was Bethel Henry Strousberg (1823-1884), who was born in East Prussia, died in Berlin and in the interim acquired British nationality. After living in London and New Orleans, he settled in Berlin and in 1861 won the concession to build the *East Prussia Southern Railway*. He subsequently built several lines in northern Germany, Hungry and Roumania as well as owning vast support industries such as locomotive works, rolling mills and coal mines. At one time he employed more than 100,000. But one project, funded by the *Roumania Railway Loan 7.5% bond issues of 1868/70,* went badly wrong and after being accused of fraud he was forced into bankruptcy. His collapse triggered a stock market crash and ultimately resulted in the nationalization of German railways.

Later Developments

The intensive period of industrial growth during the latter part of the nineteenth century was closely followed by the establishment of numerous towns with their localised businesses. As a result, many bonds were issued by cities and states.

Bond for 5,000 Marks dated 1921. Originally a family concern based in Essen, Krupp became the largest company in Europe by the start of the 20th century. It specialised in steel and weapons and supplied most of the rails for the railroad companies of the US as well as most of the weapons used by Germany in both World Wars. The company was a supporter of Hitler and used forced labour. In 1906 it produced the first U-Boat and in 1921 acquired the Swedish Bofors company. After the war, the company was disbanded by the allies but eventually re-formed and in 1999 merged with Thyssen AG to form ThyssenKrupp AG.

Among the more desirable German shares for collectors are the early issues of the giant industrial companies of today, such as *Siemens, Krupp, Mannesmann, BASF and Daimler-Benz.*

The Inter-War Years and $ Bond Speculation

The annexing of Bosnia by Austria-Hungary in 1908 caused considerable concern to both Serbia and its patron, Russia. A result of this perceived land-grabbing was the assassination of Archduke Francis Ferdinand (heir presumptive to the Habsburg Empire) by a nationalist Serb, an act which directly resulted in the First World War and led to the break-up of the Habsburg Empire.

The War was devastating for Europe resulting in the death of 10 million people, with a further 7 million permanently disabled and 15 million seriously wounded. The cost of fighting and restitution was 1.5 times the total national debt of the entire world during the years 1800-1914. The economic impacts were huge not only on the losers but also the victors. As an indication, prices in Hungary were 23,000 times what they had been before the war. Britain spent more than each of Germany, France and Russia. In contrast, the creditor nations, particularly the United States, thrived from the opportunities to fund the Europeans by supplying arms and benefiting from the resurgent home market in automotive, radio and other products. From that point on, the United States never looked back becoming the dominant power in the West both politically and economically.

Like any war, its costs were enormous and the burden on the allies was as devastating as the financial penalties imposed on the belligerents. However, the latter cannot be understated. The Versailles Treaty included harsh penalties on the aggressors and France even sent troops into the Ruhr to enforce payments. In 1921 the Inter-Allied Reparations Committee required Germany to pay 269 billion marks, or 100,000 tonnes of gold. Despite being later halved, the State was unable to meet the terms and the economy suffered its most infamous bout of inflation. A visit to the shops necessitated a wheelbarrow to carry the continually depreciating currency. At its worst, the exchange rate reached one trillion marks to a dollar.

Banknote for ten billion marks issued by the Reichsbankdirektorium in 1924.

$1000 bond issued in 1930 (the 'Young Loan').

The United States stepped in and under the *Dawes Plan* (1923) established a lifeline of $110 million which enabled annual repayments to be reduced and as a result the mark began to stabilise. The bond issue syndicated by J P Morgan but managed by Bankers Trust was highly successful, paving the way for a batch of dollar issues supporting the rebuilding of cities, banks, utilities and general industries (even churches). Jack Morgan remained largely aloof from these loans and was known as a 'notorious enemy of Germany'.

There were 156 bond issues denominated in US dollars between 1924 and 1933. In total, these amounted to around $1.5 billion (equivalent to c.£21bn today). The stock market crash of 1929 on top of the earlier German crash of 1927 put a stop to this source of funding and US credit disappeared overnight. The resultant European depression

Example of US $ bond issued to help rebuild Germany during the 1920s'. This one is for the Ruhr Gas Corporation and was issued in 1928.

hit hard whilst unemployment in Germany reached 6 million. Despite the provision of yet another dollar loan (the "*Young Loan*") of $98.25 million, which reduced German indebtedness by 75%, the rot had set in and the blame for subsequent growth of Nazi power is often laid at the door of financial deprivation.

Both the Young and Dawes loans (and indeed all the dollar bonds) have been the subject of repeated speculative activity. The bonds are readily available to the collector. Repayment was possible provided the bonds themselves did not appear on a 'stolen' list. If they did, the bonds were simply confiscated, making their submission a risky business.

Two small sterling issues remain in default despite efforts to obtain a settlement by the now defunct Council of the Corporation of Foreign Bondholders[1]. These were issued by the *Free State of Saxony* and the *City of Dresden* in 1927. It has never been made clear why Germany has refused to honour these bonds.

The financial chaos following the 1st World War in the 1930s' was largely replicated after the end of the 2nd World War. Then Germany was split into 4 'zones' (British, American, French and Russian). Arguments with the Russians were rife especially when the British, American and French collectively decided to ditch the Reichsmark and replace it with the Deutschmark in their zones on 20th June 1948. The rift with Russia resulted in the Berlin airlift and ultimately the drawing of the Iron Curtain and the creation of West and East Germany.

The Reichsbank Hoard

In a book of this kind it would be remiss to omit reference to the Reichsbank Hoard of 26 million bonds and shares.

In 1939 the Reichsbank gained the right to hold all the bond and share certificates owned by German banks. This 'hoard' was supplemented by securities confiscated from Jews and also material held by foreigners who were given interest bearing bonds issued by the State in exchange. Most papers were held in the Russian Zone and after the war were acquired by the Interior Ministry of East Germany until German Reunification in 1990. At that time, the material was taken-over by the Federal Government under the control of the Bundesamt zur Regelung offener Vermogensfragen (BAROV). Potential owners were given until 31st May 1995 to claim ownership but most did not and a large proportion remained 'homeless'. In fact only 4,500 individuals submitted claims.

The announcement of this hoard caused some consternation in the collectors market. Although most were believed to be for well known German companies such as Daimler, Allianz, Deutsche Bank and Siemens, foreign material was also included.

The hoard is currently in the process of being dispersed and 6 auctions, (as at December 2015) have already occurred. The first 5, which included German domestic companies, were handled by German numismatic auctioneers Dr. Busso Peus Nachfolger. The sixth, which included the German State bonds, was held by Spink in November 2015. Each item offered was identified by a small hole. The dates of the auctions and the gross value realised to date (including commissions and taxes) at each auction are shown below in Euro millions:

Auction date	Total Realised (€m)
June 2003	2.91
January 2005	2.98
June 2006	2.63
February 2008	1.98
June 2009	1.56
November 2015	0.015
TOTAL REALISED	**12.075**

The above excludes 'foreign bonds' which at date of publication have still to be auctioned.

[1] The Council of the Corporation of Foreign Bondholders was founded in1868 with the principal objective of protecting the interests of holders of sterling bonds publicly issued in the United Kingdom by overseas governments, states and municipalities.

Great Britain

Comment has already been made on the development of London as a financial centre in the early nineteenth century and its set backs during the two World Wars, by the end of which Britain was believed to be the world's leading debtor country. David Kynaston in his book *The City of London: A Club No More*, commented that it was generally calculated that Britain 'had lost a quarter of its pre-war national wealth'. Indeed, following the First World War the liquidation of its overseas investments in order to meet foreign debt had almost wiped out the country's overseas assets. As an example, Britain had "sold or pledged to the United States practically the whole of our American Railway and Industrial investment" (Robert Brand, Fellow of All Souls, Oxford). This alone was estimated to be worth almost 9% of the country's national debt.

This section will mainly concentrate on the period following the Industrial Revolution, in particular the building of the railways.

The Industrial Revolution

There is no official start date for the so called 'Industrial Revolution' but it was during the 1770s' and 1780s' that the necessary technological

Opened in 1825 the Stockton & Darlington was the world's first commercial steam railway. The preference share illustrated was issued in 1858.

and organizational innovations came together with the invention of steam driven equipment. For some years work had progressed on the steam engine but it was not until James Watt and Matthew Boulton developed a vastly superior version in 1778 that it really came into its own. This period was well before its application to transport but groundwork done by Richard Trevithick and Oliver Evans set the scene for the later work by George Stephenson and his construction of the first locomotive hauled passenger railway, the *Stockton and Darlington*, in 1825.

Why the 'revolution' began when it did is not clear but a number of factors contributed. For example, agriculture became more mechanical, releasing workers from the land, and an increasing birth rate resulted in shifts of population from country to cities and land to industry. Indeed, the urban population ratio increased from sixteen to twenty-five per cent during the latter part of the eighteenth century.

There is no doubt that the development of the steam engine was key to progress and with it came a batch of inventions initially focused on textiles such as Hargreave's spinning jenny (1767), Arkwright's spinning frame (1768) and Compton's spinning mule (1779). But steam power relied on coal and it was during the early 1800s' that these and other innovations encouraged an expansion of the mining industry. Britain's coal output rose from 16 million tons in 1815 to 30 million by 1835 and 50 million by 1848. Iron output doubled between 1835 and 1848 by which time the country was producing half the world's pig iron. By the middle of the nineteenth century, half a million people were employed in textiles, which in turn boosted the shipping industry, importing raw cotton and exporting finished products.

Britain, no doubt, benefited from the political revolutions going on in Europe and the United States, permitting it to consolidate an already powerful economic position. All this, despite the financial disasters arising from loans to South America and the activities of unscrupulous financial fraudsters. The crash of 1825 largely triggered by failing South American countries (including the infamous *Poyais*, of which more later) and the restrictive structure of English banks as private partnerships exacerbated the problem. The government looked to Scotland where its banks were "joint-stock' with no restriction on numbers of partners or shareholders. In 1826 England adopted the Scottish system and as a consequence Britain became a world leader in banking as well as industry. But nothing lasts forever and the once hungry Royal Bank of Scotland eventually denied the "too big to fail" mantra some 200 years later.

The powerful families of Rothschild (See Page 118) and Baring played major roles in stabilizing the big crashes during the early part of the nineteenth century, thus paving the way for a long period of economic progress beginning with the building of the railways.

The Coming of the Railways

Although steam power had existed for some years prior to the turn of the century, its engines were largely static. Trevithick did much to demonstrate the opportunities of mobility and his second steam locomotive, "New Castle" successfully hauled iron at the Pen-y-Darren Iron Works in South Wales. In 1808 he improved on the design and the world's first successful steam train ran on the Middleton line (near Leeds) in 1812. But in the end he was defeated by the limitations of iron track. It was not until 1825 that George Stephenson built the first moving steam engine using wrought iron rather than cast iron for his track. 'Locomotion No.1' ran

A drawing of the famous Rainhill Trials. Stephenson's 'Rocket' is in the foreground and in the background are 'Sans Pareil' (built by Timothy Hackworth) and 'Novelty' (built by Ericsson and Braithwaite).

between Stockton and Darlington carrying 500-600 passengers, mostly in open coaches - soot and all! The venture was supported by Edward Pease, cousin of Thomas Richardson, both Quakers who took a steadily increasing interest in the railways. Indeed, for a while, the Stockton & Darlington became known as the "Quaker Line" and although it experienced some financial problems in the early years, Richardson guaranteed £10,000 of its debt and by 1830 owned 141 shares in the company. Its success paved the way for the development of railways across the world.

But it was the Rainhill Trials on Merseyside which proved the real tester when 5 entrants competed over 4km to put their locomotives through their paces. George Stephenson's 'Rocket' was the clear winner and in 1830 the *Liverpool to Manchester* line (48km) was opened for public transportation – the worlds first true railway.

Over the next 20 years, 9,659km (6,000 miles) of track was laid down in Britain. In 1837, the first long distance line, the *Grand Junction Railway* which connected the *Liverpool and Manchester Railway* to Birmingham was built by Joseph Locke and in the following year Stephenson completed the first section of the *London to Birmingham Railway* which terminated at the newly built Euston Station

Although the end result was hugely beneficial to the country, on-going construction works were hardly beneficial to those living nearby. Between 1856 and 1897 four major building schemes took place within London disrupting some 4-5,000 people. Not only were those in the immediate vicinity of construction thrown into turmoil, all living close to the finished lines suffered from vibration, noise, smoke and soot from passing trains. During the early days, the general living conditions of the working class were painfully affected, despite the Duke of Wellington complaining that railways "enabled the lower orders to go uselessly wandering about the country" – unfortunately, most of the 'lower orders' could not afford the luxury.

ENTRANCE TO THE LONDON & BIRMINGHAM RAILWAY STATION, Euston Square, London.

Euston Station was opened by the London & Birmingham Railway in 1837. The famous arch was completed a year later. The arch and booking hall were demolished in 1961 and the station rebuilt between 1969 and 1979

Despite initially negative reactions to railway financing from the City which believed railways could never compete with canals, investment in the railways was immense, often led by the Quaker families. *The London & North Western ("LNW")* was capitalized at £43.7 million, whilst lesser lines such as the *North Eastern, Great Western and the Midland* were each capitalized at £20-30 million. Over the nineteenth and early twentieth centuries a vast number of lines were constructed, some very short, others more substantial. Quakers were active from the outset, for example, Edward Pease (*Stockton & Darlington*), William Rathbone and James Cropper (director of *Liverpool & Manchester*). All combined in the so called "Liverpool Party" to build the *Birmingham & Derby Junction, Midland Counties* and *North Midland Railway.* Another Quaker, Thomas Edmonson, devised railway tickets and their associated stamping machines

whilst another, George Bradshaw, published the Railway Guide. But it was not only Quakers who found the investment appealing, George Carr Glyn (Lord Wolverton) of Glyn Mills and, later, *National Provincial Bank*, became the dominant banker and George Hudson of York played a key role in early development (See page 110).

Whilst the process of financing and building the overground railways was progressing, the London Underground was beginning to take shape with two strong competitors, J P Morgan and Charles Yerkes, locked in combat to gain Parliamentary approval to construct key lines, in particular, the "Northern Line' (as it eventually became known). Yerkes, who had made his fortune in Chicago building the city tram system, eventually prevailed and although the lines he oversaw did not initially do as well as planned and his company the *Underground Electric Railways Company of London (UERL)* proved not to be financially viable, later work by Lord Ashfield saved the day and the Northern, Bakerloo and Picadilly Lines emerged – now representing a considerable part of Transport for London.

Progress

By 1948 the overground lines had grouped into a "Big Four", London & North Eastern ("LNER"), London Midland & Scottish ("LMS"), Great Western ("GWS"), and the Southern Railway ("SR") and it was then that the whole network was nationalized and remained so until returning to private ownership in the 1990s'.

Many of the shares issued to finance the railways are still around, some in pristine condition, others somewhat worse for wear. Many years ago the author spent several hours routing around under Paddington Station retrieving a few! Building a collection can be an exciting and achievable aim - however it's done.

The Banks

The first banking house in the City was established by Frances Child in the 1680s' and was eventually incorporated into Glyn Mills & Co.. Later, James Hoare and his cousin Richard relocated their business to Fleet Street in 1693 where C Hoare & Co. remains to this day, still led by members of the family.

The origins of UK banking between 1650 and 1700 lie with the Goldsmiths, one of the City's 12 major and oldest Livery Companies. The basic banking concepts of accepting deposits, making loans, issuing notes and allowing depositors to access their accounts via cheques were progressively established.

Bank of England

Following the "Glorious Revolution" of 1688 when William and Mary ascended the throne, public finances were weak just at a time when London was on the verge of tremendous expansion of trade. William III's annual revenue was a little over £2 million but by 1694 he was spending £2.5 million on the army alone. William Paterson, a Scottish entrepreneur, who later became one of the Bank of England's founders and was generally held to be its originator proposed a perpetual loan of £1.2 million at 8% interest to the Government. Funds were quickly raised to form the Bank's initial capital stock and in return, the Bank's Charter was sealed on 27th July 1694 permitting it to act as the Government's banker and debt manager. Four years later William Paterson became equally well known as instigator of the infamous Darien Project– (see page 102)

Bank of England, London

And so the world's second central bank, after the Swedish Riksbank (1668), came into being.

At about the same time, the *Bank of Scotland* was established by Act of Parliament on 17 July 1695. Its objectives were a little different to those of

Bank of England branch located in London's West End. Now a branch of Abercrombie & Fitch (progress….?)

the Bank of England, it being more focused on supporting local business. Interestingly, one of its founders, John Holland, was an Englishman, whereas the Bank of England's founder, William Paterson, was a Scot! The bank eventually formed the 'BOS' of HBOS and was subsequently subsumed into Lloyds Bank following a bit of governmental pressure.

During the 18th and 19th centuries government demands for money became more intense and the National Debt rose from £12 million in 1700 to £850 million by 1815 (Battle of Waterloo). As a percentage of GDP, this represented a rise from around 10% to over 200%.

The 1844 Bank Charter Act restricted issuance of notes by the Bank thus providing it with an effective monopoly and additionally laid foundations for the gold standard. In 1931 when the UK left the gold standard, the gold and foreign exchange reserves were transferred to the Treasury but continued to be managed by the Bank. The Bank managed the crises of 1847, 1857, 1866 and 1890 during which time funds were made available to needy City institutions and the requirement to limit monetary issues to gold holdings was lifted as and

when necessary. It was perhaps typical of the time that between 1833 and 1847 four out of eight Bank Governors suffered personal bankruptcy.

One of the more interesting crises was that of 1890 when, following the Chancellor's decision to reduce the interest rate on UK government debt, investors sought better returns elsewhere. 'Elsewhere' proved to be Argentina. Barings was heavily involved as the main underwriter of the country's sovereign debt but it was the failure of the *Buenos Ayres Water Works Company* which tipped the scales. The Bank of England was asked to step in to protect Barings. The Governor, William Lidderdale raised significant loans from Russia and France on Saturday (after his golf) to support the likely crash, forecast for the following

Specimen Argentinian bond of 1889 in which Barings were an active participant prior to their 'crash'.

Monday. The reserve fund proved more than adequate and a crisis was averted. Barings, however, ceased to be a partnership and was reconstituted as a joint-stock company.

In 1931 the United Kingdom broke from the gold standard and so it remains to this day despite a brief period after the Bretton Woods Agreement when gold was again linked to the money supply via the US dollar. In 1946 the Bank was nationalized by the Labour Government and remained a Government body until regaining its independence under a later Labour Government in 1997.

The Provincial Private Banks

These developed more slowly than the London banks and even by 1750 there were only five of any significance:

Year	Town	Name	Modern Link
1650s'	Nottingham	Thomas Smith	RBS
c.1685	Derby	Crompton, Newton & Co.	RBS
1716	Gloucester	James Wood	Lloyds
1737	Stafford	John Stevenson	Lloyds
c.1743	Dover	Fector & Menet	RBS

Source: British Museum

Amazingly none of them failed and all became joint-stock banks in the late 19th century. However, after 1750, the number of banks increased dramatically and by 1797, 230 provincial banks were in full swing, increasing to 721 by 1810. By 1830 every town of size had its own local bank with its own banknotes. Inevitably failures happened. New legislation in 1826 permitted the creation of 'joint-stock banks' which allowed individuals to combine as shareholders (proprietors).

The table below shows the first joint-stock banks:

Year	Bank	Modern Link
1826	Stuckey's Bank, Somerset	Natwest
1826	Lancaster Banking Co.	NatWest
1826	Norfolk & Norwich Banking Co.	Barclays
1827	Huddersfield Banking Co.	HSBC
1827	Bradford banking Co.	HSBC
1829	Cumberland Union Banking Co.	HSBC

Source: British Museum

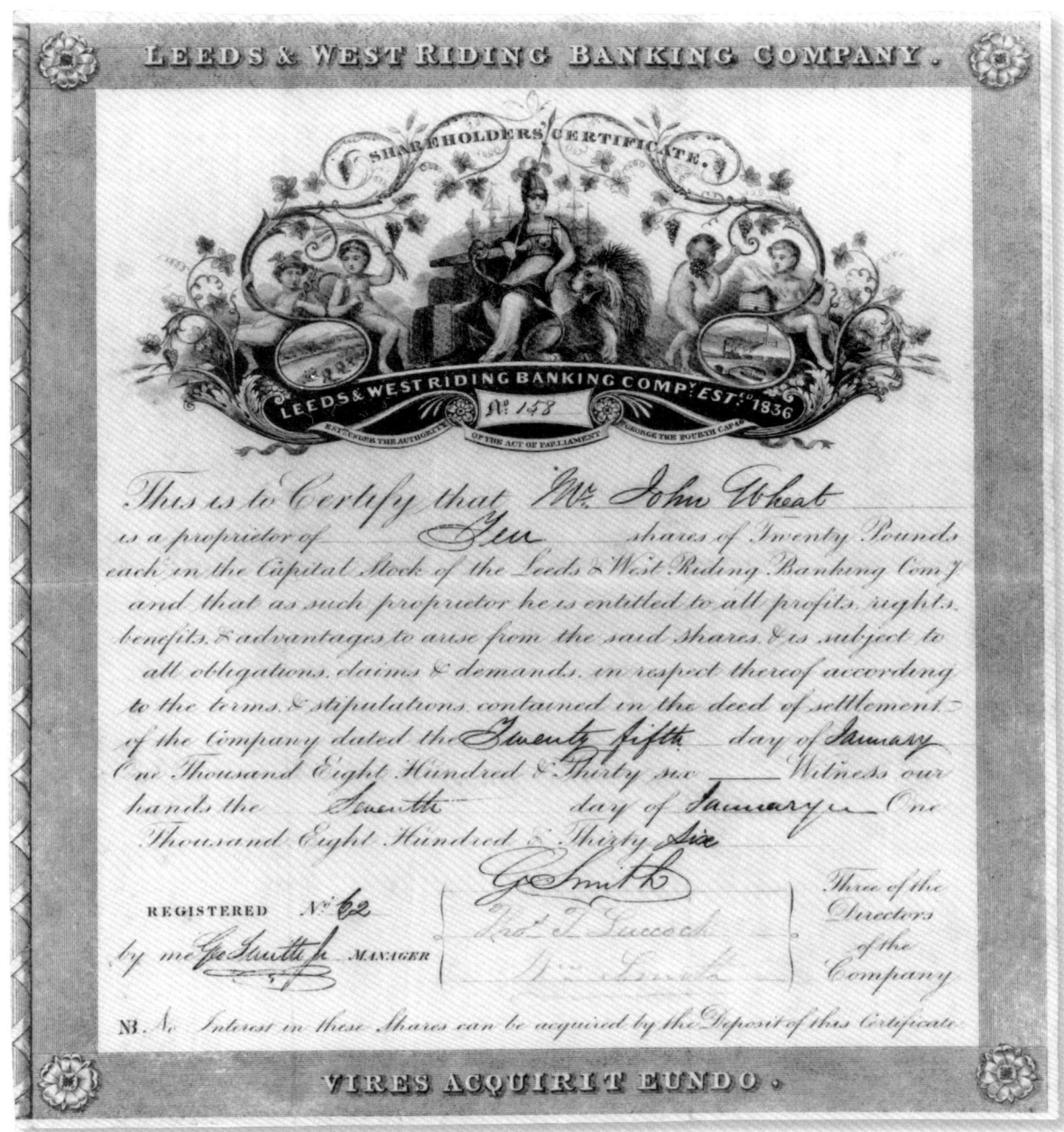

Certificate for 10 shares of £20 each dated 1836 in the Leeds & West Riding Banking Company, one of the earliest banks, which was established at the end of 1835 but eventually failed in 1846.

The Crash of 1825

1825 proved to be a dramatic year. There were 439 petitions for Private Bills for joint-stock companies. But, like all bubbles the conditions for collapse were plain to see; low interest rates, and a desperate desire to increase financial returns on capital (i.e. greed). The position was compounded by a lack of good communications and the over-optimistic (and ill informed) assessments of new markets, particularly in South America. The crash of South American investments leading to the defaults of Argentina, took place early in the year and were largely brought about by rampant promotion by financiers such as J & A Powles, a leading firm of South American merchants, and the writings of a young Benjamin Disraeli. By the time it was necessary to pick up the pieces, Disraeli was £7,000 in debt, an enormous sum in those days which hung over him for many years. Powles actively promoted stocks such as the *Anglo-Mexican Mining Association* and the *Colombian Mining Association*, just two companies who were adept at creative accounting.

The position was compounded by the demise of bankers *Pole, Thornton, Free, Down & Scott* (once one of London's largest banks), an event

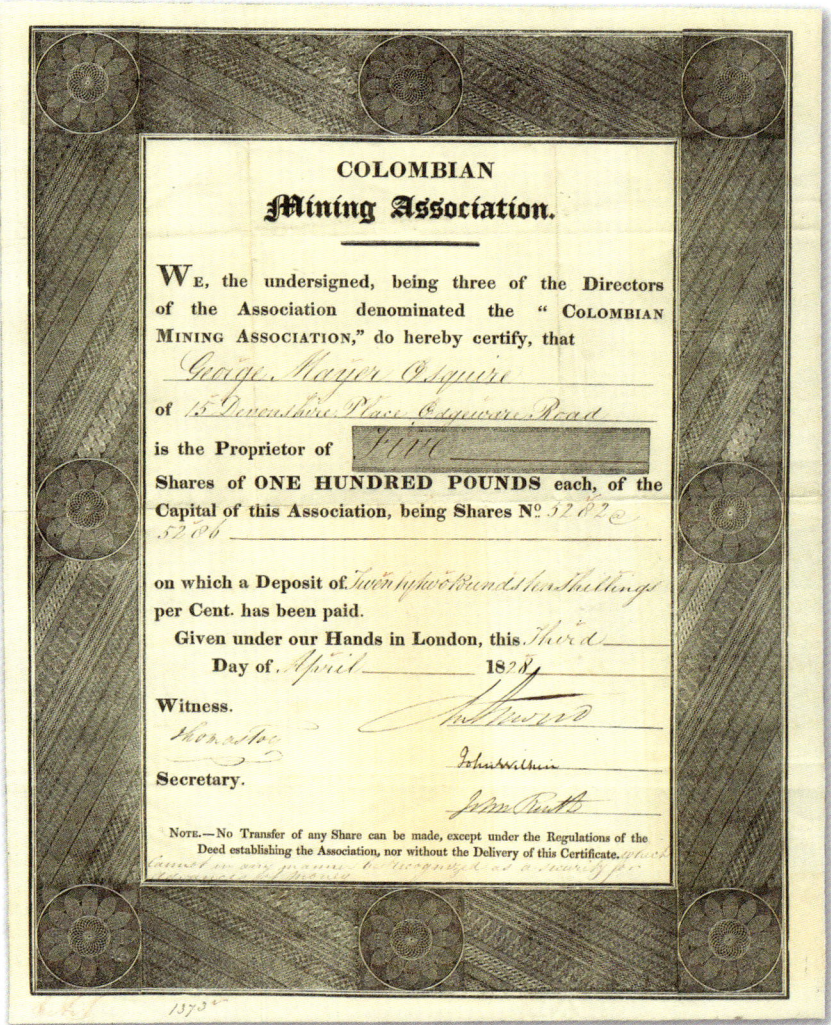

Columbian Mining Association.
Early example of speculative share dated 1828.

initiated by an unexpected withdrawal of £30,000 in December. Despite the Bank of England's efforts to stabilize the situation its efforts were insufficient. This collapse and the subsequent collapse of Wentworth & Co., a leading Yorkshire bank, resulted in 40 correspondent banks being put out of business. Banks such as Gurneys (of Norwich) resorted to placing thick piles of Bank of England notes on the counter thus dissuading customers from cashing Gurney notes. Recovery was speeded slong by a series of good harvests.

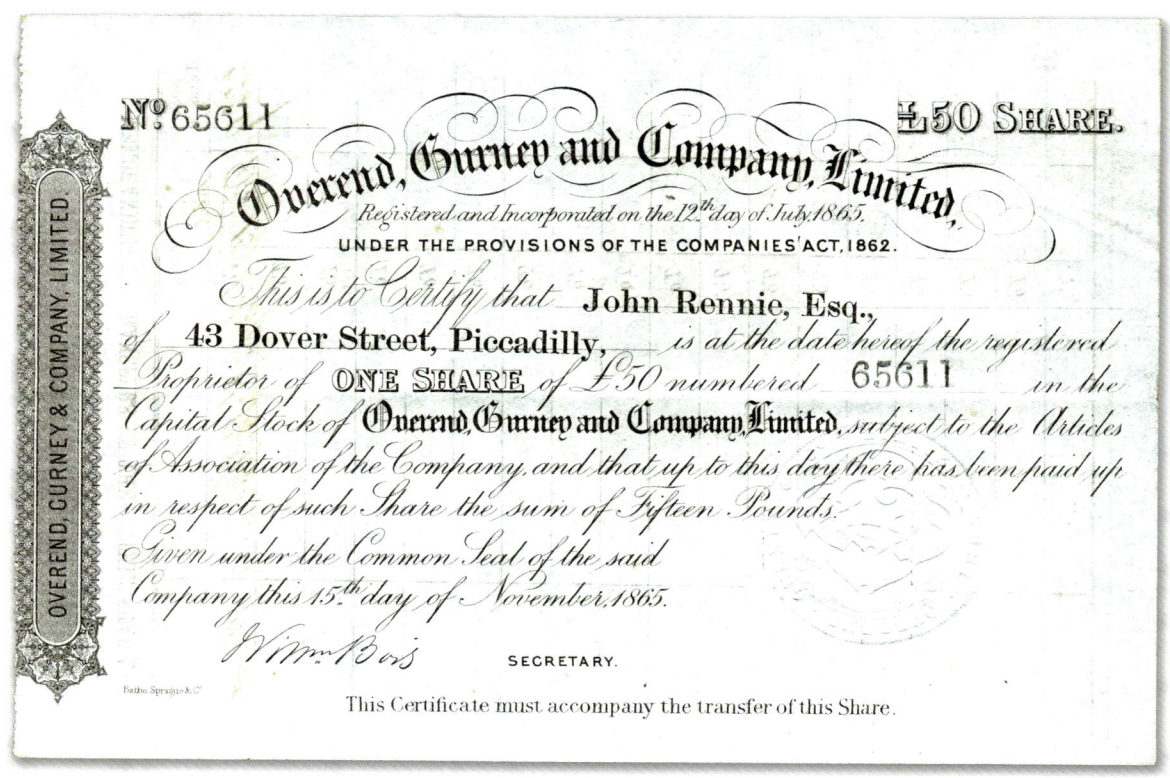

Overend & Gurney was largely responsible for the crash of 1866. This was one of the shares issued the previous year when the company went public.

Overend & Gurney

1866 proved to be a decisive year in British banking history with the failure of *Overend & Gurney*. Overend's was originally a discount house but became a lynch pin of City activity extending its interests to varied (and risky) ventures including shipbuilding, railway financing and grain trading. In its early days it epitomized sound business practice which changed the way discounting was done – no longer simply relying on the claimed strength of an *individuals* finances but by taking a commission on each transaction. Interestingly, Joseph Gurney was the largest investor in the Stockton & Darlington Railway with £14,000 of shares.

Overends was formed in Norfolk in 1770 by two highly respected Quaker families. By 1859 it was making annual profits of around £5 million, but 2 years later it began losing money as a result of taking inadequate security for loans. In1865 it formed itself into a joint stock company, largely to shore up its finances. Rumours of its precariousness abounded before and after its flotation and in May 1866 the company collapsed causing a monumental crash amongst City firms and forcing the Government and Bank of England to step in and provide support. At the time of its demise, it had debts of £11 million (equivalent to c. £1 billion today). The crash of Overend & Gurney reverberated through the City and many institutions followed including *Agra & Masterman's Bank*. One unfortunate result of the Overend & Gurney collapse was the concept of limited liability being brought into disrepute for years to come.

Later Developments

The ups and downs of financial progress, as reflected by banking development continued throughout the rest of the nineteenth and early twentieth centuries. Banks amalgamated and note issue was focused on the central bank whilst cheques began to replace banknotes as the major medium of settlement. By 1884, the picture was rather different to 40 years previously, as shown in the table below.

Amalgamation was the principal activity over the next century. Today there are 6 major independent retail banks, HSBC, Lloyds Banking Group, Royal Bank of Scotland Group ('RBS'), Barclays, Santander and Standard Chartered. The crash of 2008 resulted in considerable shuffling of ownership with the

Government taking controlling stakes in Lloyds and RBS. The big six are not the only banks however, several others are owned by major retailers and a host of smaller specialist banks such as N M Rothschild, Close Brothers and Charity Bank flourish, all carefully regulated of course. Most of the largest building societies have been absorbed by the big banks but still 50 independent Societies exist providing consumer banking facilities.

Industries beyond the "Industrial Revolution"

Railways and banks are far from being the only collectable themes available to the collector of British material. Railways may have eased transport problems and banks, money, but opportunities for the collector are immense with a subject for every specialist. Several are covered in later sections.

Number of Banks, 1884

Type	Banks	Branches	Banknote circulation
Bank of England	1	11	£25.1m
London private banks	35	10	
London joint-stock banks	21	52	
London & provincial joint-stock banks	6	517	
Provincial private banks	172	433	£1.4m
Provincial joint- stock banks	91	1,052	£1.5m
TOTALS	**326**	**2,075**	**£28m**

Source: Crick and Wadsworth (1936)

United States of America

If, for the sake of this book, we focus on the period from the Declaration of Independence (1776) to today, then we are looking at a commercial history stretching back less than 250 years.

Following the split with Great Britain, the USA set about firming up its borders and annexing land held by foreign powers. Thus:

- Louisiana was purchased from the French in 1803 (for $15 million);
- Florida entered the Union in 1845;
- After 9 years independence, Texas also joined the Union in 1845;
- California was secured in 1850;
- Britain accepted an extension of the 49th parallel in 1846 extending the country's border to the Pacific and effectively ceding three fifths of Oregon;
- The Treaty of Guadalupe Hidalgo (at the end of the Mexican War) in 1848 added a broad stretch of land to the US including, what is now, Arizona, New Mexico and parts of Utah, Nevada and Colorado.

The effect of these changes was to quadruple the land area of the United States. By 1850, the country's population reached 23 million, greater than that of Britain, but still 10 million short of France. But immigrants continued to flood in and ten years later, the total had reached 31 million.

Apart from international politics, three major events were primarily responsible for shaping the country's *commercial* backbone. The first of these was the building of the railroads, which began with the Baltimore & Ohio ("B&O") in 1830; the second was the discovery and mining of minerals, perhaps most glamorously portrayed by the California Gold Rush of 1849; and the third was the Civil War of 1861-5. These three events provide much of the material so avidly collected today. But before looking at these in more detail, lets consider the backdrop and, in particular, some of the characters of the period who did so much to sculpt the commercial shape of the United States.

Economic Awakenings

Although the New York Stock Exchange was only inaugurated in 1792 (as a result of the Buttonwood Agreement – see Page 11), there was little early corporate activity other than by companies formed and operated in Britain. This is not to say that US shares did not exist prior to this date, merely that they are generally rare and difficult to obtain. Interesting examples include the two companies formed by Benjamin Franklin: the *Library Company of Philadelphia* (1789) and the *Pennsylvania Hospital*, America's first incorporated hospital formed in 1751, the seal of which states "Take Care of Him and I will repay Thee" – an inscription chosen by Franklin. Other shares of the period include the *Baltimore Insurance Company* (which still exists as the *Baltimore Equitable Insurance Company*) formed in 1796 and the *Kennebeck Bridge*. The latter was chartered in Maine in 1797 to build a toll-bridge across the Kennebec River at Fort Western in Hallowell, Augusta. The bridge cost $27,000 but the share issue raised only $19,800 – result, no dividends for 8 years.

The two share certificates most frequently seen from this period are those of the *North American Land Company*, 1795 (signed by Robert Morris) and the *Philadelphia & Lancaster Turnpike Road*, 1795 (usually signed by William Bingham). Both

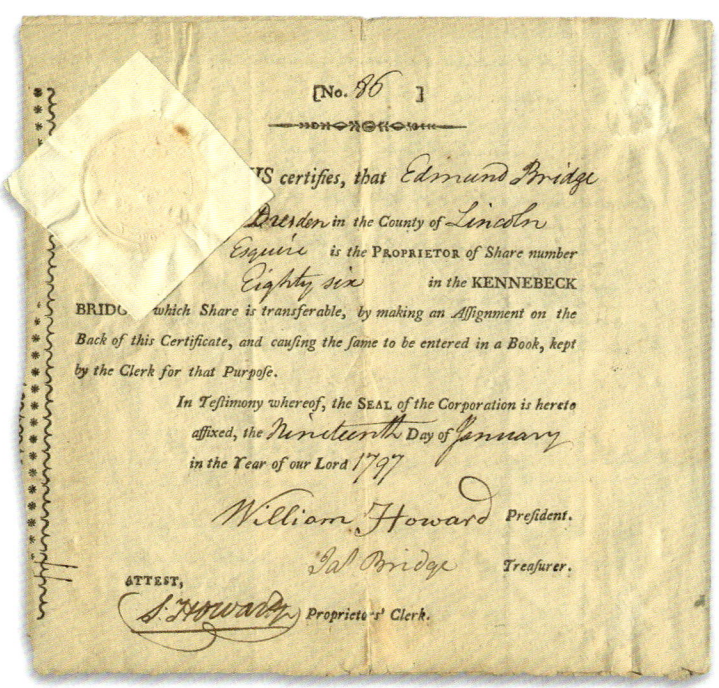

The Kennebeck Bridge located in Augusta was one of America's earliest companies. The share certificate shown here is dated 1797.

Willing, originally of Bristol, England. The Willings became one of the most prominent families in Philadelphia. Charles was twice appointed mayor and was trustee and founder of the University of Pennsylvania. On his death, Morris and the founder's son, Thomas Willing, continued to run the business extremely profitably. Thomas became president of the Bank of North America and subsequently the first president of the *Bank of the United States*, largely thanks to his colleague Robert Morris.

Morris was both a close friend of George Washington and a signatory of the Declaration of Independence. He took an active part in the War of Independence and personally funded some of the cost including the activities of the 'blockade runners' that brought needy supplies to the colonial fighters. After the war, he was appointed Superintendent of Finance and effectively became the most powerful man in America. In 1781 he set up the *Bank of North America (previously the Pennsylvania Bank)*. But, land speculation was his downfall and the *North American Land Company* was one of his prime speculative vehicles, however the days of land speculation were temporarily drawing to a close and his personal fortune was dissipated. Disaster finally struck in 1798, when creditors demanded his arrest and he was sent to the debtors' prison. Washington continued to visit him, but he died penniless in 1806.

Often regarded as the financier of the American Revolution, his name lives on in the "Robert Morris University" (RMU), Pittsburgh.

signatories, as we will see, played key roles in the financial development of the Country.

This was a time when the United States was finding its way and developing its financial structure with many individuals coming to the fore. Several have become household names and their activities are described below. The work of Alexander Hamilton, one of the most celebrated, is described in Part 6.

Robert Morris – Signatory of the Declaration of Independence, friend of George Washington, land speculator and prisoner

Robert Morris was born in England in 1734. Ten years later he arrived in Chesapeake Bay and by the time he was 16, was apprenticed to the merchant house, Willings run by Charles

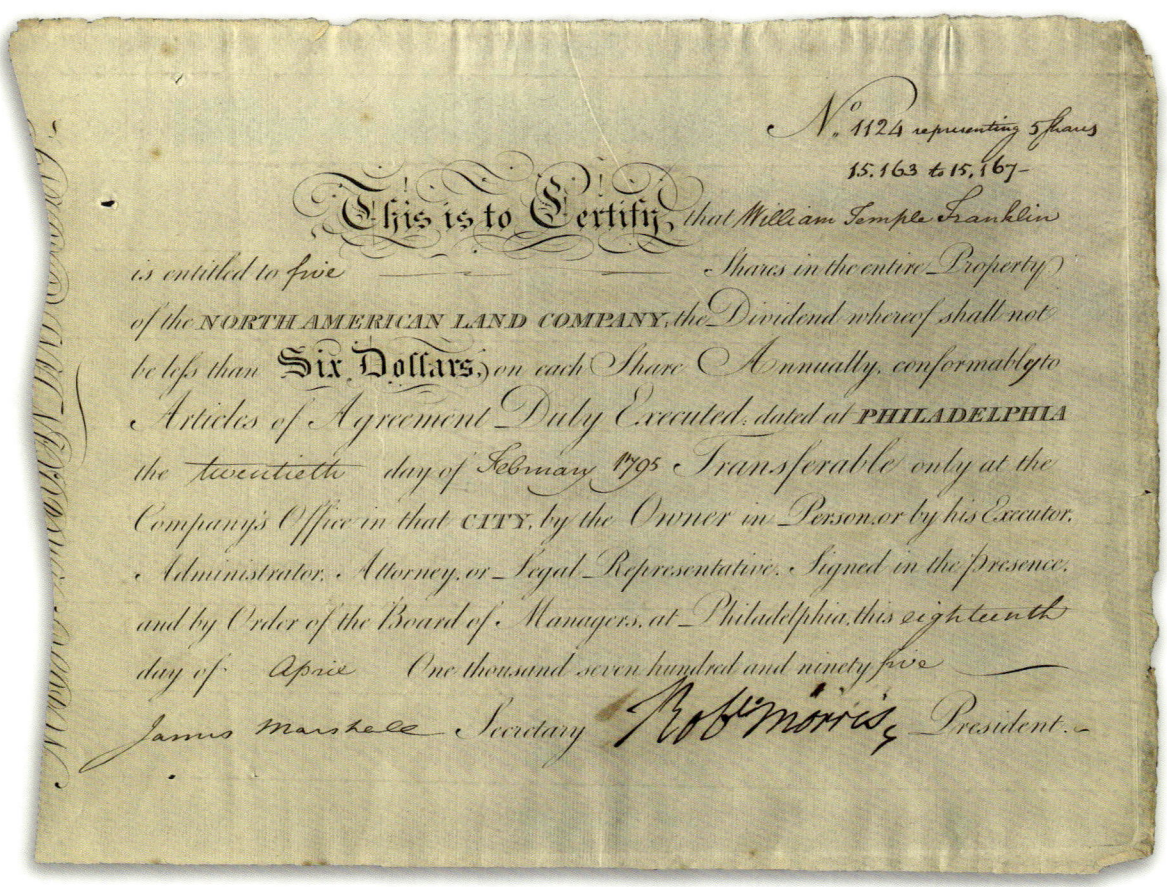

Certificate for 5 shares in the North American Land Company dated 1795 and signed by Robert Morris. The certificate is made out to William Temple Franklin, grandson of Benjamin Franklin, one of the Founding Fathers of the United States. Whilst in London Franklin was Morris's agent.

Bingham and the Barings

Born in Philadelphia in 1752, William Bingham married Thomas Willing's daughter, Anne. He was active on both sides of the Atlantic and although graduating from the University of Pennsylvania was appointed British Consul in Martinique and spent a further 4 years as commercial agent for the Continental Congress. It was during this period that he amassed his fortune chiefly through trade speculations and the tri-cornered trade that involved shipping slaves from Africa to the West Indies, trading them for sugar, then shipping it to New England to make rum for export to Britain.

He became a founder and director of the Pennsylvania Bank (later renamed *Bank of North America*), established by Robert Morris and headed by his father-in-law, Thomas Willing. He was a major landowner, founder of Binghampton, New York, and president of the *Philadelphia & Lancaster Turnpike Road*. The turnpike was the first of its kind in the United States, 62 miles long and built at a cost of $465,000. The share certificates are mostly hand-signed by Bingham, printed on vellum, usually dated 1795 and are one of the earliest to carry a vignette.

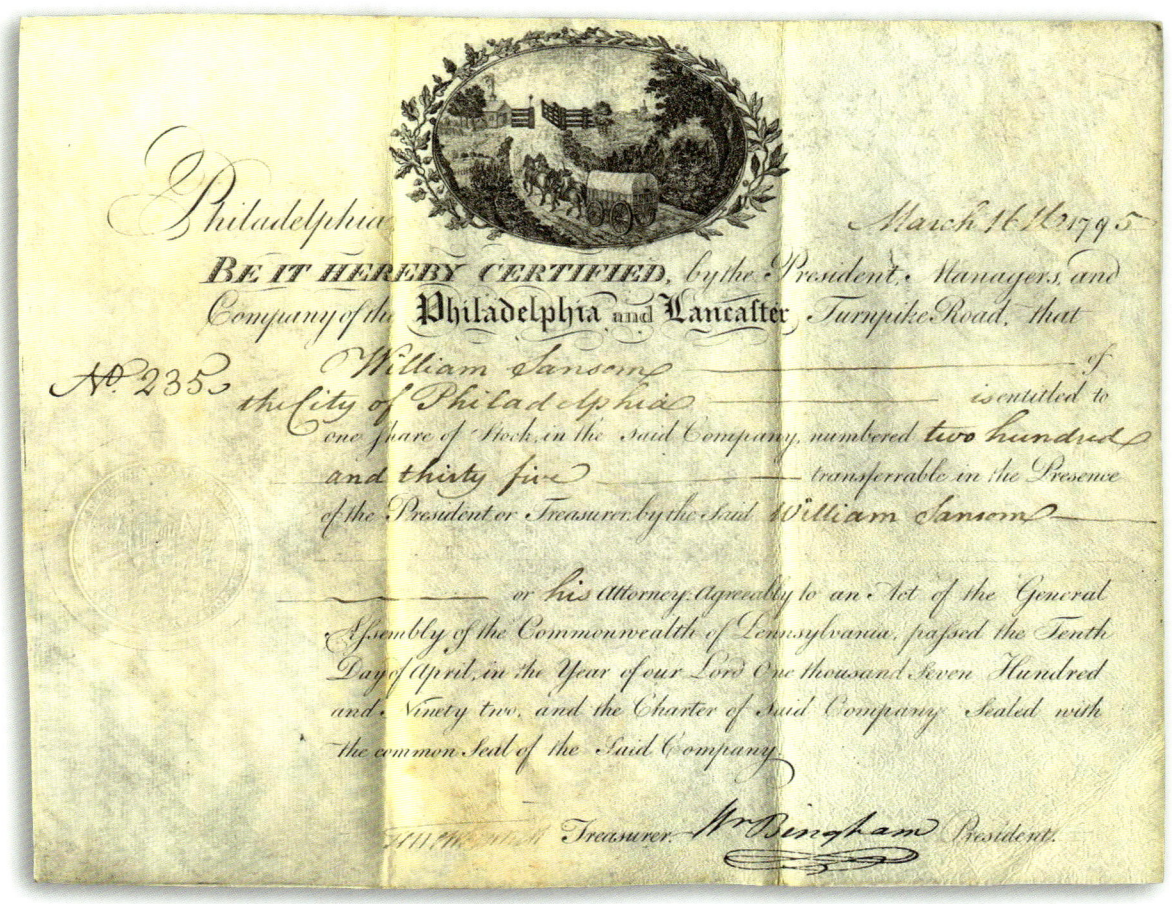

Fine example of an early American certificate printed on vellum.
Signed by William Bingham and dated 1795

Bingham was one of Philadelphia's wealthiest businessmen. His two daughters both married into the Baring family. His son in law, Alexander Baring, later Lord Ashburton, negotiated the Webster-Ashburton Treaty in 1842 that settled the US-Canadian boundary dispute.

Bingham died in England (Bath) in 1804 aged only 52. His estate was finally liquidated in 1964.

The Rocky Road towards a Central Bank

In the period between the demise of the first *Bank of the United States* and the establishment of the second *Bank of the United States* in 1816, the country suffered a complete breakdown of its banking and currency systems a situation greatly exacerbated by the war with Britain in 1812.

The Second Bank was formed in 1816 to stop the rot but in its early years was run more as a commercial enterprise than a government body; it was badly managed and plagued with fraud, despite having the strong support of John Calhoun (US Vice President 1825-32) and Henry Clay (Senator and Presidential candidate). One fifth of its $35 million capital was supplied by the government as were one fifth of its directors; the rest was in private hands. In 1819, Nicholas Biddle was named as one of the government's 5 representative directors with the backing of President Monroe and in 1822 he became president of the bank. A capable but tempestuous person, Biddle soon re-established the bank on its course as a true 'Central Bank'. Biddle did much to strengthen overseas credibility of the United States by working closely with Barings in London and Hope

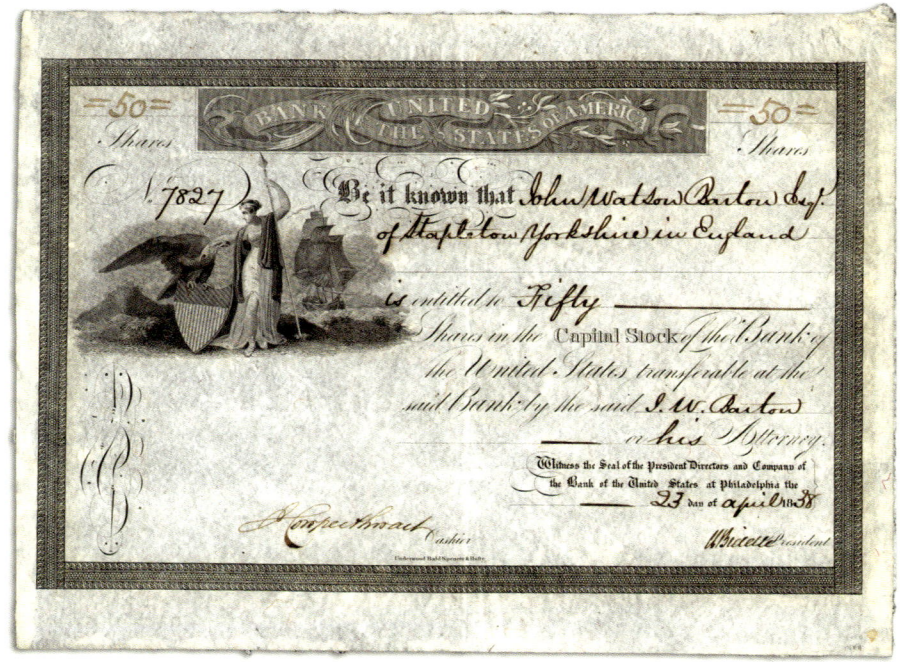

Second Bank of the United States. The bank lasted until Andrew Jackson refused to extend its charter on its expiry in 1836. Despite this, certificates continued to be issued for several years thereafter.

in Amsterdam. Around 20% of the bank was owned by European investors and many of the share certificates seen today (usually signed by Biddle) originated from this group. However, the newly elected President, Andrew Jackson, was vehemently opposed to the Bank and refused to extend its chartered life of 20 years, despite the fact that it was functioning well under Biddle. As a result, on expiry of the Bank's charter in 1836, the United States was deprived of a central bank for almost 80 years. From that date the Bank wound down, operating as the *Bank of the United States of Pennsylvania* until 1841. Interestingly (and confusingly) several certificates in the Bank of the United States are dated 1842, some years after its title was changed.

The Building of the Railways

Part 6 looks at some of the 'railroad barons' including Vanderbilt and Harriman. This section sets out the background to early development and the importance railroads played in the economic and geographical development of the United States.

The first steam railway offering both freight and passenger services, was the *Baltimore & Ohio Railroad* ("B & O"), opened in 1830, five years after Britain's Stockton & Darlington. The line was incorporated in 1827 and a year later, Charles Carroll, a director of the railroad and the last surviving signatory of the Declaration of Independence, laid the "first stone". The train, named "Tom Thumb", was built from an assortment of scrap, using gun barrels for boiler tubes. The first stretch of the line was from Baltimore to Ellicott's Mills (now Ellicott City). Six months later a race was arranged between train and horse – the horse won…just!

From then on, the race to open new lines began in earnest but it was not until the 1850s' that real progress was made. The difficult terrain and varied weather conditions of the country combined with unreliability of steam engines did not help. The *Chicago & Rock Island RR* was the first to reach the Mississippi in 1854 closely followed by the *Illinois Central* and *Chicago & Alton*. Despite violent objections by the rivermen, the river was finally bridged in 1856. Abraham Lincoln was one of the lawyers of the *Illinois Central*, which by 1856 had become the longest railroad in the world.

The Civil war spurred President Lincoln into joining the east and west of the country so preventing any breakaway from the Union by the west coast states. The *Central Pacific RR* was incorporated in 1861 and the *Union Pacific*, a year later. But it was not until 10th May 1869 that the two great lines met at Promontory Summit, Utah joining the two oceans.

The ceremony for the driving of the 'golden spike' at Promontory Summit, Utah on 10th May 1869. The joining of the of the Central Pacific and Union Pacific Railroads.

There were reputed to be over 9,000 railroad companies formed in the United States over the seventy years or so of railway expansion. Many progressed no further than the printing of their share certificates but others prospered and became targets for the financiers and railroad barons.

Eureka- Gold!

In May of 1848, the California gold rush began, the same year the state was ceded to the United States following the Mexican War. The discovery of gold had a dramatic effect on the growth of the West Coast. Its population increased from 26,000 in 1848 to 115,000 by the end of the following year. Around 25% was due to immigration from Europe, Australia and China. But it was not only gold that was discovered, originally by James W Marshall close to his partner's ranch at Sutter's Fort; coal, copper, iron ore and silver were found to be equally abundant.

Travel difficulties and doubts over 'successful' discoveries led to the grouping together of prospectors, often under the umbrella of a company, some based in California, others elsewhere; for example the *Ave Maria Gold Quartz Mining Company* and the *Anglo-Californian Gold Mining Company*, were both registered in London. Many of the companies were small with low capital and small share issues – great for today's collector. Advantages of forming a company were not limited to a sharing of risk but also gave the opportunity for overseas investors to participate at a distance.

The frantic scramble for gold and other minerals led to inevitable social problems, many of which were racially based. However, apart from these unfortunate aspects, there were a great many

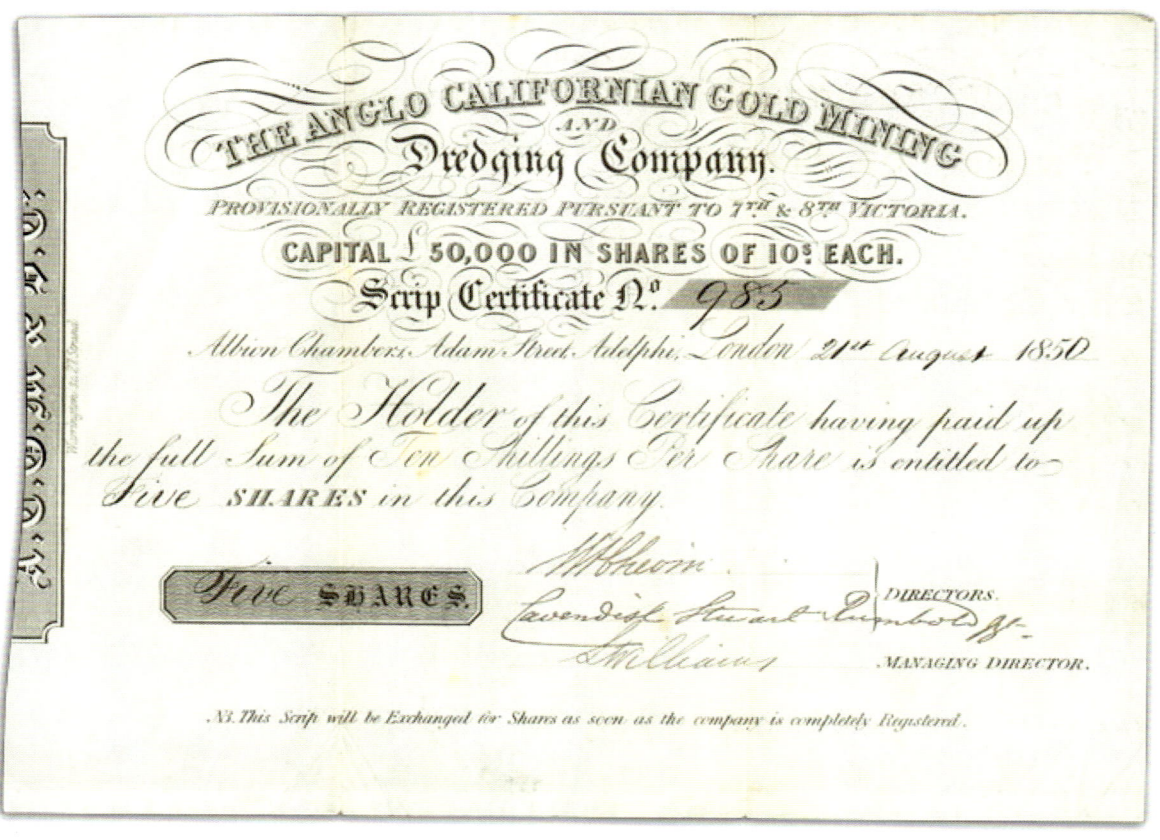

Example of an early bearer share in the Anglo Californian Gold Mining & Dredging Company dated 1850 and signed by the Managing Director Luke Williams. The company went through several name changes but was primarily involved in the mining of quartz. Regarded as a 'gold bubble company'!

positives, in particular, improved (and safer) mining techniques.

More on mining appears in Section 6

The Civil War (1861-65)

Part 7 includes a section on the design and printing of bonds issued to finance the Confederate cause and the problems even that seemingly simple task posed. Now to the war itself, the personalities involved and the impact it had on the development of the United States.

During the fifty years prior to the Civil War,

arguments over slavery, were commonplace. States were divided between "free states" and "slave states" and although the constitution had effectively stopped the 'importation' of Africans for the slave trade, very few people regarded slavery as wrong. But the "abolitionists" increased their calls and went further; for example in 1816, the American Colonization Society was formed specifically to repatriate slaves to West Africa. The nation of Liberia (from the latin, 'libertas' meaning 'freedom') was founded for the purpose and its capital, Monrovia, was named after President Monroe. The Slave States became increasingly fearful of their slaves rebelling and despite being larger in area than the Free States, their

Confederate Bond (Ball 201) with vignette of Jefferson Davis and view of Richmond. Dutch revenue stamp affixed.

In January and February 1861 seven states seceded from the Union, five weeks before Lincoln was inaugurated. The seven met in Montgomery, Alabama and established the Confederate States of America, which guaranteed the permanence of slavery. Jefferson Davis of Mississippi was elected President (Ball:16, 66, 105 and 200-210) and Alexander Hamilton Stephens of Georgia, Vice President (Ball: 113 and 165-188).

Between Lincoln's electoral victory and his inauguration and for the first month of his presidency, there was an impasse. The Southern States thought the Union would not declare war and the Unionists sought a way of appeasing the slave states. Eventually, the need to reinforce the blockaded Fort Sumter, which was located on a fortified island within the harbour of South Carolina,

population was slightly less. The disparities became more acute as the industrialization of the north encouraged immigrants, whereas few went south where industrial labour was almost non-existent.

Confederate Bond (B260) depicting the Richmond Customs House, built in 1858. Once Ricmond had been selected as the capital of the Confederate States of America, the building housed offices for Jefferson Davis and the Treasury. Ironically, it became the courthouse where Davis was eventually indicted for treason.

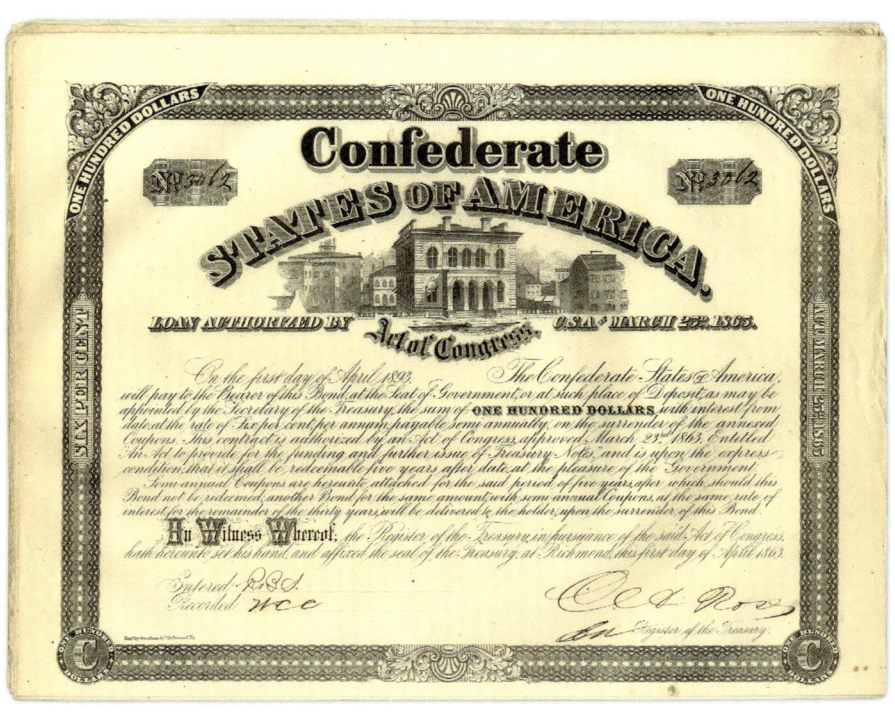

forced the pace. The South was unwilling to allow the Fort to be replenished and General Beauregard of the Confederacy commenced a bombardment – the war had begun. The first battle was over in a day and the defeated garrison was allowed to sail back to New York on 13th April 1861. No casualties this time but over the next 4 years almost a million would die, most from hunger and sickness rather than the bullet. The first seven slave states were joined by another four (Virginia, Arkansas, Tennessee and North Carolina) and the capital of the Confederacy was established in Richmond, only 100 miles from Washington.

This book will not go into the detail of the war, suffice it to say that the battles ebbed and flowed. The Confederacy sought aid from Britain and France to no avail and troops were requisitioned from volunteers and immigrants by both sides. Each developed iron clad ships, initially the *Monitor* by the Unionists and the *Merrimack* by the Confederates, something which is considered the beginning of the end of wooden warships.

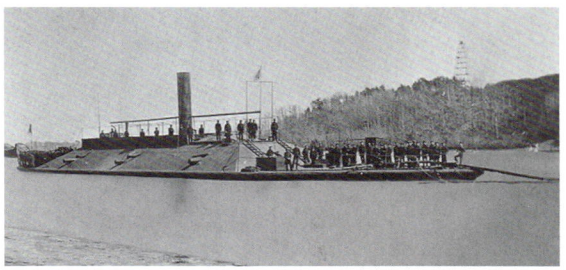

Iron Clad USS Atlanta (1864-1869), formerly CSS Atlanta (1862-1863)

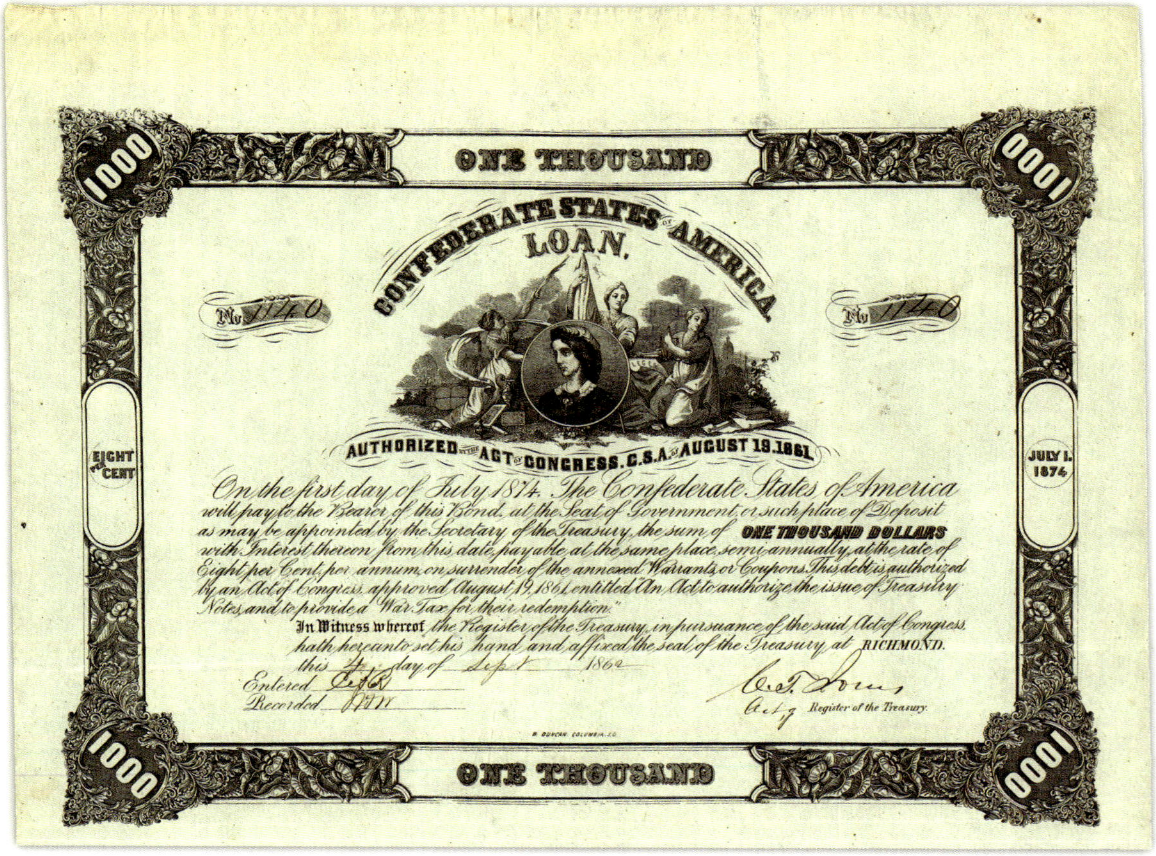

ONE THOUSAND

CONFEDERATE STATES OF AMERICA
LOAN.

No 1140

AUTHORIZED BY THE ACT OF CONGRESS, C.S.A. OF AUGUST 19, 1861.

EIGHT PER CENT

JULY 1. 1874

On the first day of July 1874. The Confederate States of America will pay to the Bearer of this Bond, at the Seat of Government, or such place of Deposit as may be appointed by the Secretary of the Treasury, the sum of ONE THOUSAND DOLLARS with Interest thereon from this date, payable at the same place, semi-annually, at the rate of Eight per Cent per annum, on surrender of the annexed Warrants or Coupons. This debt is authorized by an Act of Congress approved August 19, 1861, entitled "An Act to authorize the issue of Treasury Notes, and to provide a War Tax for their redemption."

In Witness whereof the Register of the Treasury, in pursuance of the said Act of Congress, hath hereunto set his hand and affixed the seal of the Treasury at RICHMOND, this 4 day of Sept 1862

Entered

Recorded

Register of the Treasury.

ONE THOUSAND

Confederate bond with Lucy Pickens vignette (see page 61)

An increasing number of victories for the Unionists greatly helped Lincoln's re-election in November 1864 but the war dragged on for another seven months and it was not until June 1865 that the last State, Texas, surrendered. There were no recriminations, too many had already died, but there was one more death, that of Abraham Lincoln, himself, who was shot by John Wilkes Booth on 14th April 1865.

The Bonds

Most of the Confederate leaders are depicted at least once on the bonds as are George Washington, state buildings, battle scenes and allegorical figures. The bonds were issued following the passing of 16 Acts over the period from 28th February 1861 to 28th November 1864. Some of those depicted are listed below:

Portrait	Position	Bonds (Ball reference nos.)
Judah P Benjamin	Attorney General	39, 55, 63, 68,74, 90, 111, 134
Thomas Bragg	Attorney General 1861-2	40, 59, 67, 87, 116, 122
George Washington	Confederate Bond (Ball 201) with vignette of Jefferson Davis and view of Richmond. Dutch revenue stamp affixed.	48, 296-336
John H Reagan	Postmaster	51, 71, 129
Robert M T Hunter	Second Secretary of State	54, 76, 77, 88, 92, 119, 123 125,
Christopher G Memminger	Secretary of the Treasury	56, 65, 69, 75, 91, 115, 133, 147-149, 279
Thomas H Watts	Attorney General 1862-3	57,58, 120
Jefferson Davis	President	66, 105, 200-210
S R Mallory	Secretary of the Navy	72,73, 79, 81, 96
Burton Harrison	Davis's Secretary	83, 102, 110
George W Randolph	Secretary of War	85, 103
Lucy Pickens	Socialite	86
General Winder	'Brigadier' responsible for prisoners	101
Robert Toombs	Secretary of State	108, 109
Alexander H Stephens	Vice President	113, 165-188
Edward C Elmore	Treasurer	133
Thomas R 'Stonewall' Jackson	General	240-256
James A Seddon	Secretary of War	280
Samuel Preston Moore	Surgeon General	41

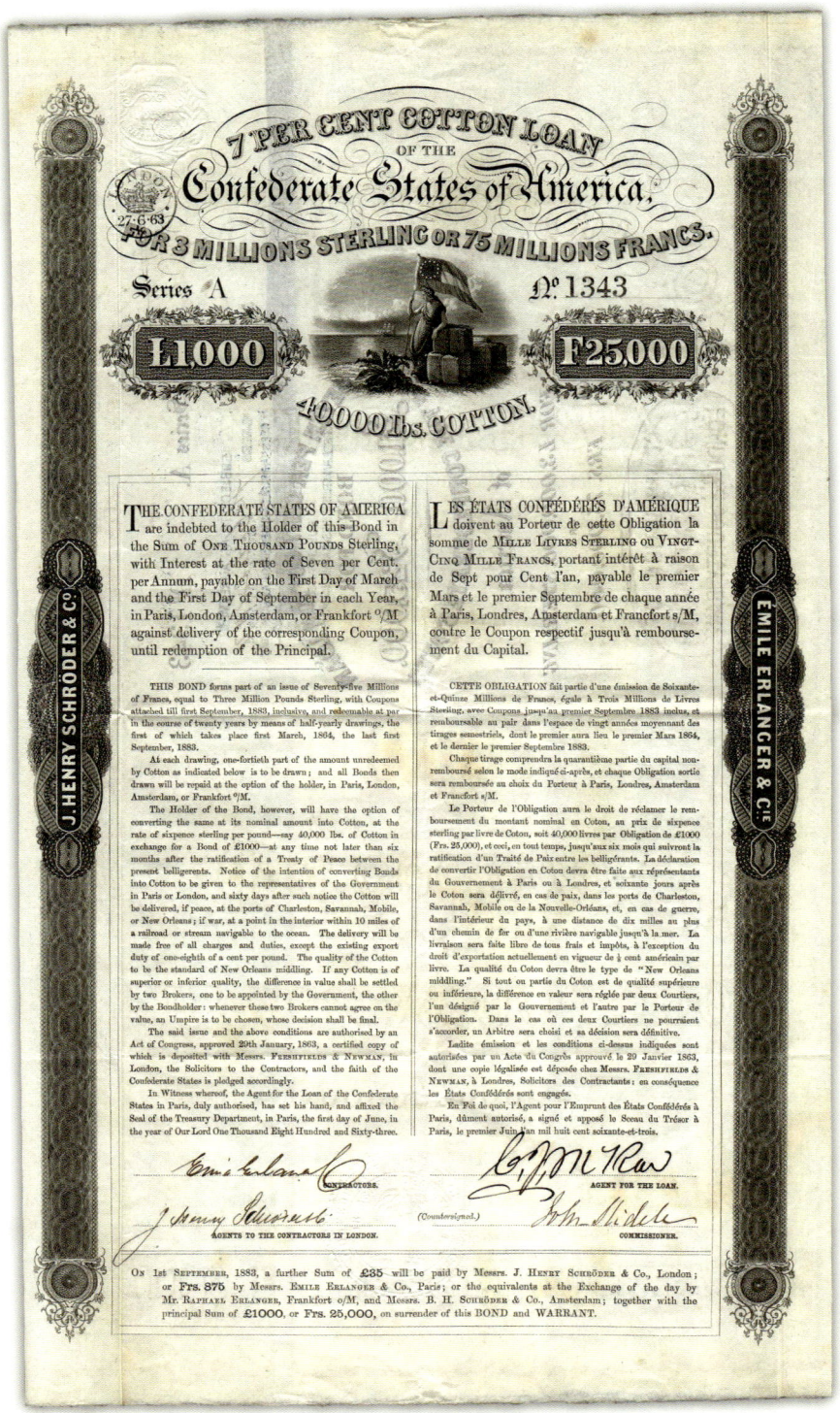

The 'Erlanger Loan' named after the bank run by Baron Emile Erlanger was isued in London and is the only series of Confederate bonds to have been engraved. The bonds were issued in denominations of £100, £200, £500 and £1,000 and the interest and principal was offered in currency or bales of cotton.

Lucy Pickens

Without examining all the characters of the war, it might be interesting to consider one, namely Lucy Holcombe Pickens who was married to Colonel Francis Wilkinson Pickens of South Carolina.

Francis was appointed US Ambassador to Russia in 1858 where he and his wife became close friends of the Tsar and Tsarina, godparents to their daughter, Douschka. Rumours flourished about the father of Lucy's child but none were proven. Lucy and Francis returned to the US just 3 days before South Carolina seceded from the Union and Francis became Governor of the State. As such he triggered the battle at Fort Sumpter and so started the war.

Lucy, known as the "Queen of the Confederacy", supported secession and a unit of the Confederate army was named after her. She is the only woman to appear on both a Confederate bond and banknotes, something approved by friend of the family Christopher Memminger (Secretary of the Treasury). It was also claimed that she sold some of the jewels given her by the Tsar to finance the Confederate cause. Following the war's loss, she sought further ways to enhance her income including visiting her many English friends, as well as Judah Benjamin (one time Secretary of State) who had escaped to Britain and become a wealthy and successful barrister. Lucy died in 1899.

Repayment

Apart from a bubbling market in Confederate bonds following the end of the war, the United States Government has always refused to consider their repayment, claiming the bonds were issued by rebels and provided no benefit to the country. Indeed the cost of the war, both in terms of manpower and money, was so great that funds were simply not there to recompense bondholders anyway. The vast majority of bonds were sold in Europe, mainly to those anxious to maintain a steady flow of cotton for the mills. At the end of the war, investors were invited to deposit their bonds in exchange for scrip certificates with a council specifically formed to administer their claims. Over the years, prices moved up and down depending on mood and rumour. The bonds themselves, were repeatedly moved, eventually ending up at Coutts Bank in London. On 24th November 1987, those bonds, numbering about 75,000 pieces, were auctioned by Sotheby's, and sold as a batch for around £350,000.

Russia

Setting the Scene

Russia's archaic social structure greatly hampered its development and whereas Britain and the rest of Europe were progressing after the industrial revolution it was not until 1861, with the Emancipation Statutes, that there was some significant progress in Russia. The key elements were freedom and land for the serfs, even though they had to pay for it. The process was complex and took several years, not helped by the Serfs basic lack of education. Nevertheless, in 1882, the Peasants Land Bank was set up to assist the transfer of land from the nobility. Inevitably there were uprisings and heavy suppressions but the Emancipation relieved the pressure and progress was made. Tsar Nicholas I pushed the button and encouraged the construction of railways despite opposition from his government. But progress was hampered, not only by serfs and nobles slowly coming to terms with the changes but also by the wars with Napoleon (which finally ended in 1812), and the Crimean War (1853-6). In 1897 Russia adopted the gold standard, which encouraged foreign investors.

The French primarily invested in the metallurgical industries of the south (e..g. *Soc. Metallurgique du Sud-Oural*), the Belgians tramways (e.g. *Tramways de Kischinew*) while Britain focused on oil (e.g. *Chatma Oilfield Co.* and *Ural Caspian Oil Corporation Ltd.*), tobacco (e.g. *Russian Tobacco Co.*), textiles and light engineering. Germany chose electricity. In 1900 Belgium was the biggest foreign investor in Russian industry.

The Railways

Construction lagged behind Europe and North America but encouraged by Tsar Nicolas I, development began with the opening of the first line in 1837. Despite being of little strategic or functional benefit, it at least provided a new way for the Tsars entourage to travel the 25 kilometres from St. Petersburg to the 'Catherine Palace' at Tsarskoe-Selo ("Tsars Village"), birthplace of Alexander II and subsequently renamed 'Pushkin', after Russia's most famous poet

Although the line was opened in 1837 it was only in the following year that steam traction was exclusively used when the train named Provorny (meaning "Agile") built by Robert Stevenson took

Tsarskoe-Selo Railway 1837

to the tracks. It was later extended to Pavlovsk, named after Tsar Pavel (son of Catherine the Great) with a station built as an entertainment centre at which concerts were given by its resident band leader, Johann Strauss. The line was built by a newly established joint-stock company headed by Count Alexander Bobrinsky whose engineer was Franz Anton von Gerstner. This line became a forerunner for the construction of commercial lines across Russia and in many respects was similar to Britain's Stockton and Darlington Railway. Bobrinsky's company employed over 3,000 workers and 17 engineers, many of whom had worked on early British lines.

The next two lines to be authorized were the *Warsaw-Vienna* (1848) and the *St.Petersburg-Moscow* (1851). The former was of immediate strategic benefit being used to transport troops to quell the Hungarian uprising.

The American engineer Major George Washington Whistler was invited to Russia to advise on construction of the all important line (in 1851 it took 22 hours to travel from St Petersburg to Moscow; today it is 4). Interestingly the Major was the father of James Abbott Whistler, the artist. The line itself was 750 kilometres and its route was determined by Nicholas I whom, fed up with endless suggestions and advice, simply drew a straight line using a ruler between the two cities; the result meant that many towns and cities found themselves some distance from the railway.

Although the Tsar was strongly supportive of railways, the government was unable to agree a single course of action in dealing with their construction and financing. The net effect benefitted the private constructors, as the government invariably shouldered the financial risk by guaranteeing dividends.

Eventually, the task of construction was taken on by the Government with the aim of selling-on finished lines to the private sector. Proceeds were invested in a new 'Railway Fund' used to finance building of further lines. The Railway Fund was initially funded by the sale of Alaska in 1867 for $7.2 million ($121 million today allowing for inflation) and the sale of the *St Petersburg-Moscow Railway* to the private sector. Further lines were similarly off-loaded including the *Kursk-Kiev* and

Nicolas Railways. To supplement income and to reduce the number of individual bond offerings, 'Consolidated Bonds' were issued in Europe between 1860 and 1901. These issues were large (see examples below) but helped restore confidence in the Russian economy:

The Consolidated Loans

Loan	Authorised Issue (c.£s'millions)
4% 1880, 6th Emission	£24
4% 1889 1st Series	£28
4% 1889 2nd Series	£12.6
4% 1889 3rd Series	£12.6
4% 1901	£16.7

The drain on government funds as a result of the many new lines was such that by 1880, it owned a mere 35 miles of operative track. The only thing it had in return was 80% of the debt.

Moscow - Smolensk bond for 1000 Thalers. 2,400 such bonds were originally issued in 1869 of which 155 were submitted for settlement in 1986.

Financing the Cities

The number of Russian cities and the quantity of bonds issued by them is appreciably less than those of railways. Because of this they make an interesting collecting theme with many issues being small (and thus rare).

Between 1891 and 1915 over 30 cities raised loans, some such as Moscow had over 40 issues, although several were replacements for earlier loans. The total number of city loans thus well exceeds 100. Of course, many issues were small with some only issued internally.

The purpose of each loan is usually described on the back of the bonds themselves. Whereas most were issued to finance typical municipal activities/debts, some more unusual objectives can be found. Thus, the 1912 City of Nicolaiev bonds were issued amongst other things, for the 'purchase of the enterprise of the *Belgian Company Limited* of the existing tramways of Nicolaiev with horse traction', and perhaps more intriguingly, 'for increasing the floating means of the municiapal pawnbrokery'.

Most external issues bear facsimile signatures of the mayor, two members of the municipal authority and the book-keeper – the latter is usually original as he no doubt "carried the can" if things went wrong. These bonds were quoted on the major European exchanges (Paris, London, Amsterdam and Brussels) and consequently are often written in four languages and denominated in at least three currencies. In view of the relatively small number of inhabitants at the turn of the century, it is a little difficult to comprehend what happened to all the money raised by these issues. In 1897, for example, the population of Moscow was about 1 million (today it exceeds 13 million).

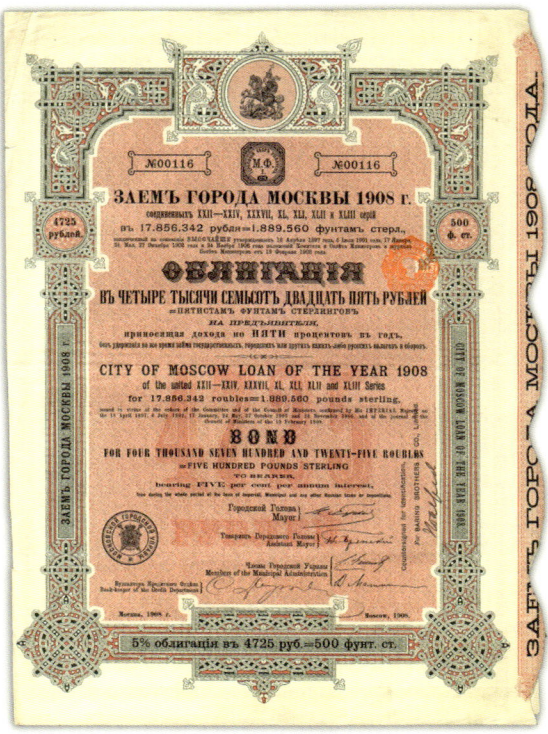

As with all pre-revolutionary Russian City issues, this £500 bond of the City of Moscow issued in 1908 depicts the city's crest (In this case, St George slaying the dragon).

With the exception of Kharkov, city bonds rarely carried views of the city but instead portrayed a municipal crest. Moscow bonds, for example, show St George slaying the dragon, a crest first introduced in the eighteenth century by Yuri Dolgurky, founder of the city. After the 1917 Revolution, heraldic symbols were banned in Russia only returning after the dissolution of the Soviet Union in 1993.

Early Industrial Development

Mention has already been made of the slow start to industrialization in Russia and the general preference of the people to trade rather than manufacture. A good example of this was the import of manufacturing expertise from Western Europe. By the time of the Revolution, not only were well over £1 billion of foreign bonds outstanding but also a similar amount in overseas equity in Russian companies. British companies such as the *Caucasus Copper Company Ltd., City of Moscow Gas Company Ltd., Cheleken Oilfields Ltd.*, and *The Russia Copper Company Ltd*, were typical examples at the end of the nineteenth and beginning of the twentieth centuries. Many companies were actually managed by the British and at the time of the Revolution there were some 30 established British families in Moscow running their businesses ranging from light engineering to textiles. Interestingly most of the families originated from Scotland or Lancashire. These were joined by many French and Belgian companies, such as *Societe des Conduits D'Eau*

The Stock Exchange in St Petersburg. Built by Thomas de Thomon, a French exile born in Berne. The building was modeled on the Temple of Hera at Paestum and completed in 1816, but only opened in 1820, presumably to give Napoleon time to move on.

a Kiew and *S.A. de la Manufacture de Moscou pour le Tissage de Laine*. One British company in particular merits more detail. This was the *New Russia Company Limited*.

"New Russia"

'New Russia' (or "Novorossiya") is the historical name, finding favour again to describe the area to the north of the Black Sea, it was also the name given to a British company formed in 1869 by John Hughes. Tsar Nicolas I (an enthusiastic anglophile who regularly visited Britain and introduced English as the spoken language of his Court) recruited the Welsh engineer to recreate the steel town of Merthyr Tydfil in the Donbas region and develop the mining of coal and iron ore. Hughes was already an acknowledged businessman and was backed by Sir Daniel Gooch*, Thomas Brassey and Joseph Whitworth amongst others.

Hughes established his operation in a new town initially called 'Hughesovka' and subsequently, 'Donetz'. The company first specialized in manufacturing armaments and munitions but with the growth of railways, it focused on rails. Machine tools were imported from Britain and in 1870 Hughes sailed for Ukraine with eight shiploads of equipment and some 100 miners and iron workers. John Hughes built the town complete with hospital and school and on his death his sons took over. But by the time of the Revolution, the town had become a centre of drunkenness and anarchy and the family was happy to leave.

*(*Gooch was a railway engineer who began his working life at the locomotive factory owned by Edward Pease and Robert Stephenson. During his career he designed over 300 locomotives, including the Iron Duke. He was responsible for laying the first trans-Atlantic telephone cable and became chairman of the Great Western Railway).*

A Waterlow engraved debenture of the New Russia Company dated 1910 and signed by Archibald Balfour. Balfour's wife was the daughter of Thomas Weguelin, then Governor of the Bank of England. The New Russia Company lasted until 1970.

Shopping

It may come as a surprise to read about some of the major retailers established in Moscow at the end of the eighteenth century but bear in mind this was a period of economic expansion and customers were not restricted to the aristocracy and immigrant industrialists. Two companies in particular are worth mentioning as both flourish today:

- GUM, and
- Muir & Mirrielees (now, TsUM – Central Universal Department Store)

GUM

Located on Red Square facing the Kremlin, GUM was first established in 1893 although its site had been used for trading since 1520. At the end of the nineteenth century it was the largest shopping center in Europe containing 1,200 shops. Stalin closed it in 1928 and used the building as the headquarters for those working on the first Five Year Plan. It was reopened in 1953 and eventually privatized in the early 1990s' and is still a flourishing emporium.

Muir & Mirrielees (TsUM)

Known locally as M & M's this major store was founded in the 1880s' by two Scottish residents, Andrew Muir and Archibald Mirrielees. Chekhov named two of his dogs after the founders and was a regular customer. In 1908 they opened the largest department store in the Russian Empire near to the Bolshoi. As with GUM, the company was nationalized during the Revolution but now has several branches holding events supported by the international retail glitterati.

GUM is still a thriving assembly of shops and restaurants in the heart of Red Square.

Rbl 1000 bearer share in Muir & Mirrielees dated 1907

Default and Settlement

Despite their default in 1917, Russian foreign bonds continued to be quoted on world stock markets, largely in the hope that a settlement would eventually come about. Stock market prices tended to fluctuate between 2% and 10% of face value depending on speculative mood but between 1978 and 1980 these levels were well exceeded as the collector market developed.

Following the signing of an agreement between Britain and the USSR on 17th July 1986, the London Stock Exchange listing of Imperial Russian bonds was at last cancelled. It was agreed that money and gold amounting to £46 million, which once belonged to the Imperial Russian Government but was frozen in Britain immediately following the Revolution, could be used to settle claims by British nationals. As with the Chinese settlement (see page 26), initial expectations were for a low percentage of the face value of bonds submitted but the final payout turned out far higher at 54.78%. The settlement was limited to UK holders but as the largest holdings of Tsarist bonds were in France and Germany, a relatively low number of bonds were submitted. Another reason for the higher payout for bondholders was the use of current exchange rates (rather than the rates ruling at the date of issue). This greatly benefitted holders of bonds denominated in sterling and severely limited claims in respect of other assets, such as property. Thus, the many foreign nationals living in Russia in 1917 were badly short-changed. Those people often had harrowing tales to tell of their escape across Russia just ahead of the Bolsheviks. The adventures of one such escapee, James Wardropper, is typical:

I was born in Riga in 1908 after my family had moved to Siberia in the 1860s'. My grandfather established a shipbuilding, fishing and forestry company at Tyumen. Father who was a zoologist and biologist ran part of the business but he spent much of his time travelling with the explorer Fridtjof Nansen, in fact an island off the Taimyr Peninsula was named after him. Whilst he was travelling I spent most of my time in Riga with my mother and grandfather who was manager of the railway. In 1914 we joined father in Tyumen.

There were already signs of revolution. One day my parents took my sister, Sylvia, into town to be christened but the Bolsheviks were closing in and father considered it best to leave immediately. Unfortunately my sister caught diphtheria and we had to stay longer. My father was looking after a nearby Yates paper factory but the Bolsheviks burned it down and decided our family should be executed by firing squad. Whilst lined up, we were saved by the arrival of the White Army.

Then followed a chase across Russia. A steamer to Tobolsk and from there a train to Omsk and another to Tomsk. Travel was difficult and diseases were rife. The ground was too hard to bury the dead. Father converted his money to sweets, as currency had little value, and was able to obtain tickets on a US Red Cross train. Fighting broke out in Tomsk, the school was torched and all the children and teachers killed. We eventually caught the train and left for Irkutsk. From there we caught the Trans-Siberian railway to Vladivostock where we stayed for some time.

With the Bolsheviks at the gates, the British Consulate evacuated the British. Our heads were shaved, clothes burned and bodies bathed in carbolic, which says something about our personal hygiene! The journey by ship to England took 8 months and when we landed were totally destitute.

Later I became a civil engineer working on the Earls Court Exhibition Centre and was later employed by the army.

James Wardropper gave this account of his early life and escape from the Bolsheviks to the author in September 1987.

Despite the existence of c.10-20 million bonds, only one million were submitted under the 1986 Settlement. The vast majority of outstanding bonds were held outside the UK but those that were handed in were mainly sterling issues used to finance railways and cities. Some of those issues were small at the outset and the settlement led to a significant increase in rarity of those remaining. The table below illustrates the impact on a few of these issues:

Some of the Russian Bonds submitted for Settlement in 1986

Description	Denomination	Number Issued	Number Submitted	Max Remaining*
Cities				
Baku 1910	£20	71,432	6,519	64,913
Baku 1910	£100	12,860	4,519	8,341
Baku 1910	£500	285	87	198
Kiev XXII 1914	£20	6,558	964	5,594
Nicolaiev 2nd issue	£20	401	77	324
Kiev XXII 1914	£500	262	33	229
St Petersburg 1913	£100	14,500	4,506	9,994
Moscow 1912	£20	50,001	19,570	30,431
Railways				
Consolidated 2nd Series 1889	Rbl 125	771,319	70,548	700,771
Eisk 1909	Rbl 500		17	
Kahetian 1912	£500	300	57	243
Moscow Smolensk	Th 1000	2,400	155	2,245
Black Sea Kuban 1913	£500	400	79	321
Triotzk 1913	£100	18,000	8,354	9,646
Wolmar 1910	£20		518	
South Eastern 1914	£100	19,363	9,370	9,993
State Loans				
1909 4.5%	Frs 500		104,264	
1894 Gold Loan 4%	Rbl 125		8,373	

Figures only take account of the settlement and do not reflect prior redemptions or loss.

Source: Price Waterhouse analysis of bonds received under the foreign compensation order 1986.

This section has looked at the paper generated by governments in their never ending quest to raise funds for infrastructure, war or simply balance of payments. In Part 3, attention turns to the individuals who did so much to finance their projects, each of which has had a major impact on our modern world.

THE FAMOUS ...

and

... THE 'INFAMOUS'

Over the years many people have been involved in finance. Some are better known than others, eventhough in their time they may have been headline news. Not all did good works, indeed many did the opposite and were branded fraudsters, but their activities, good and bad, have helped shape world finance. The fact that many of these names are captured on early share certificates, sometimes with an original signature, helps bring their stories to life. This section looks at a few of the famous and infamous, grouping them by subject (such as mining), their inventions (such as cycles) and their reputations (such as they were).

Entrepreneurs & Inventors

Edouard Empain

Born in 1852 Empain became one of Belgium's greatest entrepreneurs, ultimately involved in a vast number of companies. Having started life as a draughtsman, by the time he was 29, he was a director of La Mettallurgique and was on track to founding his own companies.

He had the idea of a 'secondary' railway network linking the small towns with the main railways, an idea which led to his interest in the construction of power stations, tramways and the chemical industry. He established his own bank (Banque E.L.J. Empain) and on its

One of Empain's early companies, Tramways Electriques de Gand. This bearer share is dated 1930 well after the company's formation in 1898.

conversion into a public company in 1919 became the main shareholder. Empain's European tram empire included *Tramways Bruxellois* (1899) and *Tramways Electriques de Gand* (1898), but he established many more companies in France including the *Compagnie du Metropolitain de Paris*, which built the first line of the Paris Metro.

However, his interests were not limited to Europe. In the Belgian Congo he developed the railway connecting Stanleyville with Lakes Albert and Tanganyika. The concession granted by King Leopold II gave him the rights to 4 million hectares thus opening the way to mining companies such as *Co. Miniere des Grands Lacs Africains* and the holding company *Auxilacs.* Between 1895 and 1908 The Congo was the personal property of King Leopold. It was rich in resources, particularly rubber. The inhabitants were treated despicably and during his tenure the population declined by some 10 million. It was eventually bought from Leopold for £2 million in 1908 by the Belgian Government.

In Egypt Empain initially focused on tramways and having been awarded the concession in 1894 he strengthened his involvement by co-operating with his main rival, the Societe des CDF Economiques, and creating the S.A. des Tramways du Caire a year later. The company was successful, building over 50kms of track by 1930 and raising profits from Frs.500,000 in 1897 to Frs.54.3 million in 1928. Several other companies were established, not all

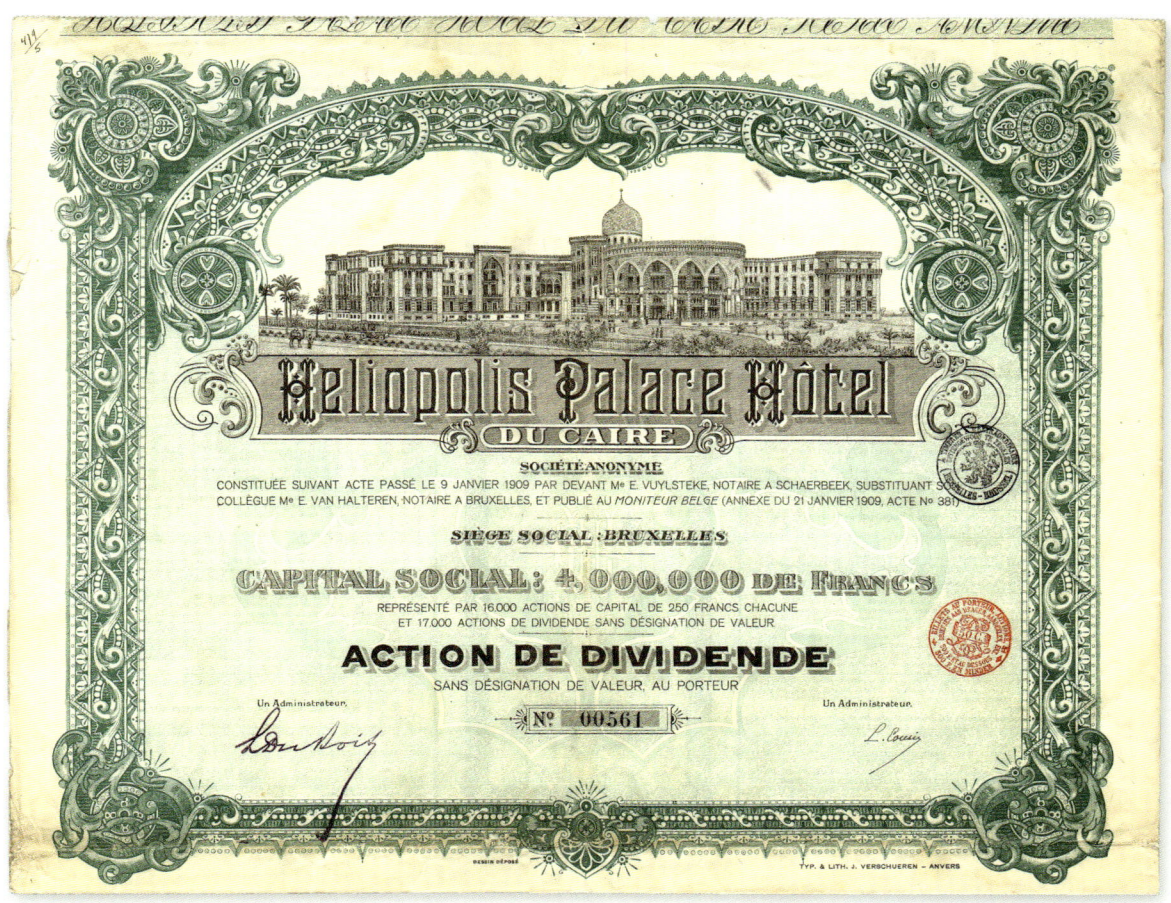

An 'action de dividende' entitled the owner to dividends but had no capital or voting rights. This example depicts the 400 room Heliopolis Palace Hotel and was issued in 1909. Signed on the right by Louis Cousin, Company Administrator and Professor at the Universities of Louvain and Santiago, Chile.

were successful but many names will be familiar to collectors of Egyptian material, for example CDF de Basse-Egypte, a railway from Mansourah to Materieh which was completed in only two years.

The Egyptian Mail Steamship Company (see Part 7) targeted the growing tourist industry and provided a service for those travelling from Marseilles to Cairo. The economic crisis of 1907 led to its downfall a year later (but not before producing some very attractive bearer share certificates engraved by Waterlow). One of his

more interesting ventures was the construction of the Heliopolis Palace Hotel 1908-10. This grand structure close to the Heliopolis Sporting Club attracted Kings and captains of industry including Milton S Hershey (chocolatier), the King of Belgium (Leopold II) and J P Morgan. Its days as a grand stop-over came to an end in the 1st and 2nd World Wars when it was used as a hospital. After the wars it was unable to compete with modern hotels and for a while became government offices until President Mubarak gave it a facelift and made it his Presidential Palace.

Tramways de Taschkent. One of Empain's many tramway companies, this one in Russia.

Empain's involvement in China was not a success. Various concessions were granted and in 1927 the Compagnie Generale de CDF et de Tramways en Chine was formed but local problems, world wars and internal civil wars all contributed to his dissatisfaction and total exit from Chinese project finance.

In 1900 Belgium was the world's largest investor in Russia. Empain could not risk not being there and established several tramway companies, the most notable being:

- Tramways de Kischinew (1895);
- Tramways d'Astrakhan (1896); and
- Tramways de Taschkent (1897).

All in all, Empain was one of the most successful and wide-ranging company promoters of his time. What ultimately remained of his companies was taken over by Paribas Group in 1981 - but there is one more twist to the tale and that concerns the kidnapping of his grandson in 1978.

In 1969 The Empain family gained control of Schneider (nowadays, Schneider Electric) and Baron Edouard Empain's grandson, Baron Edouard-Jean Empain took control. Empain Jnr was kidnapped in 1978 on Paris's Avenue Foch. The kidnappers demanded Euro 12 million emphasising their request by accompanying it with the Baron's little finger and a promise of more to come. Eventually, the police got their man and the Baron was released but his marriage did not survive and nor did his job (in fact Schneider seemed quite glad to be rid of him). The news media had highlighted the Baron's debt problems and his interest in pretty women, neither of which helped his marriage. He left the country and backpacked around the States before eventually returning.

Wells and Fargo

Of all the internationally well known signatures to be found on early share certificates, those of Henry Wells and William Fargo stand out. To many, these two people and the business they created are synonymous with the opening up of the American West.

Prior to the establishment of the 'express companies', packages and money were largely carried by friends or concealed in the hats of the stagecoach drivers. The situation became even more difficult with the demise of the second Bank of the United States, which had at least provided a secure messenger service. The subsequent lack of such a facility meant that banks incurred high costs for transporting financial instruments. The first person to recognize the commercial opportunities was William F Harnden and in 1839 he formed Harnden's Package Express based at 20 Wall Street. The company lost money until Harnden made a deal with Daniel Drew who offered him a free pass on his boats in exchange for publicity.

Henry Wells, an ex school teacher at an institution to cure speech defects and son of a pastor, learnt the express business under Harnden. In 1841 he joined forces with George E Pomeroy and Crawford Livingston of New York to form Pomeroy & Co., which not only carried valuables and currency but, for a while, even oysters (at $3 per 100) and mail. The business was centred on Buffalo. Wells, as the company's manager, shipping agent, carrier and messenger, made the first trip and many subsequently.

In 1842 Wells met and hired William George Fargo as a messenger and shortly afterwards they formed a partnership running an express line from Buffalo to Detroit. Although each went their separate ways for a time, Wells, Fargo and

Early American Express Company certificate dated 1858 and handsigned by Wells, Fargo and Holland.

Livingston eventually controlled all the express traffic in New York State. But it was at about this time that John Butterfield entered the fray. Already a wealthy stagecoach owner, Butterfield put up a strong fight to wrest the business away from our intrepid three. Eventually peace was established and they agreed to merge ('The Treaty of Buffalo"). The resultant organization was complex and relationships were not exactly friendly. Much of the competition joined forces and on 18th March 1850 American Express was formed as an "unincorporated joint-stock association" with a limited life of ten years. Butterfield owned 225 shares and Wells and Fargo about 100 each. Boardroom rows continued unabated and in 1853 the shares were offered to the public with the proviso that shares could not be sold to "married women, infants or irresponsible persons".

American Express set up many agreements with the railroad and packet companies. Wells was appointed President at an annual salary of $1,250 and in its first four months, the company earned enough to pay a 10% dividend. In 1852 Wells and Fargo wanted to expand operations to California and cash in on the gold rush but other directors opposed the idea. As a result, a new offshoot was created, The Wells Fargo Company, which became the leading express company in the West. Another equally famous off-shoot, The Overland Mail, was set up by Butterfield, running stage coaches from St.Louis to San Francisco.

By 1854 American Express had increased its capital to $750,000. Business developed fast and their messengers covered 15,000 miles a day. Headquarters were established in New York and a spur track from the Hudson River Railroad Company ran right into the ground floor permitting direct loading and unloading. After expiry of its first ten years and in accordance with the original agreement, the company was dissolved and its assets auctioned off. Existing shareholders bid for them at a cost of $600,000. In 1867 a major competitor was formed by a group of wealthy businessmen known as the 'Merchants Union Express Company'. A price war resulted in both companies making substantial losses and forced a merger. The new company was known as the American Merchants Union Express Company. Wells was replaced as president by Fargo although his younger brother, J C Fargo handled most of the detail and became President in 1881. The company name was changed back to American Express in 1873.

The development of American Express is depicted by the share certificates of which at least ten different designs have been identified. Many are handsigned by the famous pioneers.

Thomas Edison

One of the true inventors of the period, Thomas Alva Edison was not motivated by financial gain, unlike many of his contemporaries.

Born in 1847 in Milan, Ohio, Edison was not a natural scholar and was largely home taught by his mother. But he had a scientific leaning and designed a stock ticker in 1869. He failed to secure a patent as the machine was too similar to that developed by Samuel S Laws and he moved to New York to work for Laws, sleeping on the floor of the battery room of the Gold Indicator Company. The company issued gold prices to brokers but on one occasion it failed and in Laws' absence, Edison fixed the problem preventing a riot in the process. Laws was impressed and put him in charge of the whole operation with a salary of $300 a month. After leaving Laws he linked up with Franklin Pope and James Ashley setting up Pope, Edison and Company, providing telegraph lines and complex equipment. This company was taken over by the Gold & Stock Telegraph Company whose president, General Marshall Lefferts paid Edison $40,000 for rights to some of his inventions, a huge sum at that time. With the money, Edison continued to work on stock tickers and before long his product was being used in both the United States and the United Kingdom.

Stock certificate dated 1899 in the Edison Portland Cement Company made out to Thomas Edson and signed by him on the counterfoil.

In 1876 he moved to Menlo Park, New Jersey, and produced some of his most successful inventions including the phonograph, the alkaline storage battery and improvements to Alexander Graham Bell's telephone (perhaps even more remarkable in view of Edison's own hearing defect). But it was the phonograph for which he became most well known, that and the circuit permitting the connection of electric lights in parallel. To help him develop the latter, the work was sponsored by a syndicate led by J P Morgan and the Vanderbilts under the banner of the Edison Electric Light Company. Successful tests, first on a passenger steamer and ultimately at London's Crystal Palace established Edison as one of the world's greatest inventors.

In 1887 he moved again, this time to West Orange, New Jersey where he produced a string of inventions for the Edison General Electric Company. A company that eventually merged with the Thomson- Houston Company to form General Electric, now one of the largest companies in the United States.

By the mid 1890s' Edison had largely sold off his interest in General Electric and despite continuing to work well into his 80s' died in 1931, one of the most celebrated inventors of all time. Over his lifetime, he amassed over 1,000 patents.

Rogues Gallery

Inevitably, there are numerous tales of fraud in the financial world. Today we can smile but at the time many ordinary people lost their savings and future as a result of the activities of a relatively small group of criminals solely motivated by greed. Many of the frauds perpetrated then have been repeated time and time again. Here are just a few.

John Law

John's father, William, was a goldsmith and assay master for the city of Edinburgh responsible for the testing and hallmarking of silver and gold objects made in the city. In 1675 he was appointed Dean of the Goldsmiths of Edinburgh and, on the side, flourished as a money-lender. He bought Lauriston Castle overlooking the Firth of Forth but in the end died from gall stones in Paris. He left ample funds for the upbringing of his family and son John (1671-1729) who soon demonstrated a natural aptitude for mathematics, womanizing, sport and gambling (not necessarily at the same time). John eventually moved to London where he perfected his gambling techniques, which unfortunately resulted in a dual at which he killed his opponent.

Law was tried and sentenced to death. Despite earnest attempts to persuade King William to intervene, he was held at the King's Bench prison awaiting the noose, until effecting his escape with the connivance of friends. Travelling through Europe, he accumulated a fortune gambling, eventually returning to Scotland where he put forward a proposal to restore the country's finances. It was rejected. He returned to mainland Europe and significantly added to his wealth settling in The Hague. His attempts to persuade Louis XIV to follow his advice were rebutted but with the assistance of his friend, the Duc d'Orleans, he moved to Paris and on the death of Louis, Orleans became regent for the young Dauphin and Law's path was cleared.

With the help of Orleans, Law soon established himself as a man of influence arriving at a time when France was largely bankrupt. The country's debts amounted to 2 billion livres (about £1 billion) and the tax system was corrupt. Law proposed a state bank in the

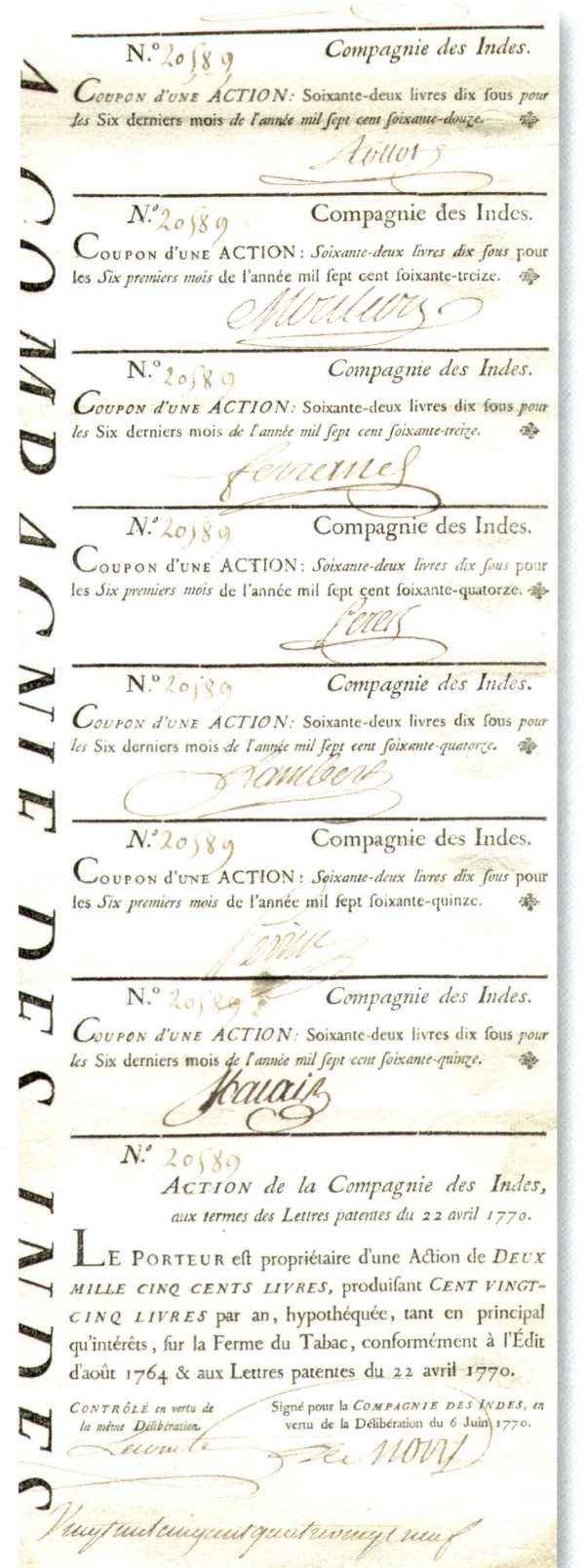

King's name which would issue paper money backed by coins – the scheme was rejected. But in 1716 Law got his own bank charter for *Banque Generale* which, two years later, as *Banque Royale*, received the royal seal of approval and effectively became the country's first Central Bank. In the following year he gained exclusive rights to exploit France's colonies through a commercial company, *Compagnie d'Occident*. Law became 'collector of taxes' and 'controller of the Royal Mint' as well as holder of the tobacco monopoly and manager of the African slave trade. On a more personal front he gained exclusive rights to develop France's interests in Louisiana through the *Mississippi Company*. He encouraged immigration but, rather like Darien, the environment was hostile with local illnesses and imported venereal disease carried by the accompanying French girls. Despite these minor problems, its share price shot up from 500 Livres to 18,000 Livres making many millionaires in the process. However, hopes of discovery of gold and silver came to nought and the venture collapsed causing a major financial crisis with French investment re-focussing on London's South Sea Company. Law was forced to emigrate as his empire crashed around him. Some believed the Revolution was a direct result of his financial excesses and by the end of the eighteenth century France was again on the verge of bankruptcy.

John Law died in Venice in 1729.

The Cie des Indes followed the Mississippi Company and derived its income from tobacco. The bearer share and coupons shown is dated 1770 (although the company was wound up a year earlier).

Baron Grant

Born Abraham Gottheimer in Dublin 1831, he changed his name to Albert Grant. By the time he was 28 he was already establishing companies with short life spans and huge financial benefits to him as promoter. His targets were small speculators, such as clergymen, widows and retired army officers. Grant's first failure was the Mercantile Discount Company, which collapsed in 1861 and had absolutely nothing to do with discounting. Credit Foncier & Mobilier of England (also known as the International

Land Company) was his prime vehicle and on whose board sat Lord Cranbourne (later Prime Minister, as Marquess of Salisbury). The company was involved in Millwall Docks, various railways and the construction of the Galleria Vittorio Emanuele, for which he was granted a baronetcy from the Italian King. In 1865 he was appointed a British Member of Parliament and again in 1874, although by that time accusations of bribery and corruption were rife.

By 1870 his wealth was said to exceed £20 million and despite some of his investments failing, such as Lisbon Steam Tramways, he was constantly seeking new opportunities. One of these was his purchase of Leicester Fields, re-naming it Leicester Square and gifting it to the City of London. The square still has a Shakespearean statue with an inscription flagging Grants largesse (see opposite).

However, failure was never far away and his promotion of the Emma Silver Mine of Utah was the final straw. The US Ambassador to Britain was on the Board, for which he received $50,000 and the Editor of the Financial Times actively promoted the venture. Both lost their jobs and reputations as it turned out the mine was exhausted and the one million shares sold to investors were worthless.

Grant died a bankrupt in 1899 and everything he owned was sold to pay his debts.

The inscription on Shakespeare's statue indicating Baron Grant's gift of Leicester Square to the city of London.

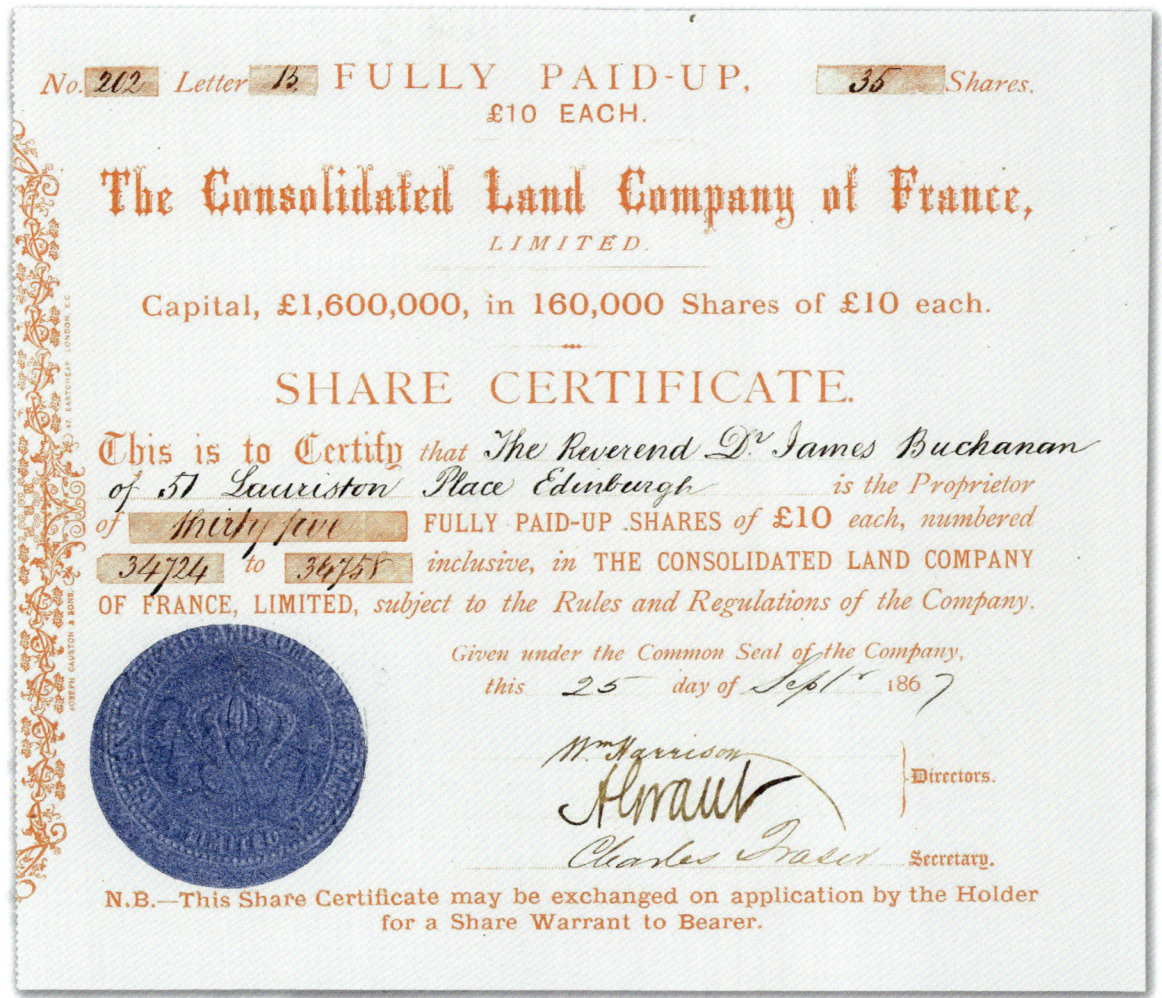

A rare example of Albert Grant's signature on this share in the Consolidated Land Company of France dated 1867.

Samuel Insull

Insull was born in England in 1859 and at the age of 21 was recruited as Thomas Edison's private secretary in the United States. He was soon appointed Vice President of the Edison General Electric Company and was responsible for the company's rapid growth both in terms of its number of employees and turnover. In 1892 it merged with its leading competitor to form the General Electric Company, a merger engineered

by J P Morgan. Insull was not a fan and left to become president of the Chicago Edison Company which specialized in power stations rather than equipment manufacture.

His company was soon the sole supplier of electricity to Chicago, a service which was gradually extended to cover the whole State of Illinois. By 1917 his company's assets exceeded $175 million. Further expansion was delayed by the war but as chairman of the Illinois State

One of many companies controlled by Samuel Insull, the Louisville & Northern Railway & Lighting Company stock certificate illustrated here is signed by him as President and issued to M E Cooley. Cooley, an ex naval officer, became Professor of Mechanical Engineering at the University of Michigan and subsequently Dean of the college

Council of Defense, Insull learned financing techniques which would ultimately allow him to greatly expand his empire. By 1930 the asset value of his companies exceeded $2 billion.

But greed took over. He created a pyramidical organization which was so complex that its structure was not fully understood for years. Cracks began to appear and when these combined with the 1929 crash, the company's downfall was inevitable. Arrest warrants for Insull, his son, Samuel Insull Jr., and brother, Martin were issued. Samuel Sr. left the country

and so set in motion a worldwide chase by the Federal Authorities who eventually tracked him down in Istanbul. He was taken back and tried yet despite one of the most complicated trials on record, he was surprisingly found not guilty. Investors are reputed to have lost nearly $800 million.

Samuel Insull died in Paris in 1938. His son eventually became president of his own insurance company, the Insull Insurance Agency.

Kreuger & Toll

The first "Ponzi Scheme" (named after Charles Ponzi) is recorded in 1919 but perhaps the most famous recent example was that of Bernie Madoff whose scheme netted losses of some $65 million and resulted in Madoff being sentenced to 150 years in prison in 2009. Kreuger & Toll was regarded as an earlier perpetrator of the crime but before outlining that case, an explanation of what a Ponzi Scheme is may be useful. Readers can then be left to their own thoughts on whether it is reasonable to believe the crime only started in 1919. Many of the tales recounted in this book would suggest a much longer heritage.

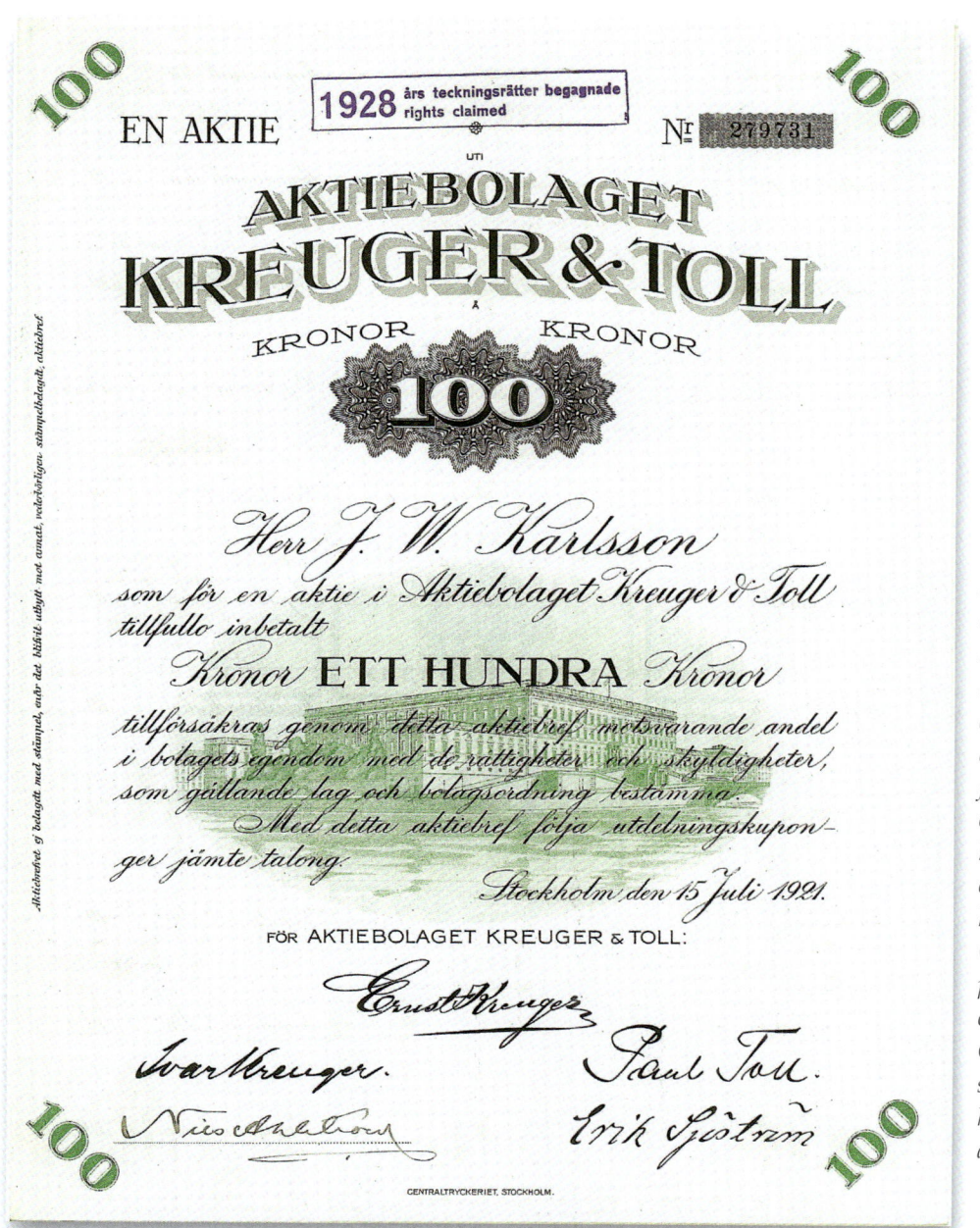

Share certificate dated 1921 and hand-signed by both Kreuger and Toll. It was quite normal for Swedish companies to have their share certificates hand signed (rather than printed) by two of its directors. Original signatures of the key protagonists are rare.

In its simplest form, a Ponzi scheme involves new money being raised purely to pay returns to existing investors. The actual business is unable to make the necessary profits to meet promised returns and as a result, it repeatedly raises more money from the public. All is fine until the music stops (that is, when the company runs out of new investors).

So, back to our friends Ivor Kreuger and Paul Toll. Kreuger & Toll was founded as a construction company in 1908. At the outset it was a kind of mini conglomerate but in 1923, Kreuger also set up the holding company International Match Corporation ("IMCO"). The Kreuger Empire became so big that in 1930 it accounted for 64% of trades on the Stockholm stock exchange. Following the First World War, European governments were cash starved and Kreuger & Toll offered loans of up to $125 million to governments in return for the exclusive right to sell matches in their countries. Resulting monopolies in 19 countries secured the company's business.

But, back to Ponzi's. Insufficient profits were made by Kreuger & Toll to pay a 'guaranteed' 20% return to investors. So dividends came out of new capital and loans, and when these dried up, disaster struck. Kreuger shot himself in Paris in 1932.

The activities of Kreuger & Toll resulted in numerous changes to US company law, in particular, the need to publish audited financial statements prior to selling securities to the general public.

Despite being famous for its match monopoly, the company had many profitable arms, owning banks, property, a mine and pulp companies, many of which have survived to this day. John Kenneth Galbraith described Kreuger as the "Leonardo of larcenists".

Clarence Hatry

Born in Belsize Park, London in 1888 to a wealthy silk merchant and a French mother, Hatry was deprived of his education following the early death of his father. Being unable to run the family company due to illness, the company failed and Hatry was made a bankrupt but within 2 years had paid off its debts.

His first business venture was as an insurance broker and his first financial "killing" was the acquisition of City Equitable Fire Insurance Company Limited from its German owners for £60,000, then turning it round and on-selling for a near £200,000 profit. From then on his focus was on reconstruction and consolidation. Some ventures were successful, others were far from it. A few are listed below:

- Amalgamated Industrials Ltd.
- Jute Industries Ltd.
- British Glass Industries Ltd.
- Commercial Banking Corporation of London, and
- Drapery & General Investment Trust Ltd., (successfully sold to Debenhams).

These were supplemented by Photomoton Parent Corporation Ltd., Associated Machines Corporation and a raft of London bus companies which eventually formed the basis of London Transport.

During this manic period, Hatry lived in style, owning houses in London's Mayfair and the largest yacht in Britain. His collapse largely came from his obsession with acquiring and consolidating the major steel companies of United Steel and United Strip & Bar Mills. His early backers backtracked and in order to raise the necessary funds he resorted to a complex fraud involving the issuing of stocks twice. This

The Commercial Bank of London, one of Hatry's ventures which eventually failed. The share certificate bears a facsimile signature of Hatry

improper activity combined with the crash of 1929 led to his downfall with debts of some £14 million. The presiding judge commented that Hatry stood convicted of "the most appalling frauds that have ever disfigured the commercial reputation of this country" (The Times 25 January 1930). He was sentenced to 14 years but after 9 was released from Brixton prison thanks to his influential friends. Those 9 years involved hard labour, sleeping on bare boards and crushing rocks.

On release, he moved to Europe until the outbreak of war. On his return he acquired Hatchards bookshop and by 1950 the business was reputed to be making substantial profits. He continued to follow his philosophy of reconstruction and consolidation well into the 1960s' indeed until his death in 1965. Despite the fortunes made, his final estate only totaled £828.

Alfred Loewenstein

Despite being one of the world's richest men at his peak, the most fascinating part of Loewenstein's life was his death. Did he kill himself, was he murdered or did he fake death in order to live a new life?

Born in Brussels in 1877, Loewenstein was only 21 when he started his first business venture. Within a year he co-founded a company which built Belgium's earliest power stations. He later teamed up with Sir William Mackenzie and Fred Stark Pearson to build electric tramways across the world. Loewenstein raised the necessary funds for these Canadian registered companies, the principal of which were the Barcelona Traction, Light & Power Co., and the Brazilian Traction Light & Power Co.. During the First World War he established Societe Internationale d'Energie Hydro-Electrique (SIDRO) and after the war became the leading name in the artificial silk industry. At the peak of his career he owned a castle in Brussels and eight villas in France. He frequently travelled across the Atlantic invariably preceded by a huge press entourage. However, a riding accident resulted in a tendency to behave in an eccentric manner and failure to take over the Banque de Bruxelles was the beginning of his financial demise. His business activities were often considered border-line and no financial chicanery was too extreme for our intrepid entrepreneur!

On 4th July 1928 he took off from Croydon airport (the precursor to Heathrow) accompanied by six of his staff. Whilst the aircraft was airborne he visited the toilet in which was an external door. After a while, a staff member checked to make sure he was all right, but there was no response only the noise of the door flapping in the wind. His body was found two weeks later in the sea off Calais and he was buried in an unmarked grave in Brussels. An inquest ruled accidental death but many questions remained unanswered. Although his wife met the plane on landing, she did not attend the funeral.

Loewenstein's death led to a panic sell-off of shares in his enterprises but despite rumours to the contrary his affairs were generally found to be sound, indeed SIDRO was still trading in the 1970s'. Interestingly, his son retained his valet, whom 4 years later was found dead with a gun in his hand.

We will never know what really happened!

Whittaker Wright

Born in England in 1845, Wright became a millionaire in record time. At the age of 21 he went to the United States and was a key player in the mining boom of Colorado but his American exploits ended with the collapse of the Gunnison Iron & Coal Co., which prompted a hasty return to London in 1889.

Back in England, he turned his attention to floating mining ventures on the stock market. Early successes were the West Australian Exploring & Finance Corporation and the London & Globe Co., two holding companies, which he amalgamated into the London & Globe Finance Corporation Limited in 1897 appointing the Marquess of Dufferin as its Chairman and a raft of the aristocracy as its other directors. Company promotions continued unabated. First up was the re-floatation of the Ivanhoe Gold Mine in London followed by the British & American Corporation, both in 1897; the latter was formed to acquire London & Globe's mining rights in British Columbia and the Yukon. Numerous other (often dubious) mining companies followed including the

A bond for the Barcelona Traction Light & Power Company, dated 1911 and engraved by Waterlow. Bears the printed signature of Loewenstein's partner, Fred Stark Pearson.

London & Globe Finance Corporation share dated 1899. Key holding company established by Whittaker Wright whose facsimile signature can be seen bottom right.

Nickel Corporation, Caledonia Copper and Rossland Great Western.

In 1900 one of London & Globe's directors, Lord Loch (former High Commissioner of South Africa) encouraged the company to finance London's underground Bakerloo Line.

Whilst other businesses were in full swing his three major vehicles, London & Globe, British & American and Standard Exploration proceeded to buy one another's shares in what can only be termed a gigantic ramp. Not all went to plan and losses hurt many small shareholders. Deficits were concealed and in 1903 Wright fled first to Paris and then to New York from where he was extradicted. At his trial, the prosecution demonstrated that the 1899 and 1900 accounts of London & Globe were seriously inaccurate and he was sentenced to seven years imprisonment. He met with his lawyer, gave him his watch and swallowed cyanide.

Jabez Spencer Balfour

Born in London in 1843, Spencer Balfour, as he preferred to be known, was educated in Europe and started his working life as a parliamentary agent. His mother was a Nonconformist temperance campaigner, something which Balfour used to his advantage in later life.

When only 25, Balfour and his associates took over the Liberator Building Society, whose investors were mostly Nonconformists. He sourced customers, board members and deposits from the Nonconformist and temperance circles encouraging ministers to praise the benefits of investing in his Society.

Church halls became effective branches where he and colleagues preached the benefits of thrift and housing. By 1879 the Liberator had become the largest building society in the country whilst at the same time, Balfour had accumulated 14 directorships as well as being appointed a Magistrate, the Mayor of Croydon and Liberal MP for Tamworth (and later Burnley).

In order to overcome restrictions placed on building societies preventing them from carrying out building projects, he set up the Lands Allotment Company in 1867 and provided Liberator customers with mortgages to enable them to purchase that company's newly built houses. In 1882 he formed the London

Share certificate in Liberator Permanent Building Society signed by Spencer Balfour and dated 1879

& General Bank and two years later acquired the construction company J W Hobbs & Co. Ltd., under the name of the Building Securities Company. During this time he constructed the Hyde Park Hotel and Whitehall Court. The latter now houses the National Liberal Club at one end and residential housing at the other – once home of several famous faces including George Bernard Shaw, H G Wells and Stafford Cripps, it was also used as the headquarters of M16 at the end of the First World War.

Balfour's various companies became a complex financial web but provided the Liberator continued to grow, nothing appeared remiss. However, with the collapse of the London & General Bank, things began to unfold. Complex accounting fraud, such as one company boosting another when its audit came round, led to two of his associates, Hobbs and Wright, being arrested. Balfour headed off to Argentina from where he was extradited, tried and sentenced to 14 years, of which he served 11, mostly in Parkhurst prison where he was both librarian and organist. Thousands of Liberator depositors lost their life's savings and many feared the workhouse as the their only place of retirement. On release he travelled the world seeking employment and finally died of a heart attack on the London to Fishguard express in 1916.

As with all such frauds, some good came out of the Liberator crash. Building society reform followed with the 1894 Act and relief funds were set up for the deprived depositors – at least until the beginnings of the 1st World War. Nevertheless it was a sad episode of financial history.

It would be a gross exaggeration to say that this section has covered all the 'famous and infamous' characters who did so much to create the framework for today's business environment. But hopefully, the 'sample' will encourage collectors to look twice at names on certificates.

Part 4 _____

"BIG DEALS!"

Many historical events are reflected in bonds and shares. Some were of huge importance, others were less so but at the time had devastating consequences. Several have already been referred to, such as the building of the railways or the development of banking, but this section highlights a few more which have left their mark on today's world. Although these may pre-date the period principally covered by this book, their stories are relevant to financial history and in many cases tie the political and military events of the time to the world of finance. Lets take a quick look at:

- The South Sea Bubble;
- The East India Companies;
- De Lesseps and his Canals; and
- The Spanish Royal Trading Companies

The South Sea "Bubble"

For those who find modern financial chicanery easy to understand the South Sea Bubble will pose no problem; for the rest, indeed the majority, that may not be the case. In many respects the antics of Robert Harley and his company reflect the worst excesses of financial skullduggery. As it is of major significance and known, by name at least, to all those who were at school in the 50s' and 60s' lets try and make some sense of it.

Founded by Robert Harley, Earl of Oxford, in 1711, the company was promised a monopoly on all trade to the Spanish colonies in South America in return for taking over the UK's National Debt. The full name of the company was *"The Governour and Company of Merchants of Great-Britain Trading to the South Seas and other Parts of America, and for Encouraging the Fishery"*, but known more commonly as "The South Sea Company". A large part of the National Debt was made up of annuities known as 'irredeemables' and, as their name implies, the government was unable to do anything with them to reduce their liability. The only option was to encourage holders to transfer into an alternative investment.

Between 1711 and 1719, the Government exchanged over £11.8 million of annuities for South Sea Company shares, which left the Company having to find ways of compensating the new shareholders with dividends. The idea was that the Company would generate profits from trade but with the Spanish wars still going strong this was not an easy task. The Company had hoped to win the contract to supply slaves to the Spanish colonies but various wars put their plans on hold and the Directors concluded that the only way they could generate sufficient profits

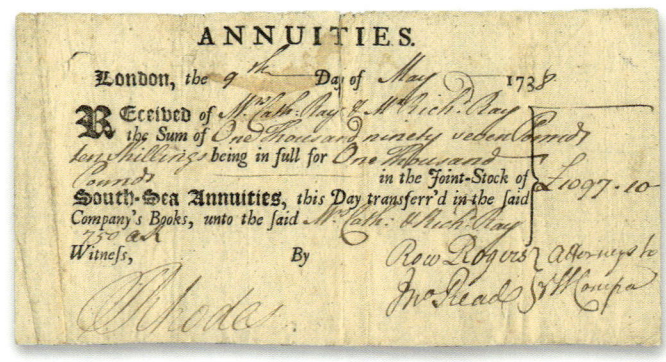

An inscribed stock receipt of the South Sea Company for £1000 dated 1738

would be to ramp the Company's share price so that the 'cost' of the annuities/National Debt acquired from the British Government would be less in real terms.

In January 1720, South Sea stock was trading at £128 but bolstered by Company claims of success and dubious tales of south sea riches, it rose to £330 within 3 months. By May, it hit £550 and with the granting of its Royal Charter, it reached a peak of £1,050.

However, a sudden realisation that the Company was not going to achieve its stated objectives resulted in the price collapsing to less than £100 - the bubble was burst.

Following subsequent investigations in 1721, "a web of deceit, corruption and bribery" (Harvard Business School) was uncovered leading to the prosecution of several company and government officials. Thereafter, with the cessation of Spanish hostilities, the Company resumed its original objectives of supplying slaves and establishing trading links. Amongst other things it supplied silver to the Royal Mint and entered the whaling business. Disputes with Spain continued but by 1750 the initial venture was wound up although the Company itself continued as a financial corporation until 1856.

Collectors of South Sea material will generally only find powers of attorney, inscribed stock receipts for transfer of annuities, or shares. Share certificates of the South Sea Company entitling the owner to shares in particular voyages have never been seen. Shareholders were recorded in the company's register and evidence of their holding is often only apparent from receipts.

The East India Companies

The East Indies proved to be a magnet for European trading nations anxious to acquire the silks and spices of the Indian subcontinent. Although trade was the prime motivator, the Portuguese and Spanish were keen to spread Christianity and whilst the former were led by the Jesuits, the Spanish expeditions were joined by Franciscan and Dominican missionaries. By the end of the 1500s' over 200,000 Japanese had been converted and the 'new' states of Goa and Macao were largely Christianised. The Portuguese, with one hundred years experience, tended to dominate trade between Europe and the Far East often working with the Dutch, at least until the Portuguese army was itself largely destroyed in a failed attempt to wrest Morocco from the Spanish in 1578. The expertise gained by the Dutch from their association with their erstwhile partners resulted in the formation of the *United East India Company,* or *Vereenigde Oostindische Compagnie* ("VOC") in 1602.

The Dutch were not alone in seeking trade with the Far East. In 1600 the *Company of Merchants of London trading into the East Indies* (the "East India Company")

was formed to allow the British to enter the fray. Founded by Royal Charter from Queen Elizabeth I, the new enterprise had 218 subscribers (shareholders) and was managed by a Governor and 24 Directors. Despite its seemingly grand beginnings, its rival, the VOC, started with ten times as much capital. The English Company was granted a monopoly on all trade in the Asia and Pacific regions. Its shares were held by the wealthy and the government had only indirect control.

The East India Company was not the first royally chartered joint stock company. The Muscovy (or Russian) Company had this honour, being founded in 1555 and was followed by the Levant Company in 1580. The first Governor of the East India Company, Sir Trevor Smythe had previously been governor of both earlier companies and later obtained the charter of the Virginia Company, which founded the colony of Virginia. Until 1657, each voyage of the East India Company was separately funded and on return the profits were divided amongst the shareholders. The first voyage largely turned into a piracy exercise as the goods taken for trade (English cloth) were unsuitable. However, in 1603, the ships brought back a million pounds weight of pepper on which the owners made a

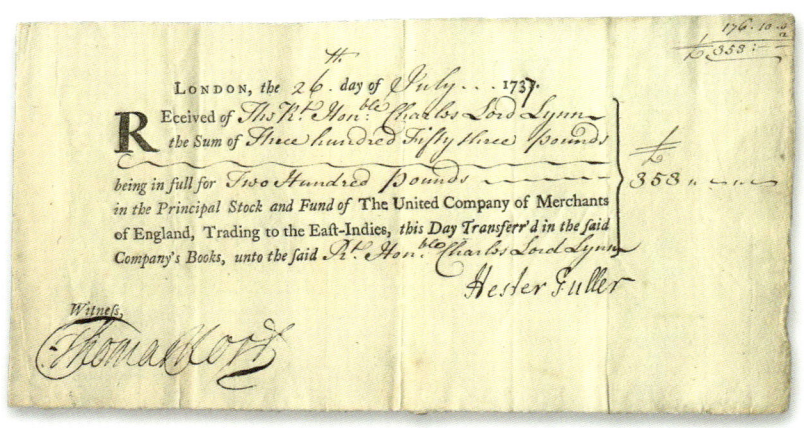

Inscribed stock receipt dated 1737 in the East India Company.

hefty return. Trade was centered on the town of Bantam (which gave its name to the small chickens stocked by sailors for their voyages – a kind of 'packed lunch'…). At its height Bantam was a great international port and its kingdom comprised most of western Java and southern Sumatra. It had existed as a city of the Sundanese kingdom of Pajajaran from the eleventh century. The Dutch later set up camp in 'Batavia' (now, Jakarta), and although the Dutch and English worked together for a time at Batavia, they once again fell out and Britain re-established its own trade centre at Bantam in 1628 (today the town is nothing more than a small port).

By 1621, one in 2,000 of England's population is estimated to have been in the company's service. The original company faced opposition as a monopoly and a rival was set up, into which both companies merged in 1708. The 'new' company, officially entitled the *United Company of Merchants of England trading to the East Indies* (known as the *United Company*) lasted over 150 years until 1873. Its Indian adventure resulted in the Company ruling large areas

of the country and culminated in its control of Bengal in 1757. These activities led to a gradual loss of power and influence with the British Government, which eventually withdrew the Company's commercial monopoly in 1813.

Very few financial papers exist relating to the original English company and evidence of shareholdings are limited. However, some stock receipts do come to light, such as that shown top right dated 1737 and the rare Power of Attorney signed by Horatio Nelson.

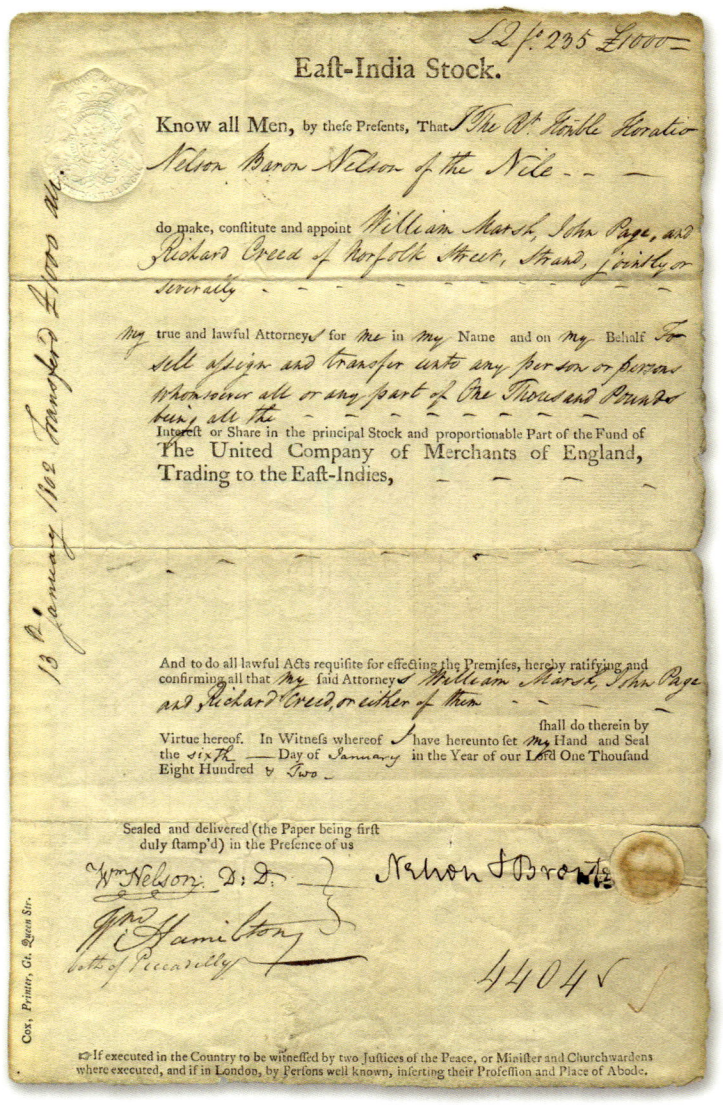

Printed power of attorney for £1000 of East India Stock handsigned by Horatio Nelson (created Duke of Bronte by Ferdinand 1 of Naples) and Sir William Hamilton, husband of Lady Emma Hamilton (Nelson's mistress) as a witness.

De Lesseps and his Canals

Not only did canals generally pre-date railways, being once the main means of transporting goods, they continued to be built well after the railway booms. Three of the most famous are the Suez, Panama and Corinth, all of which were initiated by Ferdinand de Lesseps, although he was successful with only one.

Born into a family of career diplomats in 1805, Viscount de Lesseps spent time as a diplomat in several European and Middle Eastern countries, including Portugal, Spain and Holland but the most significant proved to be Egypt. It was there that he established a friendship with Muhammad Ali, the Turkish viceroy of Egypt and his son, Said Pasha. His diplomatic career came to an end following a failure to reconcile differences between Rome and the French Legislative Assembly. Fortunately his friend Said Pasha, newly appointed viceroy (or 'Khedive') of Egypt invited him back to Egypt to commence work on the Suez canal. The results and financing of the canal are summarized below as are the trials and tribulations of his later venture – the Panama Canal. De Lesseps and his son, Charles, were eventually sentenced to 5 years imprisonment for bribing government officials. De Lesseps avoided imprisonment but died penniless in 1894.

A fine looking certificate relating to the Suez Canal.
This Frs 500 bond is dated 1885.

Suez Canal

Following Napoleon III's abandonment of plans to connect the Mediterranean with the Red Sea via canal, de Lesseps decided to pursue the project and in 1856 pulled together a group of specialist engineers. In 1869 the canal was opened by the Empress Eugenie of France, wife of Napoleon III. Funding came from the Khedive and the French Government as the British initially had no faith in the venture believing it to be an impossible engineering project. However, the Khedive became heavily in debt, a predicament discovered by Lionel de Rothschild in 1875. In view of the ultimate obvious success of the canal, Disraeli asked his friend Lionel to put forward a proposal to acquire the Khedive's 44% holding. The Cabinet agreed the plan and the deal was done for £4 million. Rothschilds profited to the extent of £100,000 but the British taxpayer made considerably more, as the shares rose from £22.5 to £35.

The canal was forcibly nationalised by Nasser during the Suez crisis of 1956, a crisis which resulted in the eventual downfall of British Prime Minister, Sir Anthony Eden.

Early share certificates of the Suez Canal are generally rare, surprising perhaps as most should have been stored in London following the British purchase.

Certificate for one fifth part of a share in the Suez Canal dated 1882. Various shares were issued in respect of the canal, this one is highly decorative with an underprint of the Sphinx.

Panama Canal

Overflowing with confidence after his success with the Suez, de Lesseps, aged 74, turned his attention to Panama. However, this task was not so easy and required construction of numerous locks as well as dealing with the torrential Chagres River and the Culebra Cut. His company, Compagnie Universelle du Canal Inter-Oceanic

de Panama was incorporated in 1881. The first share issue was not a success and subsequent ones only got off the ground with the help of favourable press comment and sizeable bribes. Construction proved too difficult and despite 1.3 billion francs having been raised via shares, bonds and 'lottery issues', the company crashed in 1889. A subsequent investigation turned up all kinds of nasties implicating many politicians and famous

De Lesseps failed to complete the Panama Canal leaving the task to the Americans. Despite that he raised vast sums from French investors. This bearer share for Frs.500 was issued at the outset and bears the printed signature of De Lesseps.

figures. Some 800,000 French investors lost their money.

Completion of the canal was left to the Americans with the first ship (the SS Ancon) passing through in 1914, over 100 years ago. The opening coincided, almost to the day, with the beginnings of the First World War. Construction of the Canal was a major engineering feat that ultimately permitted 65,000 ton ships to be raised 26 metres to a man made lake ("Gatun Lake") via a series of 3 locks and thereafter returned to sea level via two further locks. The Canal knocks almost 3 weeks off the time it takes to get from one side of the continent to the other and contributes a useful $1 billion per year to Panama's piggy bank.

But construction was not easy and it still took ten years and the lives of 28,000 men. Despite being relatively untouched for a century it is now about to be enlarged with new locks permitting much larger ships to pass through.

Corinth Canal

De Lesseps Suez success encouraged construction of yet another famous canal, this time at Corinth. Work began in 1882 but the collapse of the Panama Canal Company also caused the eventual downfall of his Societe Internationale du Canal Maritime de Corinth after 8 years of work. The work was finally completed by a Greek company and opened by the King of Greece in 1893.

Today the canal is too narrow and shallow to be of much commercial value. The steep sides are subject to rock falls and funnel high winds making it largely redundant for uses other than for the benefit of passing tourists.

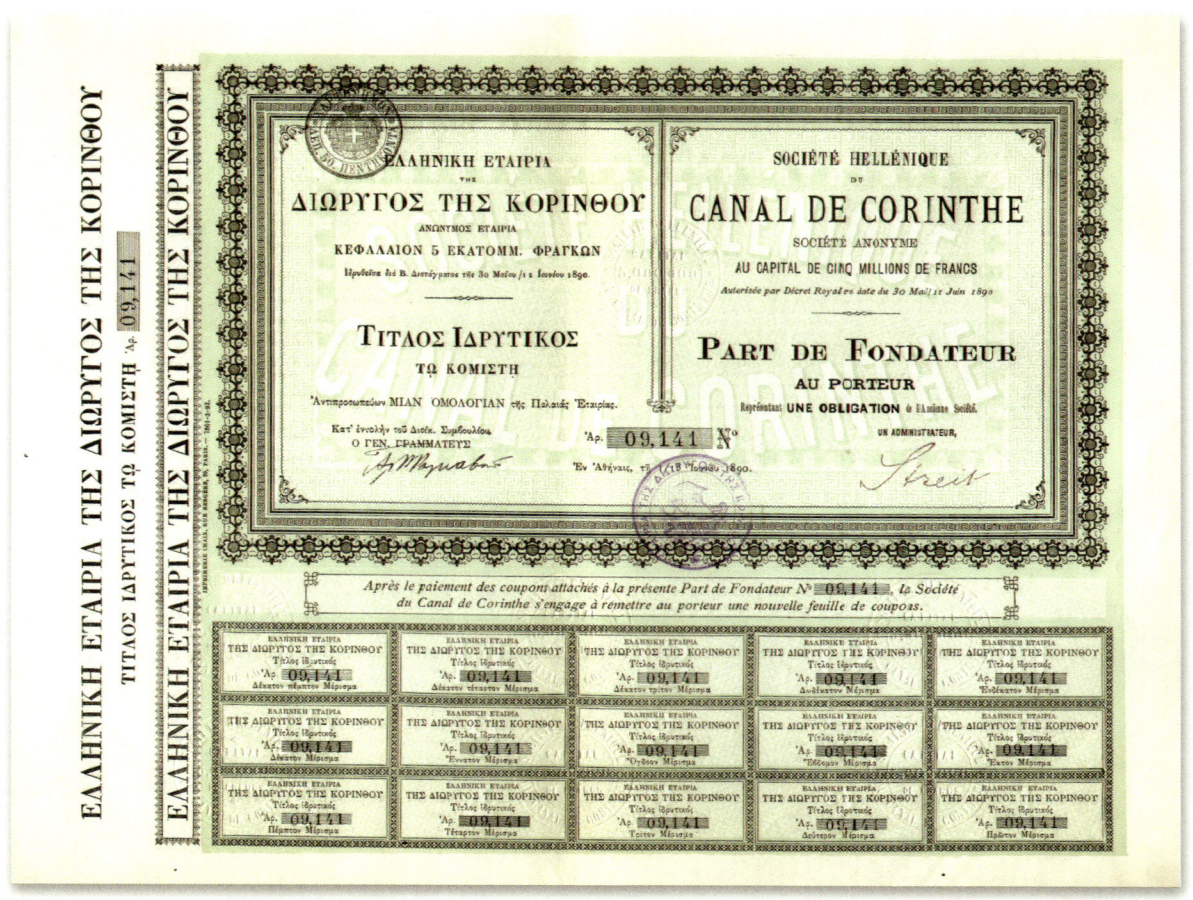

Following the failiure of de Lesseps original company to construct the Corinth Canal, work was taken over by the Societe Hellenique de canal de Corinthe and completed in 1893. Depicted is a founders share in the Greek company dated 1890.

Early Spanish Royal Trading Companies

Perhaps, in looking at the Spanish Royal Trading Companies, we are taking a step beyond the set parameters of this book, at least in terms of years. But the stories are such and the share certificates so magnificent that it would be remiss to omit the sector. The shares themselves are large, often printed on vellum and always extremely decorative.

Formed under Royal patronage, the trading companies were created in the eighteenth century to rival the activities of the Dutch and British East India Companies. Each was granted a specific monopoly, either by product, or more usually geographic trading area, thus giving them a significant competitive advantage. There were two groups: those principally formed for overseas trade, for which they were granted exclusive rights, and those formed for internal trading within Spain. Most were racked with malpractice and subsequently failed.

The first group includes the following:

Real Compañia Guipuzcoana de Caracas
Formed by Basque merchants in 1728 to trade with the Province of Caracas, it had the specific tasks of breaking the Dutch monopoly of the Venezuelan cocoa trade and developing its agriculture. The Company was able to send two ships each year from San Sebastian or Pasajes in Spain carrying Spanish goods suitable to trade for metals, cocoa, sugar, tobacco and leathers. It set up trading posts along the Venezuelan coast and in 1732 obtained a trading monopoly whereby it was the only company to be able to import and export goods from Europe. The Company was profitable in its early years and its initial capital base was increased nine-fold by 1776. Abuse of its monopoly resulted in itd forfeiture, partly as a result of international pressure and partly

due to King Carlos III's free-trading policies. In 1785 it was absorbed into the Royal Philippine Company (*Compañia de Filipinas*).

Real Compañia de Commercio de la Habana
Based in Havana and formed in 1740 the company was granted a monopoly on trade between Spain and Cuba (Spanish textiles in exchange for Cuban tobacco and sugar). The company was corruptly run and its director, Martin de Arostegui used its monopoly for his own ends, shipping tobacco to British colonies and trading in slaves. Its monopoly was rescinded and this together with the English occupation of Havana resulted in major losses. Despite this, the company survived until the early nineteenth century.

Real Compañia de Commercio de Barcelona
Possibly the best know of all the Spanish trading companies of the period. It was initially granted a monopoly on trade with Santo Domingo, Puerto Rico and Margarita Island. The monopoly was subsequently cancelled in exchange for new trading concessions with Cumana and Buenos Aires. Eventually, it merged with the *Compañia de Filipinas* in 1785. The shares are printed on vellum and are the most common of this genre.

Compañia de Filipinas
Following the assimilation of the *Compañia Guipuzcoana de Caracas* and the *Compañia de Commercio de Barcelona*, this company was formed in 1785 and was given the rights to trade with the Philippines for 20 years despite considerable international objections. Its shareholders included the Spanish King and Banco de San Carlos. By the time of the 1796 war with England the company was in poor shape and by 1834 it was dissolved.

Certificate for one share dated 1749 in the Real Compania de San Fernando de Sevilla, one of Spain's early royal trading companies. Printed on vellum the certificate depicts the port and city of Seville

The second group, generally regarded as the 'internal trading companies' include:

Compañia de Zarza la Mayor

Established in 1746 to manufacture textiles and sell them in Spain and Portugal the company abused its priviliges and was forced to merge with the *Compañia de Extremadura*, which subsequently failed.

Real Compañia de Commercio y Fabricas de Zaragoza

Formed to promote industry in Aragon, the company was a fraudsters paradise and failed in 1774, lasting less than 30 years.

Real Compañia de San Fernando de Sevilla

Its objective was to expand the textile industry and was formed in 1747. It also had the right to export produce to South America and to import raw materials at advantageous prices. Most capital came from Flemish merchants but progress was slow and like so many of its fellow trading companies, it was corrupt and subsequently failed in the 1780's.

The Spanish companies described here are not comprehensive but will hopefully give an idea of the trading activities of Spain in the eighteenth century. The certificates themselves are exceptionally decorative and although rare, several have turned up over the last few years.

This section on the Spanish trading companies owes much to the research of Howard Shakespeare and the articles published in the Bond & Share Society Journals in 1989.

Part 5 _____

THE EXOTIC

Over the years there have been many 'exotic' investment schemes, some successful, some disastrous. Collectors will come across many and those described here do no more than scratch the surface.

Four have been selected:

- The Darien Project;
- Poyais;
- Bank of Siberia; and,
- The Jewish Colonial Trust.

The Darien Project

William Paterson (1658-1719), who was generally regarded as the originator of the Bank of England, was very aware of the dire financial straits his home country of Scotland was in at the turn of the seventeenth century. So, once the Bank had been established he returned home to set about improving its financial standing.

A chance discussion with a sailor (Lionel Wafer) made him aware of a 'wonderful paradise on the Isthmus of Panama, with a sheltered bay, friendly Indians and rich, fertile land – a place called Darien'. One would have thought that the man who founded the Bank of England would have had the sense to check the story of his sailor friend before proceeding to raise an expedition – but no. However, his enthusiasm to establish a new colony on what he rightly perceived to be a key crossroads of trade between east and west, was not fired by personal gain; he was anxious to create revenue for his country which would give it international standing as well as help balance the books.

In 1695 Paterson set about raising the necessary funds for the *Company of Scotland Trading to Africa and the Indies'* (the Darien Company). The idea was extremely popular and Scots, rich and poor,

keenly contributed £400,000 in share capital to equip the expedition, despite best efforts by the English East India Company to block the project, viewing the new company as a potential rival. Consequently, the British did nothing to help which proved sufficient in the end to ensure the expeditions failure.

The first expedition of 5 ships set off in 1698 with a pile of useless gifts for bribing the local Indians. These included the usual combs, mirrors and wigs. Of the 1,200 'settlers' on board, only the captain knew their destination. After making landfall at Darien, they built huts at 'New Edinburgh', soon discovering that heavy rains and disease were not conducive to colonization. They had little food and were surrounded by unfriendly Spaniards. The expedition, now reduced to 300 due to cholera, headed home. Amazingly, a second expedition set off a year later being unaware of the failure of the first, which was still on its way back. The Spanish were unimpressed….again, and drove the new settlers away. Only a handful survived.

The net result was a loss of £232,884 out of the savings of the people of Scotland. Despite its disastrous adventure in Darien, the company continued to cause problems for the East India Company whenever they transgressed into Scottish waters. Eventually the English agreed to pay the company's debts together with other elements of Scotland's National Debt. The amount of £398,085 (known as the 'Equivalent') was agreed after 3 months of debate in the Scottish Parliament and 3 days of debate in the English. The new result was formation of the Union in 1707. Holders of 'Equivalent' debt, taking the form of debentures established the 'Equivalent Company' out of which emerged today's Royal Bank of Scotland in 1727.

Today the Darien National Park is one of the largest and most protected areas of Central America.

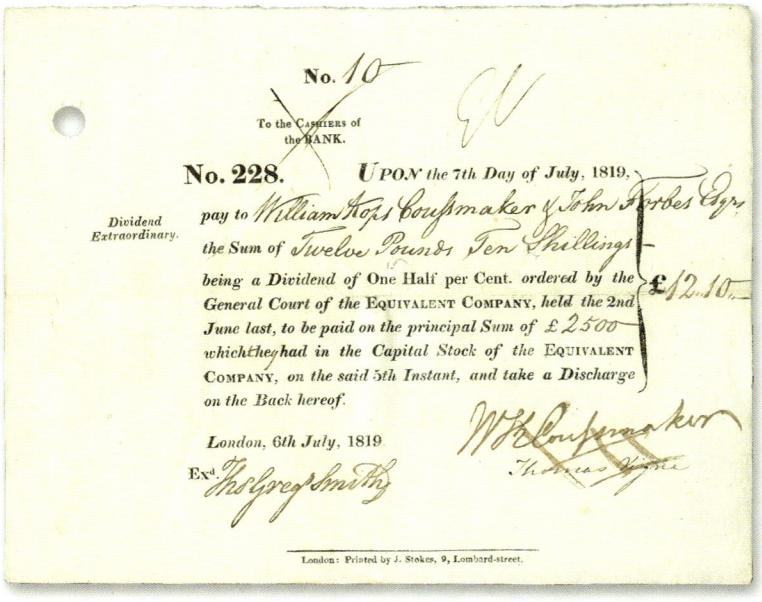

Dividend warrant of the Equivalent Company dated 1819 and payable at the Bank of England. Issued to and signed by William Kops Coussmaker. The company was the precursor to the Royal Bank of Scotland.

Poyais

Not all exotic investments and their advisors originated in Scotland, although the previous section on Darien and the earlier piece on John Law (Part 3) may suggest otherwise.

There is, however, a tendency for the country to produce a number of entrepreneurs and adventurers. One of the 'greats' was Gregor

MacGregor born in 1786 to a captain of the East India Company. His grandfather was a nephew of the famous (or infamous depending on your point of view) Rob Roy MacGregor. Gregor was a professional soldier, a Captain in the British Regiment of Foot, a Major in the Portuguese 8th Line Battalion and, ultimately, a General in the Venezuelan army under Simon Bolivar – his first wife's uncle.

Following an adventurous life in the Caribbean, Florida and Panama, MacGregor obtained a land grant from King George Frederick Augustus II of the Mosquito Shore and Nation, located in Central America in what is now Honduras and Nicaragua. The grant gave him the rights to an area of 8 million acres – later described as 30 million acres…

Poyais banknote for One Hard Dollar

Discontented Scots at home were enthused by his tales of fertile soil, gold nuggets ('as plentiful as pebbles') and an already civilized society. They were soon pressing to emigrate and in 1822 land grants and a bond issue for the State of Poyais, consisting of 2,000 bonds of £100 each, bearing 6% were offered through bankers, Perring & Co., with payments by installments. The bonds have never been seen but the installment certificates ('scrip') and the land grants are still around. Additionally, 70,000 bank notes were issued denominated as "One Hard Dollar" and these were exchanged for English pounds.

The 1822 bond was the first issue and this was followed up in 1823 by a second raising £200,000, a third 'Redemption Loan' in 1824 and a fourth in Paris two years later.

The first batch of 70 intrepid pioneers arrived in February 1823 followed by a further 170 a month later. What they found was not what it said on the tin! Antagonistic Indians, no food, fever and mosquitos. Despite brave attempts by the nearby Governor of British Honduras to rescue the duped settlers, over 200 died.

Despite serving prison sentences in London and Paris, MacGregor was still selling Land Grants in 1837. But two years later he gave up and moved back to Venezuela where the government acknowledged his past services. Gregor MacGregor died in 1845. His daughter married into the Laird shipbuilding family and her son became managing director of the African Steam Ship

Company, later to become Ocean Transport & Trading Ltd.

The bonds and land grants issued over a period of some 15 years often bear the signature of MacGregor which greatly adds to their glamour. But signatures aside, the certificates make fascinating and amusing reading demonstrating the ease of perpetrating a fraud in a world limited by poor communications.

Opposite page: £100 bond in Gregor MacGregor's 'Kingdom of Poyais' dated 1823. Note the opening words: "We, Gregor the First, sovereign prince of the independent State of Poyais….."

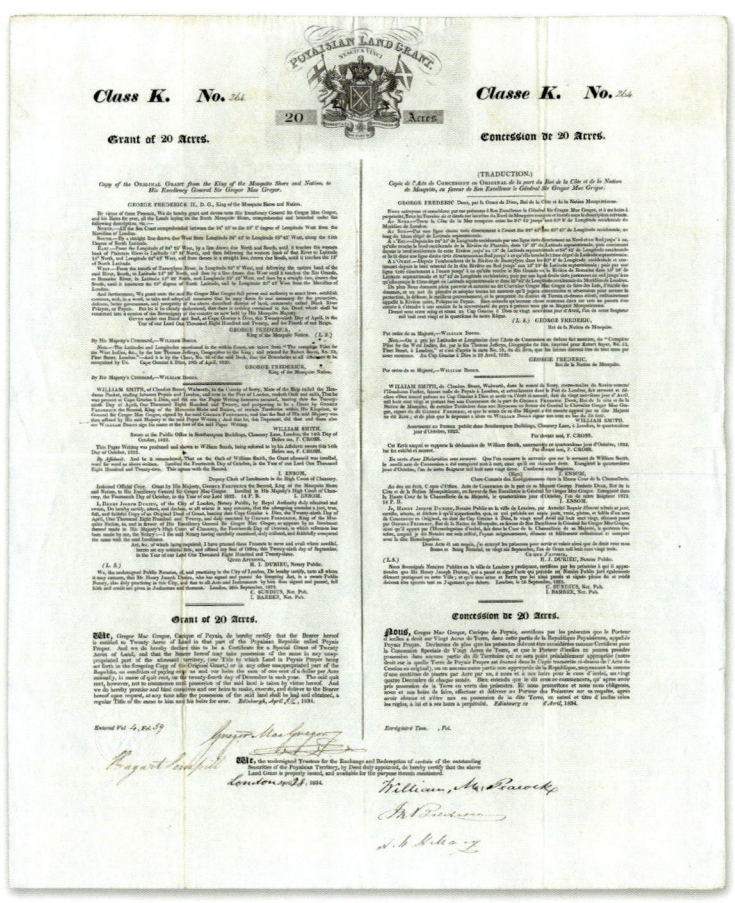

A Poyaisian land Grant for 20 acres (of mosquito infested swamp!). The certificates were rather more attractive than the land itself

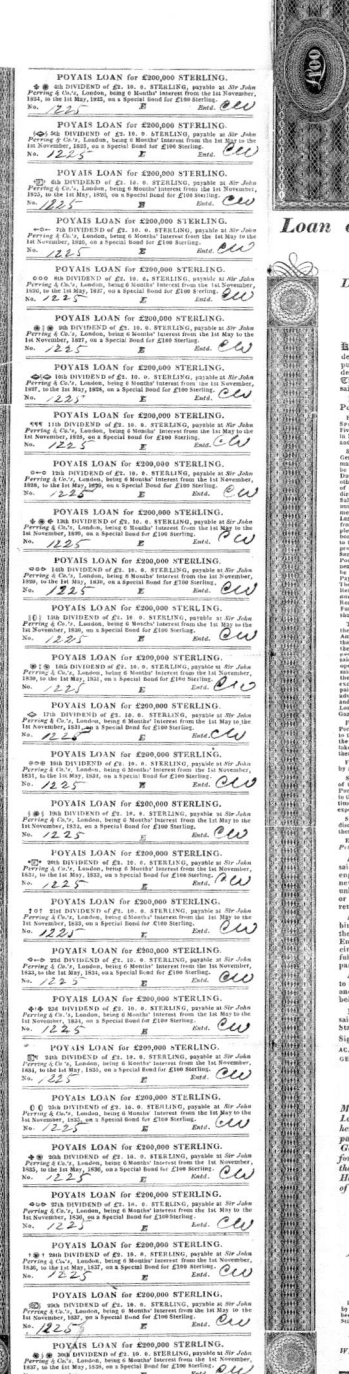

The Bank of Siberia

Many banks operated in Russia prior to the Revolution. Two of the most famous were the Peasants Land Bank and the Land Bank of the Nobility, which were involved in the transference of land from aristocracy to peasants. Both were major bond issuers and by 1917 they jointly defaulted on £100 million.

Grain was a key Russian export, a trade which was largely controlled by 6 banks; *Commercial & Industrial Bank, Russian Bank for Foreign Trade,* the *International Bank,* the *Commercial & Industrial Bank,* the *Volga-Karma Bank* and the *Commercial Bank of Siberia.* Acquisition of these was viewed as strategically essential to the British objectives of undermining the Bolsheviks wherever possible, keeping assets out of German hands and maintaining trade with Russia after the war.

This book is not intended as a general receptacle for all things interesting to the historian so we will not dwell too long on Britain's spying activities around the Revolutionary period. Bruce Lockhart who was appointed Vice-Consul in 1912 and subsequently lost his job due to an extramarital affair, returned to Russia in January 1918 as Head of Special Mission, a role which included co-ordination of MI6's spy network in Russia. One of his 'spies' was Sidney Reilly ("Ace of Spies"). Lockhart's involvement in an attempt to assassinate Lenin resulted in his arrest, interrogation by his one-time 'friend' Felix Dzerhinsky (Chief of Soviet secret police) and detention at the Lubyanka until a prisoner exchange was arranged by MI6 (then, 'SIS').

Whilst this was going on, Britain's General Poole conceived a plan to take over the Russian economy through acquisition of the six aforementioned grain-banks of Siberia. The plan was approved by the British Government, ahead of the Germans who were planning much the same. At the end of the day, majority shareholdings were achieved in two of the banks and a deposit of £300,000 paid on the Commercial Bank of Siberia shares. Needless to say, when the Bolsheviks realized what was going on they immediately blocked the purchases and Poole had to telegram London that the bank directors were forced to sign over to the Russian 'Government' all the balances and valuables held.

The tale does not end there, however, as the Managing Director of the Commercial Bank of Siberia, who escaped from Russia, turned up in London after the war and claimed his £3 million! The Treasury, apparently, was forced to pay up.

Interestingly, 25% of the share capital of the Bank of Siberia was found in storage at London's Law Courts in 1981.

Opposite page: Share certificate in the Commercial Bank of Siberia dated 1910.

The Jewish Colonial Trust

Fine and early (1900) example of a bearer certificate in the Jewish Colonial Trust. Vignettes depict trade, industry, agriculture and religion (the "wailing wall").

Formed in 1899 and incorporated in London the Jewish Colonial Trust ("JCT") represented the aspirations of Theodor Herzl for the formation of a Jewish state. It was intended as a financial vehicle to gather money for building industries, railways and the buying of land in Palestine. There were over 100,000 shareholders, however, the majority were relatively poor and this is reflected in the disappointing £395,000 raised as compared with the targeted £8 million.

The bank's activities in Palestine were carried out by its subsidiary, the Anglo-Palestine Bank, which opened its first branch in Jaffa in 1903 and subsequent branches in Jerusalem, Beirut, Hebron and several other cities. The bank

provided farmers with long-term loans and managed to survive the 1st World war despite efforts by Turkey to close its branches. In 1934 the JCT ceased its direct banking activities and remained a holding company for Anglo-Palestine Bank. During the 2nd World war, the Anglo-Palestine Bank financed companies supplying the British army and on the formation of the State of Israel, it was given the concession to issue the country's banknotes.

In 1950 the Anglo-Palestine Bank became Bank Leumi. Original holders of JCT shares may claim restitution from the "Company for Location and Restitution of Holocaust Victims' Assets".

Part 6

GREAT COLLECTING THEMES

Building a collection by country or signatory are not the only choices. There are many themes ranging from the big (such as railways), to the small (such as theatres). This section looks at some but it should be stressed that these are not comprehensive. Indeed, whatever takes your fancy….!

Railways and their Barons

George Hudson – The "Railway King"

Despite coming from a drapery background, Hudson soon became a major figure in the British railway industry and was known as the "Railway King". He inherited £30,000 from a distant relative when 27 and by 1833 was managing the *York Banking Company* as well as running his family business. Twice elected Mayor of York, he realized that many small railway lines would never be economic and so from the 1840s' began buying shares on a large scale with the object of amalgamation. Thus, during the 1840s', he gained control of the *Newcastle & Darlington, Newcastle & Berwick, York & North Midland, Leeds & Bradford and Eastern Counties Railway* companies. By 1844 he controlled over 1000 miles of railway and by 1846, his companies controlled over a quarter of the railways then built in England. On top of this he also found time to become a Tory Member of Parliament.

Hudson attempted and failed to consolidate the railways under his control into the *Great Northern* (originally named 'London & York'), being caught on a legal issue trying to use proceeds of a new stock issue to pay dividends (sounds a bit like a Ponzi scheme…). This led to his financial collapse and a spell in prison.

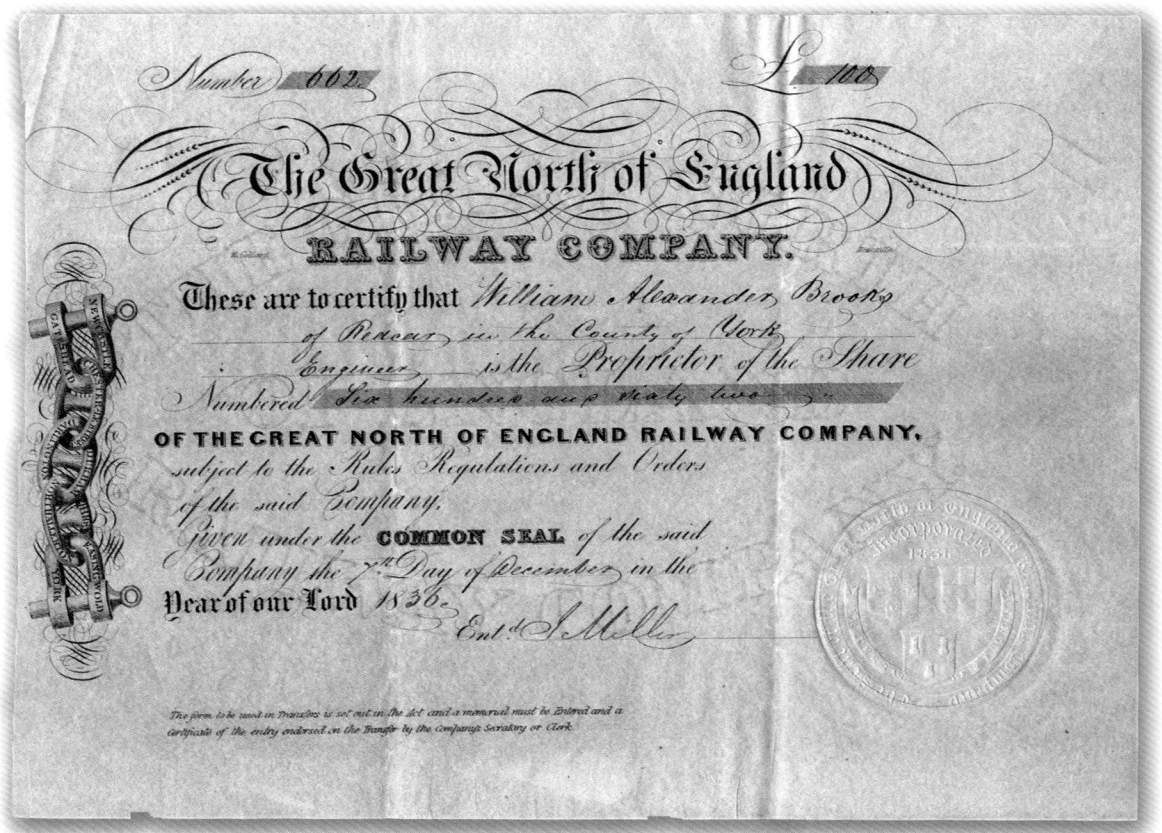

Dated 1836, the Great North of England Railway opened in 1841 connecting York and Gateshead. Hudson was a large shareholder and director. The line was eventually transferred to the Newcastle & Darlington Junction Railway in 1846.

Once a millionaire, he died in 1871 with an estate of only £200. He was so discredited that a wax effigy of him at Madame Tussaud's was melted down!

Jim Fisk, Daniel Drew, Jay Gould and the Erie Railroad

Perhaps one of the most flamboyant of the "railroad barons", Jim Fisk was undoubtedly a rogue of the first order but despite that he enamoured himself to the public, such that 25,000 people clamoured to get to his funeral.

Born in 1835 Fisk was the son of a peddler, a business which he helped develop so fast that by the time he was 21, the one wagon his father had started with had become five. Later, working for Jordan Marsh of Boston, he supplied textiles to the soldiers fighting the Civil War. He did not shy away from lavish entertaining nor the odd bribe, and in no time had been granted a partnership with his employer. Buying cotton from the South and using attractive ladies to move it to the North were par for the course. At the end of the war, Jordan bought Fisk out of the partnership for $65,000 enabling him to move on to New York and the world of finance. His first killing was in Confederate Bonds. Feeling that the collapse of the South was inevitable he set up a communication system with London which would enable him to sell bonds short the moment the war ended ahead of everyone else. When Lee surrendered, Fisk pocketed the difference between $22 and $80 on $5 million of bonds. But his gains were soon dissipated on Wall Street.

His next venture netted him a fat commission on the sale of Daniel Drew's fleet of nine steamers and with that came a long association with one of the least liked railway barons.

Perhaps of all US Railroads, the *Erie* is the one which attracted most 'barons' – nearly all of whom pulled in opposite directions. Drew's antics with its stock gave Fisk another opportunity to act as broker and earn fat commissions. Drew launched a bear raid on the Erie, dumping his shares and selling short, forcing its price down from $80 to $55; then he bought back. One of the biggest losers was Cornelius Vanderbilt which pleased Drew who had previously lost heavily as a result of a similar raid by the Commodore. By 1867 Fisk was reputed to be a millionaire, owning a sizeable block of Erie shares and buying his wife a $75,000 mansion in Boston.

Vanderbilt was not happy about the *Erie*, which was a direct competitor to his own line, the *New York Central*. He appreciated the importance of establishing a railroad entrance to New York City and he was also not happy about Drew. There were three opposing parties vying for control of the Erie in 1867:

- Drew and Fisk;
- Vanderbilt; and,
- John S Eldridge with a group of Boston speculators.

Eldridge & Co. controlled the *Boston Hartford & Erie Railroad* ("B, H & E"), which had loads of debt and little else. He was keen to find a way of passing off the debt on to the Erie.

After their first tussle and much negotiation, Vanderbilt agreed to let Drew continue as a director of the Erie – one of his few errors of judgement. The Erie assumed the debts of the B, H & E and Fisk and Jay Gould were appointed directors. Vanderbilt assumed he had control but it proved not to be - the others were turned by Drew. Drew then printed 100,000 more shares and dumped them on the

$1000 bond in the Boston Hartford & Erie Rail Road Company dated 1866 and signed by John S Eldridge.

market (the "Erie Panic") forcing Vanderbilt to pick them up. A blatant fraud, as the money merely lined the coffers of Drew and not the *Erie*. The ensuing battle nearly broke Vanderbilt but his resources and cunning were a match for Drew, Fisk and Gould and although he failed to gain control of the Erie, he eventually saved his own fortune. Initially he lost $8 million in the process but the battle was far from over. Drew's partners fled to New Jersey and left Jim Fisk to do the talking.

In the meantime, Vanderbilt was still losing money. He was not averse to sending a mob of kidnappers to New Jersey to bring Drew and Fisk back to the jurisdiction of New York, but neither were they averse to sourcing their own 'army' from Jersey City's police department. The battle continued with free drinks for the police, hefty bribes and a barrage of legal actions. By the end of the day Vanderbilt recovered about $5 million of his losses, Eldridge gained $4 million for $5 million of dubious stock in the *Boston Hartford & Erie* (the railroad was never completed), Drew was allowed to keep his speculative earnings after paying $540,00 in costs, and Fisk and Gould were left with the *Erie*; Gould as President and Fisk as Comptroller. The two raised even more funds, shorting stock and printing more shares such that the company was able to rebuild some of its decrepit lines (prompted by a major disaster at Carr's Rock when coaches left the lines and over 40 passengers died) and at the same time keeping themselves in the life they expected. Legal actions continued with judges bribed and individuals threatened.

Fisk and Gould continued to take what they could from any railroad that came their way. The

Albany & Susquehanna was next on the list followed by a foray into the gold market. Fisk's long time mistress, Josie Mansfield, eventually fell into the hands of rival business associate and heavy gambler, Ned Stokes. In 1872 Stokes shot Fisk dead at the Grand Central Hotel; Fisk was 37. The hotel was renamed 'Broadway Central'. It collapsed in 1973 and the site now houses a hostel for NYU students.

Share certificate in the Missouri Kansas & Texas Railway Company handsigned by Jay Gould and dated 1880

Jay Gould was ousted from the Erie board in a stockholders coup but continued to profit from stock market dealing. He died in 1892 aged 56, leaving a fortune in excess of $70 million.

'The Commodore' – Cornelius Vanderbilt

Born 1794 on Staten Island with no money, he died 83 years later, the wealthiest man in America. He left most of his $100 million fortune to his son William, who was the child who worked most closely with him.

Cornelius married his first cousin, Sophia Johnson when he was 19 and over the next 25 years they had 13 children. Initially working for his father on the ferry serving Staten Island, he persuaded his parents to lend him $100 so he could buy a boat to start his own service. Despite competition he was sufficiently successful to be able to repay the loan within a year and add to his fleet whilst gaining a reputation for punctuality whatever the weather. During the war with

Britain in 1812 he significantly expanded his operations and won a government contract to supply the forts around New York harbour.

After the war, he sold his sailing vessels and became a steamboat captain for Thomas Gibbons who operated a ferry service between New Brunswick and New York City. Vanderbilt greatly improved the business and added six more steamers. He got on well with Gibbons but after eleven years, in 1829, he went solo. During this time, his wife, apart from having a baby every two years, made their tavern ("Bellona Hall") famous for food and service. Vanderbilt continued to expand his new passenger and freight service such that by the 1840s' he had 100 steamships and was the largest employer in the United States. But during the Civil War he lost his youngest and favourite son, George.

The California Gold Rush brought more opportunities and soon the Commodore owned the principal transportation business on the East Coast to San Francisco route via Panama known as the Accessory Transit Company.

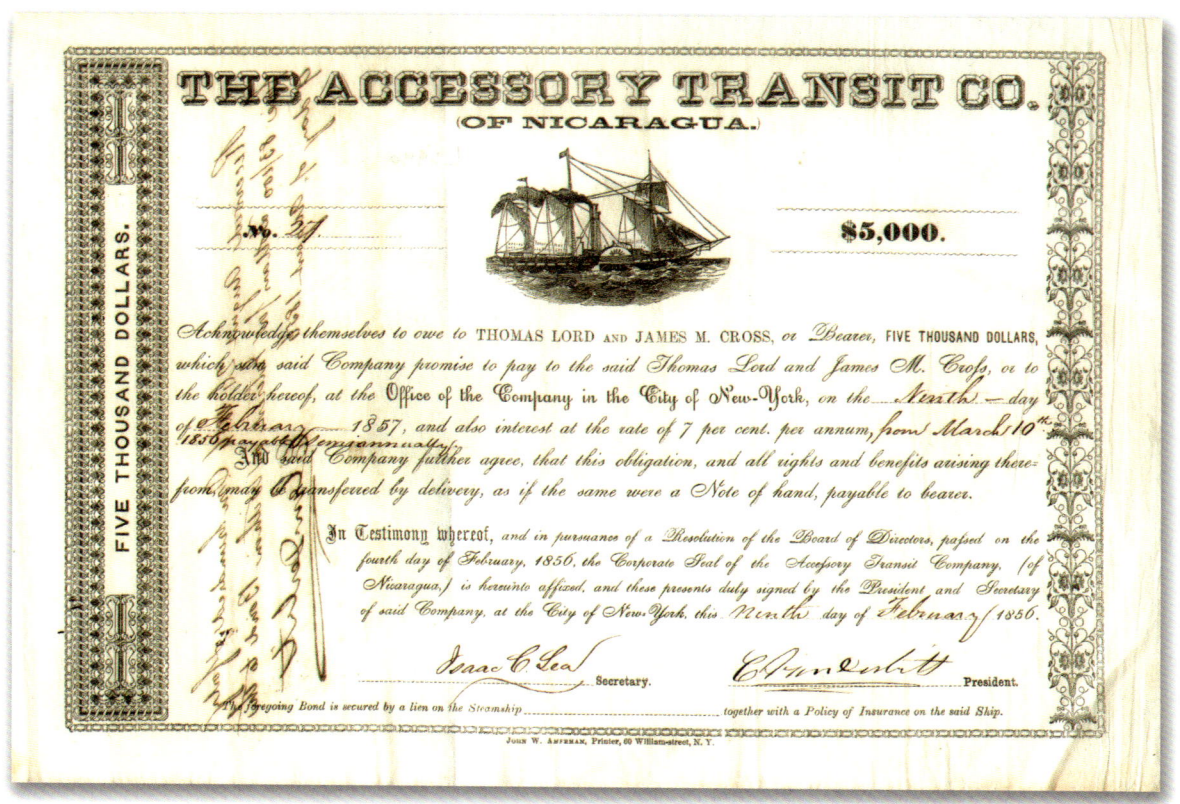

The Accessory Transit Company was set up by Vanderbilt in 1851 to facilitate transportation of miners to the gold fields of California..He left its management to Charles Morgan and Cornelius K Garrison whilst he travelled to Europe. The pair took advantage but were eventually ousted by Vanderbilt and friends following war in Nicaragua. A resulting collapse in the price of its stock allowed Vanderbilt to buy back heavily. The certificate pictured is for a 7% bond for $5,000 issued to Lord and Cross in 1856 and signed by the Commodore .

He entered the trans Atlantic shipping business but was unable to compete with Cunard and subsequently sold off his fleet. In the 1860s', at the age of 70, he changed horses and with his son William moved into railroads. First purchase was the *Long Island Railroad* and then the *New York & Harlem* and the *Hudson River Railroads*. In 1867 he acquired the *Central Railroad* and proceeded to improve services and consolidate all lines into the *New York Central*. William encouraged expansion towards Chicago and soon the Commodore was in control of the largest railway system in America.

1868 saw the death of his wife Sophia – a great companion and business advisor - but a year later at 73 he married again, this time, a distant cousin, Francis Armstrong Crawford, 34 years his junior. It was then that he gifted $1 million to Nashville's Central University, now known as 'Vanderbilt University' (its athletic teams today are still called 'The Commodores'). It was also at this time that his battles over the Erie took place (see previous section on Gould). He died in 1877 aged 83 leaving most of his $100 million fortune to William and half a million dollars to each of his daughters. His wife was left $500,000 in cash and 2,000 shares in the New York Central Railroad. That half million is equivalent to $130 million today.

The New York and Harlem was one of the first lines to be acquired by the Commodore. This certificate, dated 1873, is handsigned by his son and principal benefactor, William.

Edward Henry Harriman

Born in 1848 E H Harriman ("EH") began his career on Wall Street aged 14 years. In 1879, he married Mary Williamson Averell whose father was president of the *Ogdensburg & Lake Champlain Railroad*.

At 21, E H foresaw the coming of 'Black Friday' and sold the market short, netting $3,000, sufficient to buy himself a seat on the Stock Exchange. Next, a successful raid on coal stocks brought him $150,000, but it was railroads that became his prime focus. His first venture, reorganizing the impoverished *Lake Ontario Southern* and offloading it to *Penn Central* set the scene. After gaining a seat on the board of the *Illinois Central* thanks to Stuyvesant Fish, who was then Vice President and subsequently President, Harriman transformed the line with

a keen attention to detail, which surprised his contemporaries. When the line expanded to Iowa a clash with J P Morgan and Vanderbilt was inevitable but Harriman fought and won.

His next foray was the *Union Pacific*, a line in dire straights with poor track and rolling stock. In 1893 it fell into receivership. He set up a syndicate to run the line under his control as Chairman. His obsession with detail paid off and he eventually re-integrated the *Oregon Short Line* and gained control of the *Oregon Railway & Navigation Company* at the same time. Towards the end of the 1800s' he took control of the *Central Pacific*, a railroad built in 1862 by Leland Stanford, Collis Huntington, Charles Crocker and Mark Hopkins. But it was his battle with Jim Hill which proved most bloody. Hill and Morgan worked together in securing the reorganization of the *Northern Pacific* but

An initial tussle over the *Chicago Burlington & Quincy Railroad* was won by Hill, however, the main 'war' was over the Northern Pacific itself and its extension through California to San Francisco. Men died and the lawyers got rich before a truce was called but not before Harriman had lost the war. A struggle that precipitated the stock market panic of 1901.

E H Harriman died in 1909 leaving an estate valued at over $70 million. His wife Averell became a dedicated philanthropist and donated the land that later became 'Harriman State Park', the second largest park in New York State, comprising almost 50,000 acres. EH Harriman was often regarded as the 'good guy' so far as

railroad barons were concerned and he was probably the last. Cars were set to take over from trains and by 1920 tracks were being pulled up.

His son, William Averell Harriman (1891-1986) was a well known diplomat whose second marriage was to Pamela, nee Digby, better known as Pamela Harriman. She became US Ambassador to France and lover/husband to the great and good. Averell Harriman became the American ambassador to the Court of St James (United Kingdom) in 1946 and between 1955-59 was Governor of New York prior to Nelson Rockefeller. He was extremely active during the 'cold war' period, and twice stood as Democratic presidential nominee.

Appointed to the Board of the 'B & O', Harriman was active in its running. This certificate is both issued to Harriman and bears his original signature, shown here, on the back dated 1901.

The Money Men

Great ideas (fraudulent or not) need money and none of the developments described so far, and in the pages to come, would have been possible without it. The next few pages look at some of the 'money men' giving a brief insight into their modus operandi and their own ups and downs. As with all sections of this book, there is only space to describe a few and even those are much abbreviated. Readers are encouraged to research further.

George Peabody. Peabody accumulated enormous wealth from international banking and in his latter years gave some $9 million away to worthy causes. Housing estates built for the poor at the time of Charles Dickens are dotted around London today (one is opposite Selfridges). Peabody died in 1869 having survived the 'Panic' of 1857 (thanks to an £800,000 loan from the Bank of England). On Peabody's death, Junius Spencer Morgan (JP's father), who had become a partner in 1854, took

J.P. Morgan signed few certificates and this one, only on the reverse as a Trustee. The New Jersey Junction Railroad was incorporated in 1886 and provided an interchange for traffic between various railway systems. Terminating at Jersey City

John Pierpont Morgan

Coming from a wealthy family, J P Morgan ("JP") began his banking career with *George Peabody & Co.*, a company which had been founded in London in 1837 by the philanthropist

over the firm changing its name to J S Morgan & Co.. On Junius' death in 1890 the company eventually became *Morgan, Grenfell & Co.*.

Junius' son JP returned to New York in 1858 and initially worked for the American branch of George Peabody & Co.. In 1871 with his business partner Anthony Drexel, he founded *Drexel, Morgan & Co.*, renaming it *J P Morgan & Co.* after Drexel's death 22 years later. Both he and Drexel became deeply involved in railroads with Morgan able to use his British connections to sell stock outside the United States, thus protecting the local share price. Such operations brought him close to the rather more brash Cornelius Vanderbilt and ultimately a directorship with the *New York Central.*

Morgan had an innate interest in railway companies, perhaps stemming from his grandfathers early investments in the *Baltimore & Ohio* ("B&O") and *New Haven & Hertford.* J P reorganized numerous railroad companies including the *West Shore & Buffalo, the Philadelphia & Reading* and the *Chesapeake & Ohio Railroad.* He was highly respected, this at a time when the more unscrupulous were also making their fortunes, people such as Daniel Drew, Jim Fisk and Cornelius Vanderbilt. His association with Vanderbilt in disposing of his interest in the *New York Central Railroad* to English investors, resulted in his appointment to the Board. But it was not only his involvement in railroads which made him both money and reputation; his association with Thomas Edison led to the formation of *General Electric* (see Page 77) and his interest in the steel industry, resulting in his acquisition of Carnegie Steel for the (then) huge sum of $480 million, ended in the creation of the giant *US Steel Corporation*.

From an early date, his expertise was called upon by the Government and in 1895 when the country's gold reserves were rapidly disappearing following the panic of 1893, Morgan formed a syndicate to supply the Government with $65 million in gold, mostly sourced from Europe. His subsequent involvement in the rescues of the US Treasury,

New York City and the banking industry in the financial crises that plagued the end of the last century were perhaps his greatest contributions. Today the firm continues to be highly regarded and is often the first port of call by a government in trouble.

J Pierpont Morgan died in1913 aged 75 one of the wealthiest men in America. Interestingly, his son, John "Jack" Pierpont Morgan Jr., who took over also died at 75.

The Rothschilds

Perhaps the most well known of all the great financiers were the Rothschilds who established their reputation on integrity, communications and contacts. By the time Nathan Meyer Rothschild, son of Mayer Amschel Rothschild, died in1836 his estate amounted to almost 1% of the British National Income. Even by 1825 the combined wealth of the 'House' was nine times greater than that of Barings and the Banque de France combined.

By 1769 the family under its head and banking founder, Mayer Amschel (1743-1812), was already well established in European finance. As Court Agent to William of Hanau (said to be the richest man in Europe) they managed his fortune, the interest from which provided the basis for the family's great wealth. Mayer Amschel had five sons, Nathan, Amschel, Salomon, Carl and James. Nathan was the first to leave Frankfurt at 21 and initially lived in Manchester as a textile and general merchant. In 1809 he moved to London and set up offices at New Court in the City (still the bank's offices today). He dealt in Bills of Exchange and arranging foreign loans. The expertise he developed brought him to the attention of the British Government.

Nathans four brothers followed his lead and set up branches around Europe: James in Paris, Salomon in Vienna and Carl in Naples, whilst Amschel, the eldest, headed up Frankfurt.

Nathan proved to be the more adventurous (and profitable). His most successful venture revolved around bullion dealing on behalf of the British Government facilitating payment of the army towards the end of the Napoleonic wars in 1812. The operation was not only successful for the Government but also for the family becoming the prime source of its wealth, netting around £1 million for the bank. Nathan was clearly the senior 'partner' and his brotherly communications were often direct and to the point. His next major deal involved a loan of £5 million for the Prussian Government, a fairly typical transaction for which the House became famous. Nathans brothers were equally active in funding railways, engineering and mining ventures across the world. Nathan successfully raised funds for Russia in 1822 and the bonds around today usually bear his signature, although the paper on which they are printed is soft and not of the highest quality.

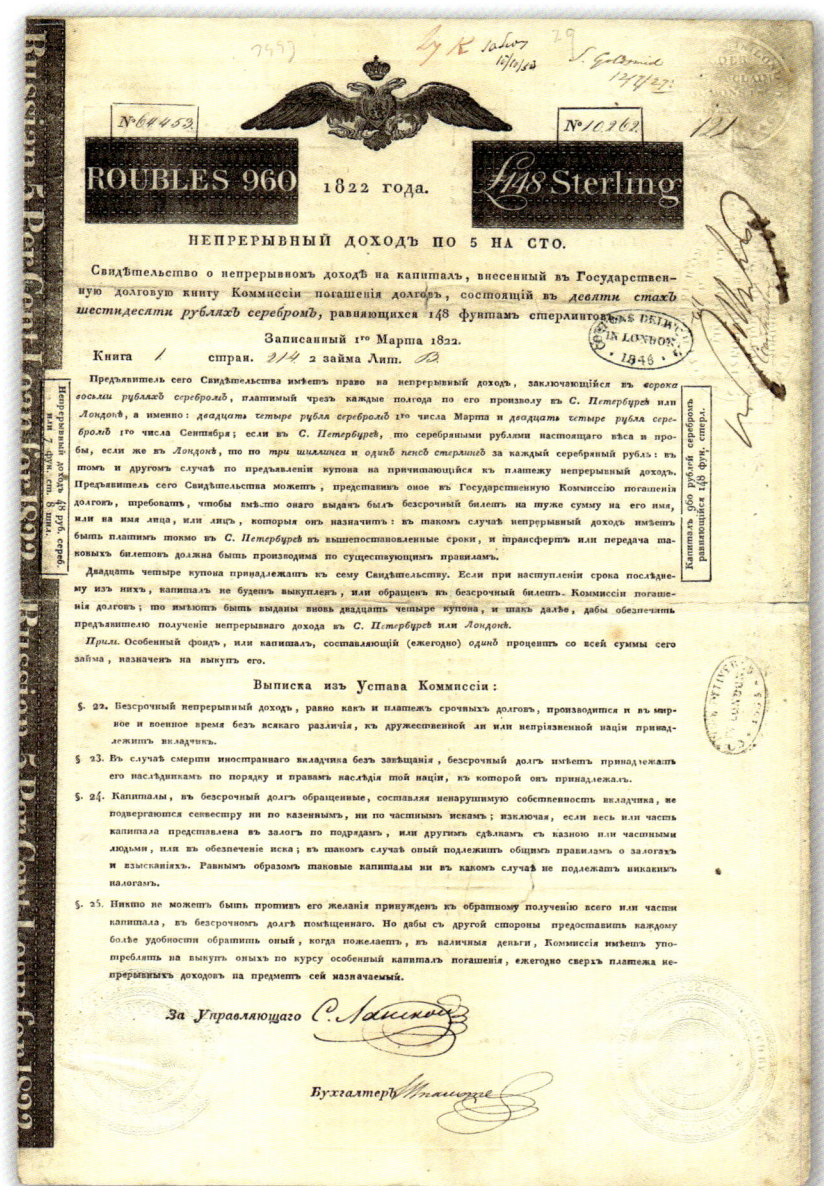

The Russian State Loan of 1822 was issued in four denominations (£111, £148, £518 and £1036); the bond shown here is for £148 (Rbls 960) and bears the hand signature of Nathan Rothschild (top right).

Nathan died in 1836 having established Rothschilds as the foremost international bankers in the world. His son Baron Lionel Nathan de Rothschild (1808-1879) took up the reins and although less adventurous than his father became instrumental in the purchase of the Khedive's 44% holding in the Suez Canal (see Page 95). In 1840, N M Rothschild & Sons became the Bank of England's bullion brokers and was active in mining especially gold, mercury and precious stones throughout the world. In 1887, the bank together with Alfred Beit, financed the formation of De Beers. Development of the oil fields of Baku in Russia, along with the Nobels, were also key investments. Uprisings in Europe during the mid nineteenth century did not cause the family too many problems although the Unification of Italy in 1861 led to the closure of their Naples bank.

In 1919 they chaired the new daily fixing for the world gold price, something which continued until 2004.

John D Rockefeller

"John D" was born in Richford, New York in 1839, his family came from Germany in the mid to late eighteenth century. After leaving school he began his business career with Maurice Clark, an Englishman, taking commission on agricultural produce. Despite a starting capital of only $1,000, borrowed from his father (at 10% interest), in their first year of business they turned over $450,000 making a net profit of $4,400. This was just the beginning and the partners benefitted hugely from the Civil War. John D invested his returns in railroad stocks and land.

In the 1860s' he was attracted to oil, initially in refining, but the business expanded vertically as John D added storage and transportation.

Share certificate of 1878 signed by John D Rockefeller and Henry Flagler. Not only was this the world's largest oil company it was also America's largest monopoly.

He also found a new and dynamic partner, Henry Flagler, and in 1870 the two of them converted their firm into a joint stock company – *Standard Oil of Ohio*, capitalized at one million dollars with Rockefeller as President and Flagler, secretary-treasurer.

Refining 1,500 barrels a day, the company became the world's largest oil producer. It rapidly acquired most of the country's refineries by fair means or foul and by 1880 controlled 90% of the US oil business. In 1882, the group was further consolidated under the title *Standard Oil Trust* but its obvious domination of the oil business eventually led to a forced break-up under progressive anti-trust legislation.

Between 1875 and 1882 the company increased its capital from $1 million to $3.5 million. During this period share certificates bear the signatures of Rockefeller and Flagler. As the number of shareholders was tightly controlled (only 5 in 1870 and 41 in 1880) relatively few certificates are believed to exist from this period but later certificates in *Standard Oil Trust* (an "alliance of companies") are appreciably more common, as well as carrying the signature of John D.

Rockefeller was a philanthropist and gave huge sums to charitable causes, hospitals and libraries. In 1889 he founded the University of Chicago, initially with a gift of $600,000 but ultimately over $80 million.

After his retirement the business was run by his brother William and later by his son, John D Rockefeller Jr..

The successful dynasty continued. Nelson Rockefeller, grandson of J D became Vice President of the United States but never achieved his ultimate aim of the top job.

Alexander Hamilton

Of all those involved in the Financial development of America since the war of Independence, Alexander Hamilton must rank No.1.

Hamilton was born in Nevis in the British West Indies in 1757 to a Scottish born father and a French Huguenot mother. His mother died

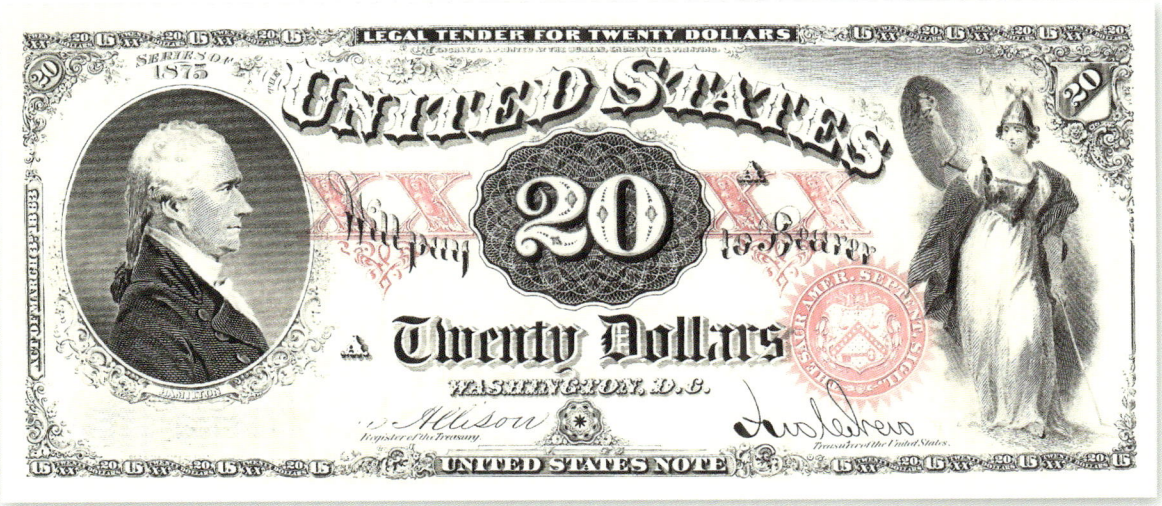

Banknote for $20 with vignette of Alexander Hamilton

when he was 11 and as his fathers business was not successful, he went to live with his maternal relatives at St.Croix in the Virgin Islands. From there he was sent to Columbia University (then, 'Kings College') and became a 'revolutionary'. In the course of fighting for the cause, he attracted the attention of George Washington and in 1777 became his private secretary. Four years later, he resigned and Washington secured command of a field regiment for the young Alexander (still only 24). In the same year he married Elizabeth Schuler, the daughter of one of Washington's Generals.

At the end of hostilities, Hamilton practiced law and when Washington was made President he was appointed Secretary of the Treasury with the task of settling war debts and reorganizing public finances. He was a controversial and aggressive operator who went about his tasks with enthusiasm. In 1791 he persuaded Congress to incorporate the country's first national bank ("Bank of the United States") despite considerable opposition from Thomas Jefferson and the southern states. The bank was reasonably successful in its aims but its chartered life of 20 years was not extended. Hamilton fought repeated battles over taxes and tariffs designed to protect agricultural industries but by 1795 he resigned and returned to private law practice in New York where he handled most of the City's important commercial cases. He was never wealthy but became the figurehead for capitalism in the United States. He died in a dual at the hands of Aaron Burr, whom he had attempted to prevent taking control of the democrats. He fathered eight children and was reputed to have had more than one affair.

Possibly the most famous of all America's capitalists.

Miners and their Mines

Second only to railways in terms of volume and variety of material, 'mining' offers the collector a vast range of material with choice over mineral or geographical location. It's not hard to understand why so many individuals headed for the hills with a spade and a pick-axe; initial investment was minimal and the sense of adventure and potential rewards, huge. Hordes of gold diggers simply moved from one location to another following the rumour of the moment. It was not unusual for the same people panning for gold in California in the late 1840s' to reappear doing exactly the same in South Africa years later. Not all, by any means, formed companies, indeed this tended to be the last step on the road to wealth, but once on that road and once discoveries were made, the end goal was worth all the hardship.

This section looks at some of the miners and minerals sought, particularly gold, silver, diamonds and copper. But very often the location and the mines would throw up a combination. A book of this kind cannot describe all the attempts to become rich and readers with a fascination for the subject are encouraged to read more in the many excellent (and often, exciting) histories. Here we look at a few of the big guys and their explorations.

A Step towards the Presidency

Herbert Clark Hoover was born 1874 in Iowa and orphaned at the age of nine. He scraped a place at Stanford University and majored in geology, paying his way by establishing a student laundry service. Starting work as a surveyor and working 70 hours a week on a gold mine near Nevada City, set his path. In 1897 he was employed by the British engineering firm

Certificates siged by Herbert Hoover are scarce. This one in the Maikop & General Petroleum Trust is dated 1910 and is signed by Hoover as a Director.

of *Bewick, Moreing and Company Ltd.*, initially to investigate and manage its interests in Western Australia. He also led a major expansion programme for the *Sons of Gwalia Gold Mine*.

In 1899 Hoover moved to China where he became chief engineer of the *Chinese Bureau of Mines* and later, General Manager and Director of the *Chinese Engineering & Mining Corporation*. He was drawn into the Boxer Rebellion of 1900 and helped the local authorities withstand the siege. He was actively involved in local coal mines, railways and shipping companies and became a partner in Bewick, Moreing & Company Limited which acquired the Chinese Engineering & Mining Company in 1900. Leaving the company in 1908, he set up his own consultancy practice and within 5 years was employing some 175,000 men. He also established *Zinc Corporation* which eventually formed part of *Rio Tinto Zinc Corporation* ("RTZ').

During the 1st World War Hoover provided food for the Belgians and following the entry of the United States into the War, Woodrow Wilson appointed him Head of U.S. Food Administration, controlling profiteering and distribution of food to the allies. Amongst other things, he set up the Sugar Equalization board and bought up the

Share certificate dated 1919 in the Chinese Engineering & Mining Company of which Hoover was the General Manager.

whole sugar output of Cuba for distribution at reasonable prices. This was just the beginning of Hoover's public life, in 1921 he was appointed Secretary of Commerce and in 1929 won the Presidency by a landslide, serving 5 years during one of the most difficult periods of history – the Great Depression.

Despite a poor relationship with Roosevelt, Hoover regained his influence with the appointment of Harry Truman and continued with government and humanitarian projects until his death in 1964. His son, Herbert Clark Hoover Jr. was appointed

special advisor on international petroleum problems with much of his time spent in Iran sorting out the disputes over the oil fields and the fallout of the ousting of the premier by the CIA in 1953.

A Family Concern

Born in Norwich in 1779, John Taylor and future generations of Taylors, established their initial reputations in Devon. John was a mining engineer and when only 19 took over the management of *Wheal Friendship*, famous for copper but also a source of arsenic, lead and iron. The village of Mary Tavy (now Blackdown) was home to the workers, who lived in extreme poverty. The mine owners were slow to pay their workers and Taylor, along with other businesses of the time (1811-1820) created a local currency, known as the 'Tavistock Token" which acted as a credit buffer enabling the miners to live whilst their wages were processed. The Government banned such tokens in 1820.

A 'Tavistock Token" dated 1811 for one penny.

John's interests and abilities were broad. He oversaw the construction of the *Tavistock Canal* and in 1807 was elected a Fellow of the Geological Society. Five years later he struck up a partnership with his cousin, John Martineau of Birmingham. The Martineaus' were a wealthy family from Norwich involved in local politics and early surgery (is there a difference?....). Thomas Martineau, John's brother, was the uncle of Prime Minister Neville Chamberlain. The two Johns set up a chemical plant to manufacture vitriol but the relationship did not last and Taylor turned away from vitriol and reverted to mining. In 1819 he reopened the *Consolidated Mines* in Gwennap, Cornwall, which employed over 3,000 people.

In 1825 he was elected a fellow of the Royal

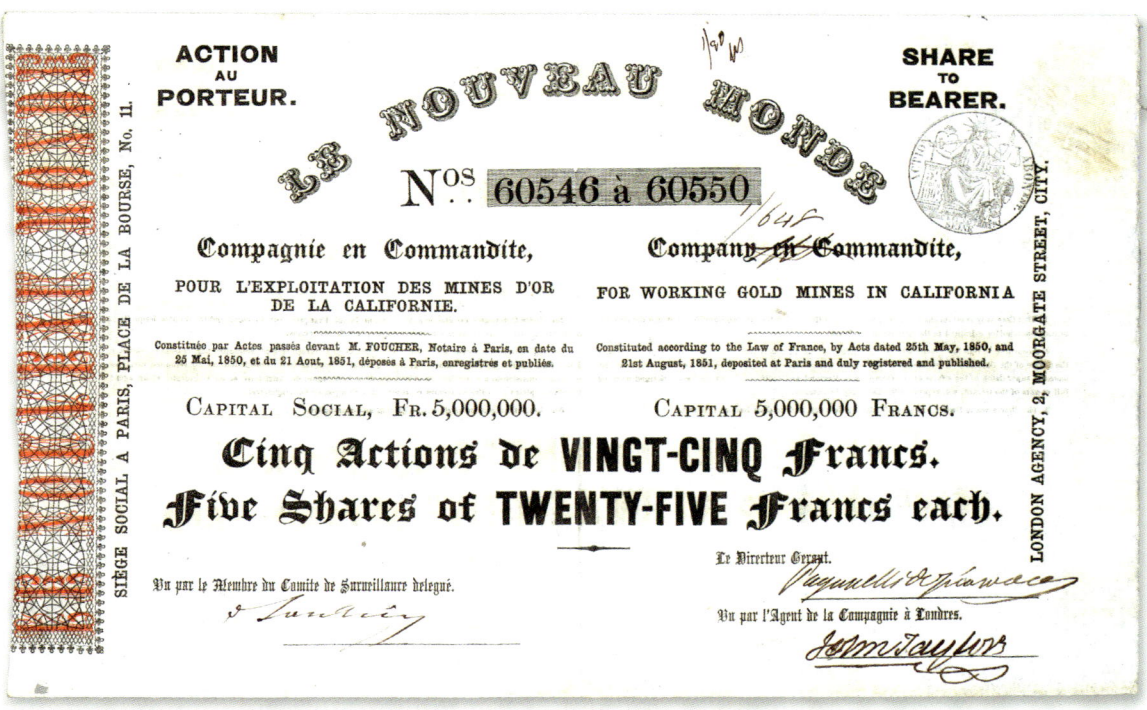

One of several enterprises in which John Taylor was involved, this time as trustee and technical manager. Formed as a French company to ensure its shareholders benefited from limited liability (not then available to British companies). The company sought gold in California but was unsuccessful and later operated in Central America. But by 1857, its capital was exhausted and its claims were finally sold on to the Central American Mining Company in 1859. The certificate above is hand signed by John Taylor.

Society and was a founder of the British Association and University College, London.

John Taylor died in 1863 shortly after assuming management of the *Linares Mining Company* through his own company John Taylor & Son. His son, John Taylor Jnr., born in 1808, became manager of the lead mines of Flintshire, Mold and Halkyn. By 1845 he was a full partner of his father and his management of the Linares mines led to the formation of the *Fortuna & Alamillos* companies working with other lead mines in Spain. One thing led to another and in no time mines yielding silver, copper, cobalt and nickel were in full operation. His brother, Richard, joined the partnership in 1851 and together they developed *Cape Copper Mines* in South Africa and the *Coueron* lead smelting works on the Loire. Richard was a founder of the Royal Cornwall Polytechnic Society and a member of the Royal Institution.

John Jnr. died in 1881 and Richard two years later.

Barney Barnato and Cecil Rhodes – The Odd Couple!

Mining often brings opposites together and Barnato and Rhodes were certainly that. Born in the slums of London in 1852, Barnato (original name, Barnett Issacs) was an uneducated trader. Rhodes, born a year later, the son of a vicar in Hertfordshire, was not a healthy child and his parents sent him to South Africa to benefit from the warmer climate. There he joined his brother, Herbert, who, under a system of assisted emigration, had started to grow cotton. But Herbert was intent on bigger fish and diamond fever encouraged him to 'dig deep'; Cecil followed.

Herbert soon tired of the explorers life and left it

to brother Cecil, who, with his partner Charles Rudd began providing ancillary products and services to the miners of Kimberley. These included ice cream, cold water, cakes and pumping water from mine workings. The profits permitted Rudd to buy into the Baxter's Gully claim on the De Beers mine and Rhodes to complete his education at Oxford, dividing his time between there and Kimberley.

At the same time as Rhodes was making his fortune, Barney Barnato was setting out on his. Initially teaming up with his brother, Harry, in the music halls of London, as a prize fighter he eventually headed off to the Cape where he became a 'koppie-walloper', a small diamond dealer buying from the diggers and reselling to the market. Working with his brother, Barney made enough to invest in a block of claims in Kimberley. His reputation was constantly in question but he was sharp and understood the mining business. Whilst Harry slipped into the background, Barney accumulated more claims and eventually consolidated them under a corporate umbrella, the *Barnato Diamond Mining Company,* which later merged with the *Standard Company* and ultimately the *Kimberley Central Diamond Mining Company,* at which point he and Rhodes came face to face. Whilst all this was going on, another of Barney's relations Woolf Joel, Barney's nephew, joined the band becoming a director of Kimberley Central. The company acquired the *Compagnie Francaise des Mines de Diamant du Cap* and by 1887, Barney had agreed amalgamation of his companies with De Beers after protracted negotiations, during which, Rhodes reputedly produced a bucketful of diamonds to encourage Barney to sign. So, in 1888 *De Beers Consolidated Mines Ltd.* was formed. The deal cost Rhodes £5 million of which £4 million went to the Barnato brothers.

Barney thrived from the link and was soon a

Typical early diamond company share. This one for the Kimberley Octahedron Diamond Mining Co. is dated 1881. In fact the Kimberley Octahedron Diamond was not discovered by De Beers until 1964 and is the 14th largest gem quality rough diamond ever discovered.

Diamonds were far from the only attraction of South Africa to the men with shovels. Indeed, following their discovery and the establishment of De Beers, gold came through strongly with early discoveries in Barberton and in the hills of the Witwatersrand. Cecil Rhodes was an active participant forming *Gold Fields of South Africa* in 1887 with Charles Rudd. Other companies followed, including *Rand Mines*, *General Mining*, *Union Corporation* and Sir Ernest Oppenheimer's *Anglo American* in 1917.

The table below lists a few of the big names (other than those mentioned) and the mining companies, in which, at some stage they were involved:

member of the Cape Assembly and the stock exchange, despite his reputation. He chaired De Beers and was closely involved in the sale of the *British South Africa Company,* as well as setting up the *Johannesburg Consolidated Investment Company Ltd.,* and the ill fated *Barnato Bank, Mining & Estates Company.*

In 1897 following a series of dubious investments and legal actions, Barnato committed suicide, jumping overboard on his way to Queen Victoria's diamond jubilee in London. Despite being a 'rogue' he was loved by his family and many of Johannesburg's streets and institutions still bear his name.

Miner	Company
Max Michaelis	Werner Beit & Co.
Sammy Marks	African & European Investment Co
Sir George Farrar	East Rand Proprietary Mine
Sir Sigismund Neumann	S Neumann & Co
Adolf Goerz	Union Corporation
Sir George Albu	General Mining & Finance Company
Sir Abe Bailey	South African Townships, Mining & Finance Co.

Australia's 'Woolly' Beginnings

It would be remiss to talk about mining without mentioning Australia. Although, the country's early industries revolved around sheep, the discovery of gold in the mid nineteenth century transformed the country. In 1802, Australia had a population of 6,000. The country's formation and occupation was, by some, considered an alternative to Britain's 'lost' colony of America and/or a suitable place to park prisoners. Whatever the reason, the country became a source of wool for Britain's mills and in 1824, the Australian Agricultural Company was formed to produce merino wool for the British market.

By 1836, Brisbane, Perth, Adelaide and Melbourne had been established and the earliest bank (Bank of New South Wales) was opened in 1817 by Samuel Terry, an ex-convict.

But it was the 'discovery' of gold by Edward Hargraves which really kicked off development. Born in England, Hargraves became agent for the *General Steam Navigation Company* near Sydney. He left his wife and moved to California with the '49ers' and returned to Australia with the aim of finding gold and claiming a government reward of £10,000. Linking up with John Lister and William Tom, he employed the panning techniques he had learned in California and in 1851 announced gold had been discovered at Lewis Pond Creek. Within 5 months, over 300 diggers were on site seeking their fortunes. Hargraves received his government prize and even met Queen Victoria but counter-claims

The Australian Agricultural Company was one of the earliest Australian companies. This example is dated 1825 and depicts Sydney top centre

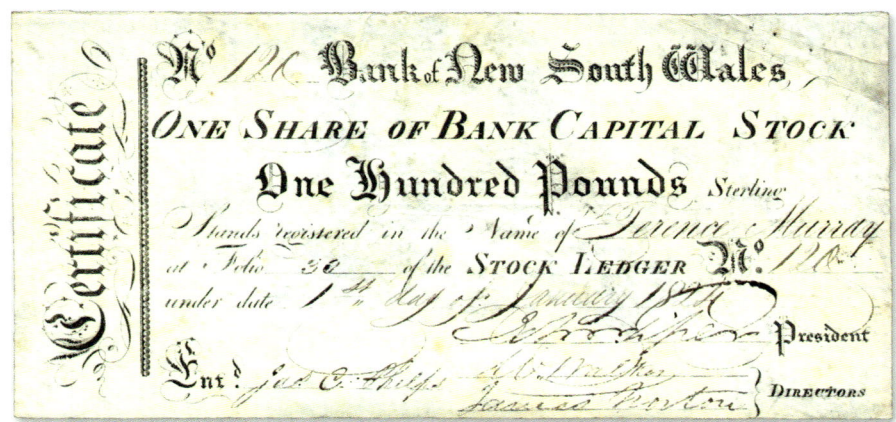

One of Australia's earliest banks. The bank of New South Wales was formed by Samuel Terry, an ex-convict.

few months *Bayleys Reward Claim Gold Mining Company* had yielded 3,000 ounces of gold (about $4 million at today's exchange rate). The company was bought by Sylvester Browne three months later and although more gold was extracted, early estimates proved optimistic.

by Tom and Lister discredited him and he died with an estate of less than £375.

Despite Hargrave's exaggerations, gold and minerals were indeed in abundant supply and mining companies (and local stock exchanges) sprang up across the fields, eventually followed by the first steam railway, the *St Kilda & Brighton Railway Company*, in 1857.

By the 1890's, rich seams had been found in the west, particularly in the Coolgardie and Kalgoorlie areas outside of Perth. It was here that Herbert Hoover was active, whilst others such as Horatio Bottomley, Claude de Bernales and Whittaker Wright played their parts; although not always in the public interest . As on the east of the country, stock exchanges sprang up, but not all were traditional institutions, indeed the preference was for 'open call'. *Kalgoorlie's Open Call Exchange* was simply a huge public auction with over 600 people trading shares on the crash of an auctioneers hammer.

Two key pioneers were largely responsible for the early finds in Coolgardie, Arthur Bayley and William Ford. Their discovery of gold nuggets in 1892 triggered a rush to Coolgardie. Within a

A series of takeovers resulted in the original mine being absorbed by *Bayley's Gold Mines Ltd* and eventually ending up under the control of one time London entrepreneur Claude de Bernales through *Phoenix Gold Mines Ltd.*. Its final resting place was with the *Western Mining Corporation.*

Inevitably 'frauds' were rife and two deserve mention; *Londonderry Gold Mine* and the *Wealth of Nations*. Initial rich finds resulted in the former being sold to the Earl of Fingall and his associate, Colonel J T North, who sealed the mine with steel sheeting and then raised £700,000 capital in London. When the sheeting was removed, there was no gold left! The *Wealth of Nations* also failed to live up to its name and after floating the company for £480,000, Colonel North advised the mine was bereft – as indeed were the investors.

Miners continued to prospect the area and three others deserve mention, Patrick 'Paddy' Hannan, Dan O'Shea and Tom Flanagan.

The miners faced hardship, particularly from lack of water, and it was not long before the nuggets that been easily picked up on the

Share certificate dated 1899 in the reconstituted Londonderry Gold Mine set up with a capital of £70,000. Lord Fingall and H Myring gave up their accrued profits in the original company.

surface ran out. Mining needed money and although the stock markets were eager to find new investments, new money disappeared and of the 800 companies floated by 1896, only 140 existed in 1891. However, the discovery of gold did wonders for population levels and the raft of industries and railway companies which followed established the country's economy.

Tin and Copper

There is a tendency to focus on the glamour of gold and diamonds when talking about mining, but there are many more minerals equally valuable and equally important. Amongst these are tin and copper.

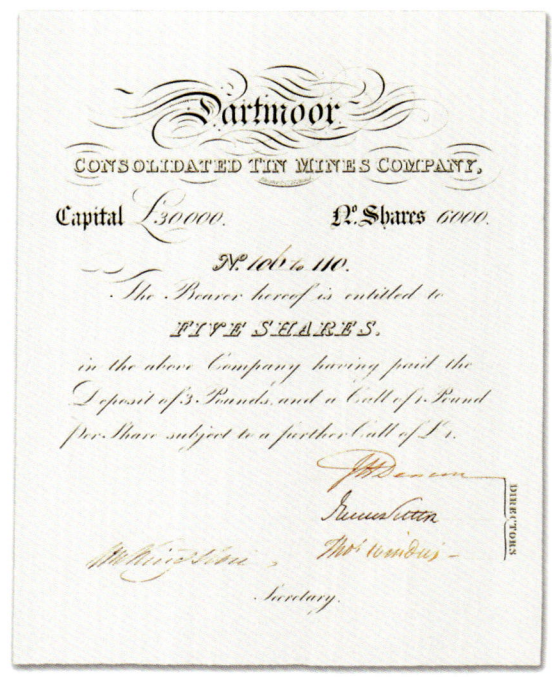

One of Cornwall's early tin mining companies dating from 1818.

Typical mining company share certificate issued by one of the many copper mining companies operating in Nevada during the early 1900s'.

Tin has been mined in Cornwall for 2,000 years. Its geology is also conducive to copper, iron, zinc, lead and silver. But it was during the early 1800s' that mining began in earnest in Cornwall and it was copper that proved most important in those early days. As copper stocks were depleted, attention switched to tin but drainage problems resulted in another kind of industrial development; the application of steam traction. Richard Trevithick, the son of the Dolcoath Mine's manager, transformed Cornish mining by designing and building 30 static steam engines (known as "puffer whims"). In 1803, he built a mobile locomotive that he drove up Tottenham Court Road in London and on a circular track near Euston (unfortunately, the track broke!). Trevithick took his engines to Peru but by the time he returned George Stephenson had taken on the railway mantle.

Copper predates tin with finds dating back 6,000 years. Since that time its uses have stretched from arms to electrical engineering. It is mainly found in the western United States, Zambia, Newfoundland and Central Canada, and the Andes regions of Peru and Chile. But it has also been discovered in Australia and Antarctica and has been mined in Cyprus since the fourth millennium BC.

Cars, Buses, Boats and Bikes

It may seem strange that all forms of 'contemporary' road transport originated at about the same time in the last quarter of the nineteenth century. Development of all, of course, was a direct result of industrialization. Each make an ideal collecting subject and these few words are no more than an introduction.

Cars

Britain's early 10 miles per hour speed limit (subsequently reduced to 4 mph) and the requirement for a red flag to preceed vehicles gave an edge to France, which in the late nineteenth century took the lead in automobile development. Thus, although Daimler (Germany) produced the first petrol driven car in 1887, it was France which rapidly took the lead in manufacturing. The most prominent French companies of the time were Rene Panhard and Emille Lavassor, whose factory in Paris employed 850 workers by 1901. Other French companies included *Mors* and *De Dion-Bouton*. The Belgian company of *S.A. Minerva Motors* was formed in Antwerp in 1903 and became famous for engine manufacture, with England as its main market. Minerva car owners included the kings of Belgium, Sweden and Norway as well as Henry Ford.

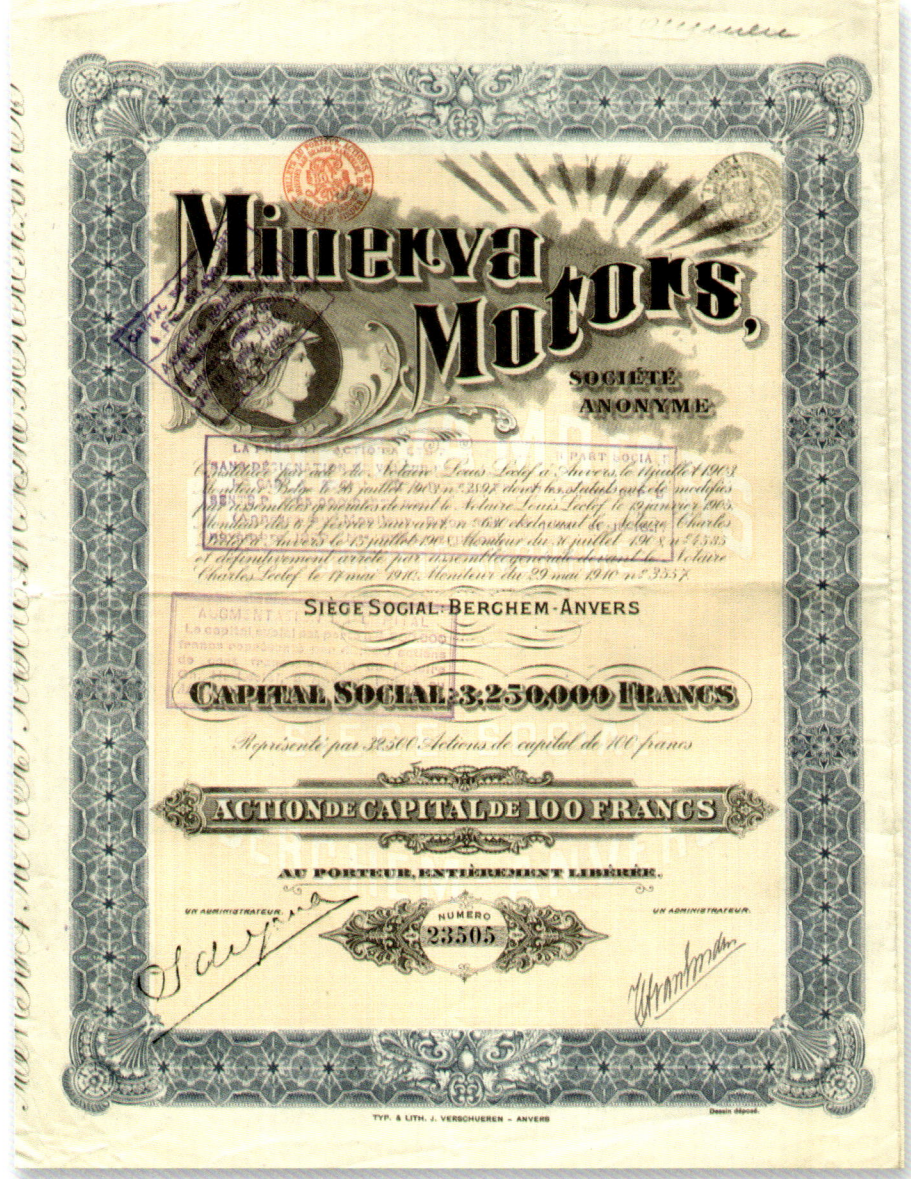

Early share in Minerva Motors issued in 1903, manufacturer of cars and bicycle.s

In Germany two entrepreneurs were well established in the motoring field by this time, Gottlieb Daimler and Carl Benz. Although they never met, both developed automobiles independently and simultaneously. Benz initially built the three wheeled "Velocipede" whilst Daimler produced the first 4 wheeled vehicle and worked with his colleague Wilhelm Maybach who invented the spray-nozzle carburetor.

Progress was fast, no doubt encouraged by an increasing number of race meetings. The first of these, sponsored by the French newspaper *Le Petit Journal,* ran from Paris to Rouen and entry requirements necessitated an ability to achieve 7.75 miles per hour. Only three contestants lasted the course, averaging 12 mph. But it was the following year (1895), which really set the standards with the inauguration of the Paris-Bordeaux-Paris race, a distance of 732 miles. Twenty-two cars took part but only nine finished with Emile Lavassor coming in first, *Peugeot* taking the next three places and Hans Thum driving a Benz in fifth place. Daimler was very active in the sports world and their racing car was commissioned by Emil Jellinek and named after his daughter, Mercedes. *(Jellinek was a successful businessman and diplomat becoming Austrian Consul General in Nice, where he sold many cars).*

In Britain, meanwhile, attitudes were mellowing and not only was the red flag abolished but the speed limit was raised to 14 mph by the "Locomotives on the Highway Act" of 1896. To celebrate, supporters organized a procession of cars travelling from London to Brighton, and so began the famous annual event. By 1913 nearly 200 British companies were producing cars – most failed. Much of the early interest came from the wealthy with such worthies as William Vanderbilt, Baron Henri de Rothschild and the Honourable Charles S Rolls, participating in early races. One classic event was the Gordon-Bennet Trophy established by the wealthy son of the founder of the New York Herald and an enthusiast of fast cars, planes and women. In 1906 he established the hot air balloon race still held today but any connection with the expression 'Gordon Bennet', is unproven. In 1926, Daimler-Benz AG was formed with the merger of *Daimler-Motoren-Gessellschaft* ("DMG") and *Benz & Cie.*

Car manufacturing was not limited to Europe and during the first four months of 1899, eighty companies were formed in the United States with a combined share capital of $338 million. By 1903, there were reputed to be 300 automobile factories across the country. But it was the appearance of Henry Ford on the scene, which not only established American dominance of the industry but also made the car available to all – not just the privileged.

Henry Ford

Ford was not the only American car company to start production in the early 1900s', Buick, Pierce-Arrow, Cadillac and Packard all began around the same time. These companies joined the already existing Oldsmobile, Studebaker, Haynes and Locomobile.

Henry Ford started out with 12 partners and $28,000 in the bank. In 1909, the 'Model T' was born and dominated the market for almost 20 years. By 1914, 250,000 of them were being sold each year, representing 45% of the American market. By the 1930s' Ford's River Rouge plant employed over 100,000 people on 2,000 acres supported by its own police force, fire department and hospital. The "Rouge" was developed between 1917-1928, the factory which had its own railroad, initially produced Eagle Boats (submarine chasers for the war effort), then tractors and then the Model 'T' from 1927. The Ford Motor Company made profits of over $1 billion in its first 25 years.

Bond for M.1,000 dated 1909 in Benz & Cie., issued in Mannheim with art nouveau border.

CAPITAL STOCK, $125,000.00

The Ford Motor Company of Canada, Limited

No 88   STOCK CERTIFICATE   6 Shares

This Certifies that Henry Ford of Detroit Michigan is entitled to Six fully paid up shares of One hundred Dollars each in the Capital Stock of the Ford Motor Company of Canada, Limited

The said shares are transferable on the books of the Company only by him or his Attorney duly constituted, and upon surrender of this Certificate, and as provided for in the By Laws of this Company

Dated at Walkerville, Ontario, this Seventeenth day of September 190

G. M. McGregor, SECRETARY.   Henry Ford, PRESIDENT.

Although separate from its US associate, Ford Motor Company of Canada was founded in 1904 to produce and sell vehicles in Canada and the British Empire. Henry Ford was one of its 12 founder members and owned 13% of the company. The above certificate is issued to him and assigned by him - a rare example. The company was originally located at Walkerville, Ontario where it continued to produce automobiles until its move to Oakville. Even in the 1970s' Ford was the largest company in Canada and today produces 320,000 vehicles a year and employs 23,000 workers - a far cry from its first years production of 117 cars.

Billy Durant and General Motors

Ford's, success inevitably brought competition and one of the most significant was William Durrant who, in 1909, began consolidating his vast combine under the title *General Motors*. Buick, Cadillac, Pontiac and Oldsmobile were soon absorbed and Dodge followed shortly after. Opel (of Germany) joined the combine 30 years later having progressed from sewing machines through bicycles to cars. William "Billy" Durant

spent $2,000 to incorporate GM in New Jersey having made his fortune from building horse-drawn carriages. Despite his initial revulsion at "noisy, smelly and dangerous" automobiles he went on to plant the seeds of a major business empire. However, his fellow investors thought him too much a spendthrift and forced him out in 1911. But Durant returned only to be forced out once again in 1920. During the Depression he suffered bankruptcy and spent his last years running a bowling alley in his home town of Flint.

Buses

The motor industry was not limited to car production. Like any new industry, catering for the mass market was essential and the omnibus was the most practical means. Most early vehicles were made by *De Dion-Bouton & Cie,* and exported worldwide to such markets as Bolivia, USA, Italy, Austria and Spain. Indeed several companies were established in Spain to run the buses including the *Sociedad Espanola de Automoviles Segovie a la Granja* which made a point of allocating one of its fleet for the sole use of the royal family.

Boats

The Builders

Early experiments on power propelled ships were carried out in France at the end of the seventeenth century, but it was in Scotland where the most significant developments took place. In 1785 James Taylor of Lanarkshire was appointed tutor to the children of Patrick Miller of the Dalswinton Estate. At the time Miller was experimenting with mechanical propulsion of ships on the Firth of Forth using manual labour to drive the paddles. Taylor suggested using a James Watt steam engine and William Symington was asked to build it. The results were tested at the Dalswinton Loch in 1788 and on the Forth in the following year where a speed of 5 miles per hour was achieved. There followed some dispute over who actually did the inventing which has generally been attributed to Symington and Miller. Following this success, steam boats were built in increasing numbers in Scotland, with the boats concentrating on coastal and short-distance transportation (for example, the *Dumbarton Steam Boat Company* founded in 1815).

In the United States, John Fitch sailed a steamboat driven by paddles rather like ducks feet in 1789 and Robert Fulton, having witnessed the Scottish experiments, built the Clermont in 1807. This was the first commercially successful steamboat in the country which plied the Hudson River between Albany and New York; a distance of 142 miles. From then on steamers began to flourish and many ships were built on the Clyde. A major improvement was the substitution of the paddle wheel by the screw propeller and it was this that was crucial in persuading the British Admiralty to adopt steam driven ships for the Royal Navy.

The Carriers

The close relationship between ship builders and shipping line managers stemmed from those early days in Scotland and the stories of Cunard and Elder Dempster are good examples. The tales are made more appealing to the collector by the availability of many share certificates.

Cunard

Coming from a once wealthy Philadelphia family, which was banished to Nova Scotia for supporting the British, Samuel Cunard created a shipping line that rivaled the companies of the railroad barons. Setting up his new home in Halifax, Samuel determined to make a living from the sea and by 1812 he and his father had acquired their first schooner. Their shipping business did well as a "neutral" carrier during the wars with France, but after 1815, Halifax was no longer a garrison town and new business was needed. Cunard sought and won a contract from the British Government to carry mail to and from Bermuda and more significantly, won a contract from the East India Company to receive and trans-ship tea from China.

Further investments in a whaling fleet, local canals, the *Annapolis Mining Company* and the *Halifax Banking Company* all created a diverse and sizeable business empire. But it was steam ships that really fired Cunard's imagination particularly the possibilities of Atlantic crossings. Such ideas were encouraged by a ride on the *Liverpool & Manchester Railway* and news of the first Atlantic Steam crossing by a Dutch ship, the Curacao. Later crossings by Brunel's SS Great Western and the Sirius in 1838 led directly to Cunard's determination to win the British Post Office contract to carry trans-Atlantic mail, despite strong competition from Cornelius Vanderbilt. Once won, he persuaded Robert Napier to design and build the three ships

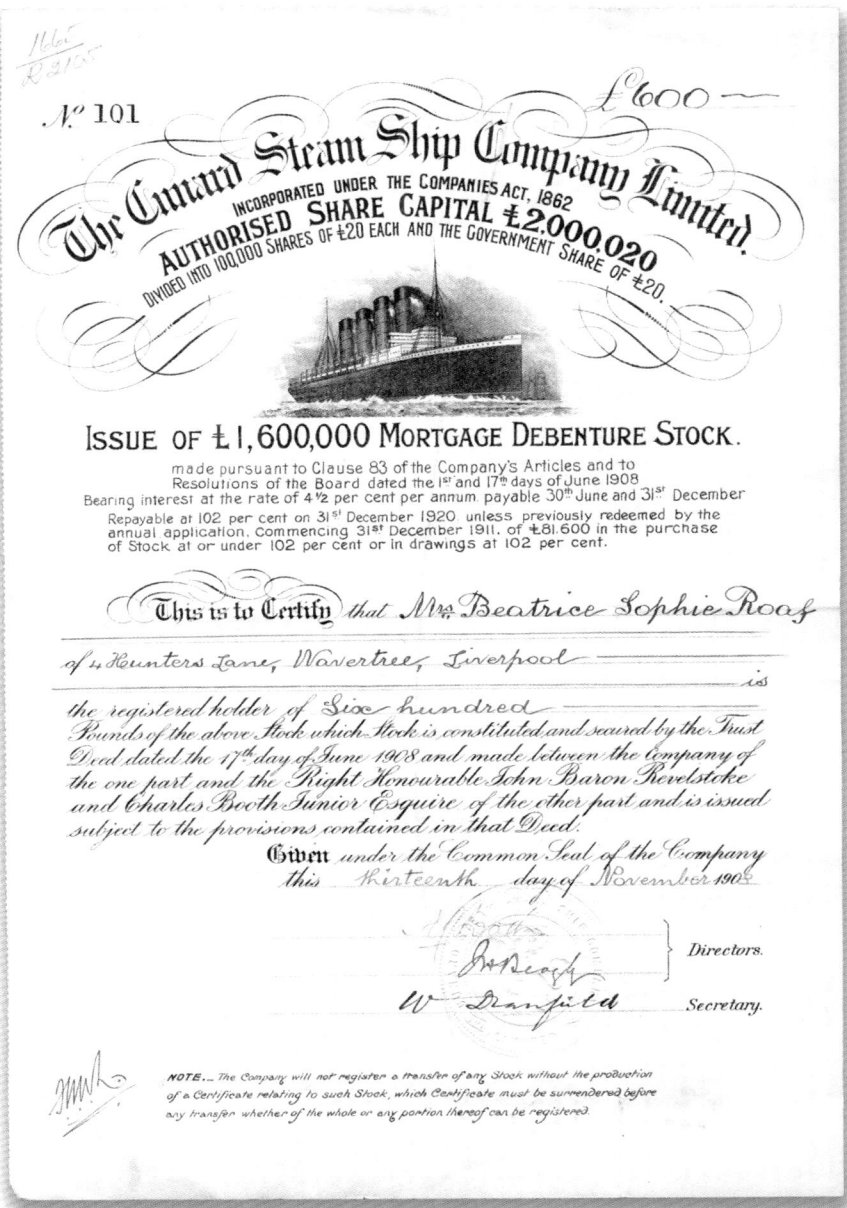

Debenture in the Cunard Steamship Company

and only then set about raising the necessary cash. The ships were ordered at £30,000 each subsequently increased to £32,000 when the Admiralty insisted on a capacity of 960 tons. The funds were raised through a newly formed company, the *British & North American Royal Mail Steam Packet Company*, a name so long that newspapers abbreviated it to "Mr. Cunard's Company" or simply "Cunard's". The first of his steamers to reach Halifax from Liverpool arrived in 1840 after only twelve and a half days at sea. Eight years later the service was extended to New York.

Preference share dated 1913 in the Elder Dempster Company signed by Owen Philips (later Lord Kylsant)

Samuel Cunard eventually settled in England and was knighted in 1859 in recognition of his contribution to the Crimean War. He died 6 years later, the same year Abraham Lincoln was assassinated.

Elder Dempster Company

Although early business with West Africa concentrated on the profitable slave trade, it was the availability of less contentious produce, such as vegetable oils, which was primarily responsible for its growth in importance. The

African Steam Ship Company founded by Royal Charter in 1852 was the first shipping company to establish regular links. Its prime objective was to carry mail for the British Government and its Managing Director and founder was Macregor Laird, son of the founder of *Cammell Laird* and grandson of our old friend Gregor Macgregor of Poyais.

Following Laird's death the company became the *British & African Steam Navigation Company*. Two ex-employees of the African Steam Ship Company, John Dempster and Alexander Elder were appointed agents and the resultant

Elder Dempster Company was formed in 1868. Sixteen years later the founders retired and Sir Alfred Jones took control of both groups.

On Jones's death, Lords' Kylsant and Pirie (the former a director of the *Royal Mail Steam Packet Company* and Chairman of *Harland & Wolff*) bought Elder Dempster for £500,000 and incorporated it in 1910. Having merged the shipping lines of Elder Dempster and the Royal Mail Steam Packet Company, Kylsant set off on the acquisition trail. Large stakes were taken in the *White Star Line* (owner of the Titanic) from *International Mercantile Marine, Lamport & Holt,* and the *Union Castle Steamship Company.* At the height of his career Kylsant controlled 560 ships and employed over 59,000 men but all did not go well. A combination of poor trade, management disagreements with his brother, Viscount St. Davids, and rumours of insolvency caused the group to collapse in 1931. Kylsant was arrested and convicted of giving false trading information in a prospectus.

Several of the certificates of companies in the group carry Kylsant's signature.

Bicycles

Like all forms of transport, the bicycle is ideal for both competition and getting from 'A to B' as cheaply as possible.

The earliest machines date from around 1818 thanks to the ingenuity of Baron Karl von Drais, but it was a further 67 years before the machines we recognize today were perfected. In the interim, progress was slow, moving from Pierre Michaux's model based on a hobby-horse through the ubiquitous Penny Farthing to the first safety cycle manufactured in Coventry by J K Starley. Throughout, sport played its part:

the first womens' race took place in Bordeaux in 1868 and Penny Farthings, achieved frightening speeds of 50kph. at Herne Hill velodrome, which became the early home of British track cycling, hosting the 1948 Olympic games.

The velodrome was set up by George Lacey Hillier who floated a company called the *London County Athletics Ground Limited* in 1891. The track was made of rolled ballast and surrounded a rugby field. During the 1920s' and 30s' meetings regularly attracted massive crowds of over 10,000. The authors father, Arthur Hollender, one of the top cyclists in Britain before the war participated, riding the 170 miles from his home in Yorkshire after work on Saturday and riding back again after racing on Sunday – people were made of sterner stuff in those days.

When it came to manufacture, safety was hardly a priority and it was not until the Rover Safety Cycle was produced by J K Starley in 1885 that we began to see something recognisable today. At around the same period, Minerva Motors entered the field and although it eventually became better known for motorized bicycles, it produced its first 'safety bicycle' in 1897. The availability of pneumatic tyres, courtesy of John Dunlop, combined with Starley's cross spoke wheels established the pattern. However, the early models were far from cheap and not built for the common man (the cost of one bicycle was equivalent to 310 gallons of beer!), but from then on, prices fell and the bike was truly established. Although Rover was acquired by BMW, Starley Bikes continues today.

Famous Signatures

By their nature (and often by law) share certificates carry at least two signatures. Nowadays these tend to be facsimiles but certainly prior to 1900, they were usually the real thing. Of course, the Company Secretary or Accountant may not add value (sorry guys) but in the past, it was quite usual for certificates to bear the handwritten signatures of a company's president and/or directors, some of whom were, and still are, well known. The presence of a famous signature can add considerably to value as well as interest. It may seem remarkable to us in the twenty first century to contemplate a busy chief executive signing thousands of share certificates, but in many countries, particularly America and Britain, it was simply part of the job. Messrs Kreuger and Toll, however, appear to have taken it in turns with their directors to sign. Interestingly, but absolutely nothing to do with this subject, the earliest known signature of a well known figure is believed to be that of El Cid, dated 1098 AD.

Below are listed a few original signatures which can be found on share certificates:

Signature	Certificate	Date
Henry Wells & William Fargo	American Express Co.	1852-70
Robert Morris	North American Land Co.	c.1795
William Bingham	Philadelphia & Lancaster Turnpike	c.1795
Nathan Meyer Rothschild	Russian State Loan	1822
Gregor Macgregor	Poyais Bonds	1820-30
John D Rockefeller	Standard Oil Co.	1870's
Cornelius Vanderbilt	New York & Harlem Railroad	c.1870
J P Morgan	New Jersey Junction Railroad	c.1886
Stephen Austin	Texian Loan	1836
Thomas A Edison	Edison Portland Cement Co.	c.1899
Jay Gould	Missouri Kansas & Texas Railway	c.1880
Max Michaelis	Du Toit's Pan Diamond Mining Co	c.1881
Bernard Oppenheimer	Central South African Lands & Mines	c.1903
Barney Barnato	Beaconsfield Diamond Mining Co	1881
Alfred Beit	Kimberley Imperial Gold Mining Co	c.1886
Kreuger & Toll	Kreuger & Toll	c.1927
Nicholas Biddle	Second Bank of the United States	c.1838
Charlie Chaplin	Chaplin Studios Inc.	c.1918
Samuel F B Morse	New Orleans & Ohio Telegraph Co.	c.1847

The above are all originals but there are also many facsimile signatures, usually on more recent material. Typical of these are:

Signature	Certificate	Date
Hugh Heffner	Playboy Enterprises Inc.	c.1977
Bernie Cornfield	I O S Ltd.	c.1960's
J Paul Getty	Mission Development Co.	c.1950's
Whittaker Wright	London & Globe	c.1899
Fred Stark Pearson	San Antonio Land & Irrigation Ltd	c.1912
Sun Yat Sen	Chung Hwa Revolutionary Party, Fund Raising Bonds	1915
Eamon de Valera	Republic of Ireland Bond	1920
Ferdinand de Lesseps	Co. Universelle du Canal Inter-Oceanic de Panama	1881

It is always worth seeing to whom a share was issued and some interesting names can be found by turning it over, as certificates would often have been endorsed by the owner with an actual signature.

Walt Disney and his brother Roy founded the famous company in 1923. It went through several name changes with Walt adapting to fast changing film technology. His greatest early creation was Micky Mouse. Following close on the heals of the film business came the theme parks, the greatest of which being the Epcot Centre, Florida, completed in 1982 after his death. The certificate illustrated is overprinted "WED Enterprises", later renamed "Walt Disney Imagineering" which was primarily responsible for development of the parks. It is made out to his grandson, Christopher Miller and hand signed by Walt front and back.
Picture provided by Fred Fuld III at AntiqueStocks.com

More Themes

There are an endless number of themes open to the collector. Some have already been covered (with a 'splash' of history) but space does not allow similar treatment for all. A few more are listed below:

Bridges	Insurance & Banking	Food	Cinema & Theatres
Textiles	Libraries	Tea and Coffee	Tramways
Oil	Lumber	Wine and Water	Heraldry
Sport	Publishing	Coal	Banking & Finance
Aircraft	Rubber	Shipping	Cinema & Theatres

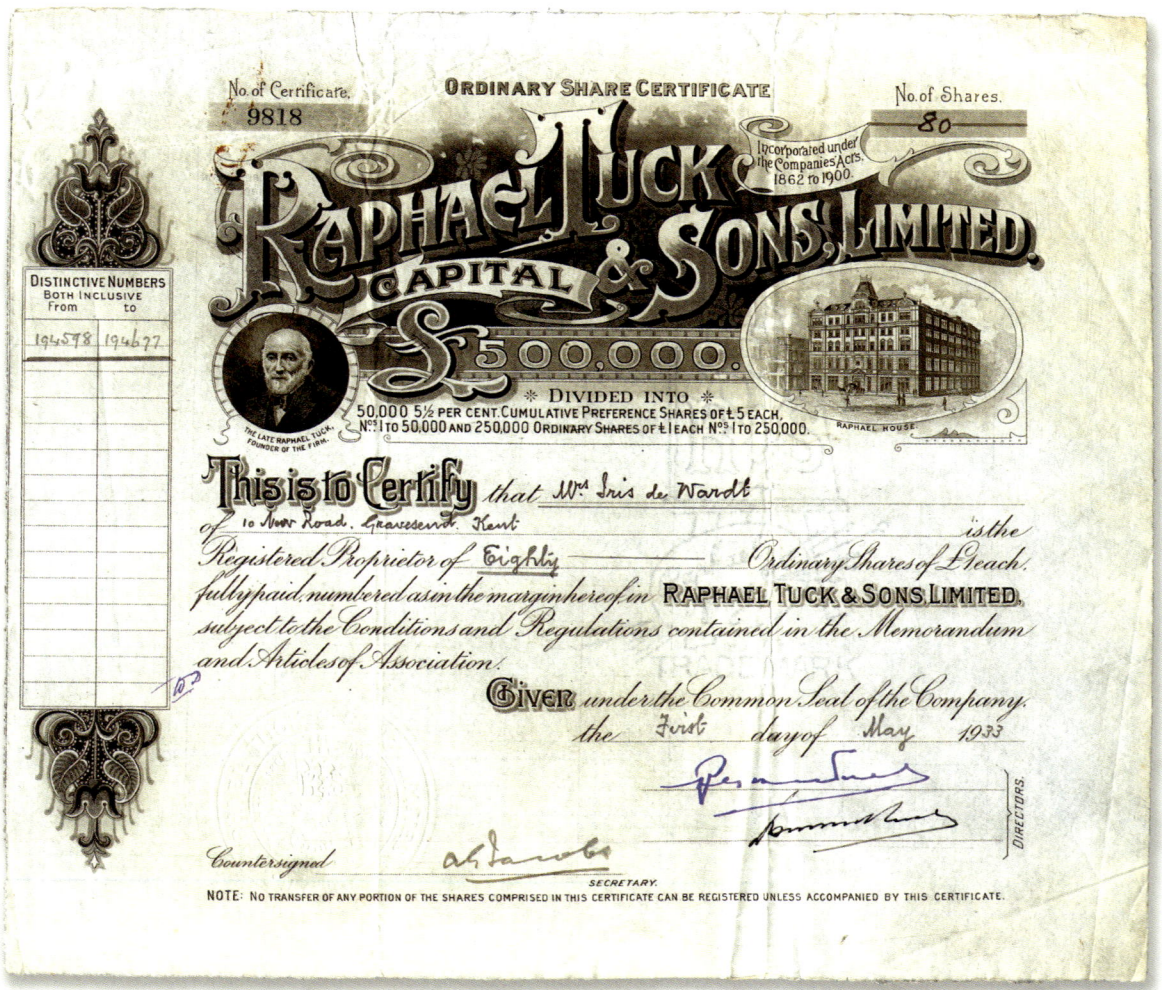

Raphael Tuck & Sons was the foremost producer of postcards in the 1930s' having specialised in all forms of graphic art. The business was started by Raphael Tuck, who is pictured on the certificate, and carried on by his sons. Despite their Jewish origins the company was a major publisher of Christmas cards. It eventually became part of British Printing Corporation (1959) and was subsequently absorbed into the Maxwell empire.

Part 7

PRINTING & DESIGN

Not all bonds are "bearer" and not all shares are "registered", but the vast majority of bonds, which appeal to the scripophilist (and criminal fraternity), are bearer and this inevitably raises concerns over forgery. The theft and illegitimate use of bearer bonds has been the basis of book plots and Hollywood movies for years. Thus, in "The Great Gatsby", which is set in the 1920s, author F. Scott Fitzgerald has his main character involved in a scheme to sell 'bearer bonds' of questionable origin. In popular modern movies like "Beverly Hills Cop," "Die Hard" and "Heat," the villains are out to steal millions of dollars in 'bearer bonds'.

Just as the printing of banknotes is regarded as the domain of the specialist security printer, the printing of bonds and bearer shares falls into the same category. Apart from the danger of forgery, the engraving on a bond or share often suggests the solidity of the company and may even portray the company's trade. Remember, photography and other modern media were not available in the early days.

The most effective deterrents to prospective forgers were a combination of high quality paper, skilled engraving and intricate design. The same companies, which printed banknotes and postage stamps were used to produce bonds and share certificates.

Here are a few examples:

Engraver	Example
Waterlow	Egyptian Mail Steamship Co. Ltd
	Canton Kowloon Railway
	Buenos Ayres Lacroze Tramways Co.
Bradbury Wilkinson	Chilean Northern Railway Co.
	Genoa District Waterworks Co.Ltd.
American Bank Note Co. ("ABNC")	Playboy Enterprises
	Carthage & Adirondack Railway
John A Lowell Bank Note Co., Boston	Hereford Railway Co.
Imprimerie Chaix, Paris	Chemins de Fer Ethiopiens
Eden Fisher & Co. Ltd.	Costa Rica Railway Company
International Bank Note Co., New York	Baltimore & Ohio Railroad Co.
Archer & Daly, Richmond, Va	Confederate States of America Loan
Evans & Cogswell, Columbia, S.C.	Confederate States of America Loan
H Rateau, Paris	Banana du Rio-Grande

The Techniques

Early engraving techniques involved cutting into a copper or steel plate (also referred to as "intaglio") using tools such as a *burin* or *graver*. Skilled engravers knew how deep to cut the plate in order to create different depths of design and perspective. Prior to the early nineteenth century copper plates were used being softer than the steel plates used thereafter.

The most frequently encountered engravers are Waterlow & Sons, Bradbury Wilkinson and De la Rue of Britain and the American Banknote Company of the United States. From 1858, the latter acquired several competitors and in 1879 took over the Canadian Bank Note Company. In 1986 De la Rue acquired Bradbury Wilkinson.

In the early nineteenth century the American, Jacob Perkins, who later settled in England and formed Perkins Bacon, Crown Agents, invented the transference method of security printing. This permitted the production of large numbers of certificates while still maintaining the individuality necessary to prevent easy forgery. Each engraver worked on a separate plate and the engravings on each was then transferred to a master plate. Colours were applied by means of separate plates or by use of the lithographic method whereby a 'stone' is waxed and the areas which will later take the ink are scraped away.

Another mechanical process was instrumental in the engraving techniques used for bonds and share certificates from about the mid nineteenth century which helped make forgery even more difficult, if not impossible. This was the introduction of the geometrical lathe for making ornate borders and was invented by Asa Spencer, a founder of the American Bank Note Company. Using discs and gear wheels moving together (rather like the childrens' toy, 'Spirograph'), a

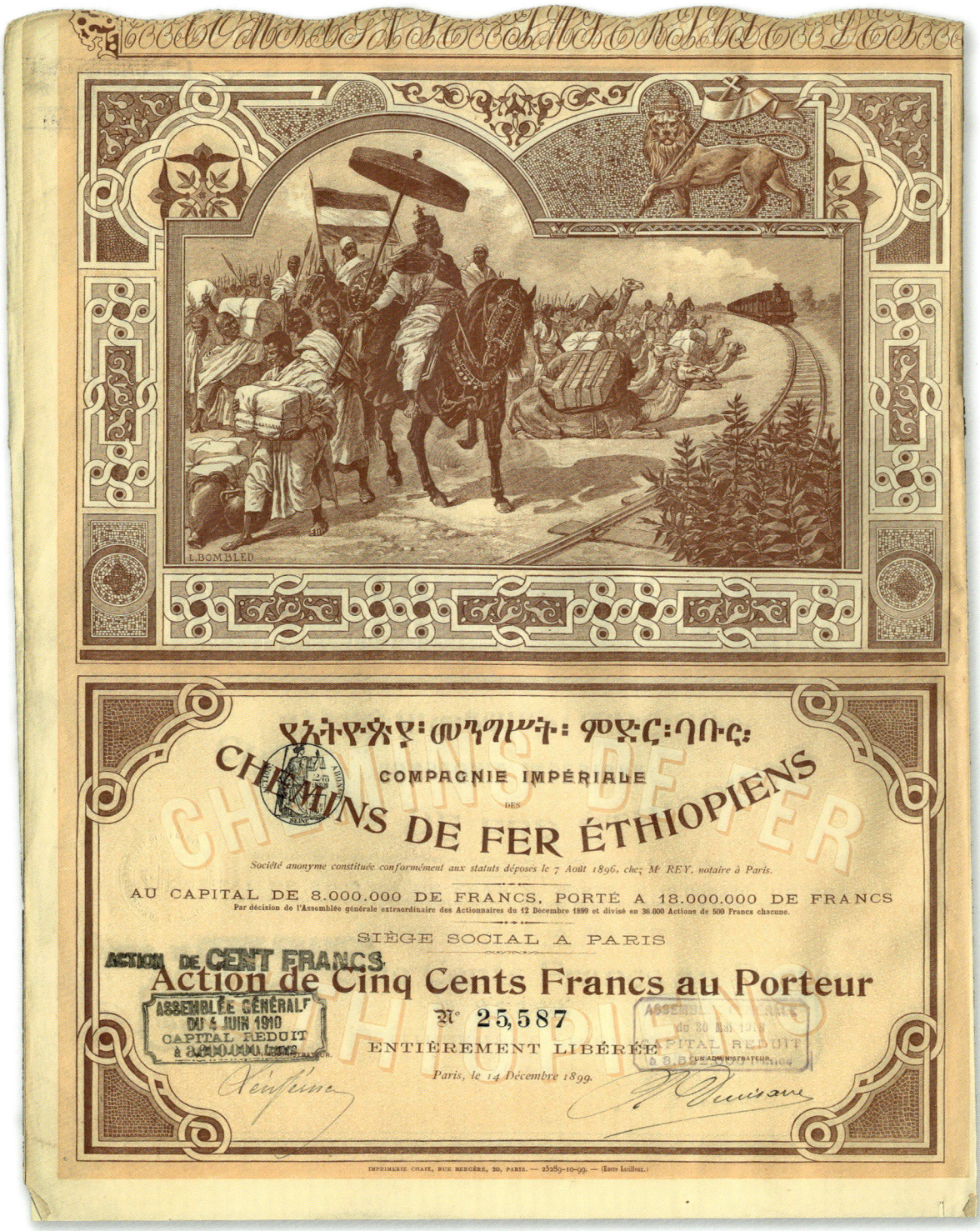

Fine example of the printers art (and imagination). Bearer share in the Chemins De Fer Éthiopiens dated 1899

Waterlow engraved certificate for 5 'Deferred' shares dated 1907 in the shipping line which ran between Marseille and Alexandria (depicted in the vignettes).

series of complex patterns were formed using a diamond tipped point moving over a plate. The method provided the opportunity to create an infinite number of patterns.

Confederate Bonds

An interesting period of print and design occurred during the American Civil war, when the Confederates raised large sums through bond issues. Shortage of material (particularly, security paper) and other hazards of warfare, placed considerable pressures on the printing companies to physically produce the bonds. Enormous efforts were expended on finding suitable paper, some being imported from Europe, but there were repeated quality problems and a tendency to disintegrate after a short time. For example, the pink paper used for the 7% February 20 1863 bonds (Ball: B.212-B.256) came from the Belvidere Mill in Richmond but even they had great difficulties making it and countering its natural tendency to disintegrate in the vats or printing presses. The typical holes through ink signatures bear witness to the problem.

Douglas Ball in his *Catalog and History of Confederate Bonds* identified 12 people or companies who were instrumental in the printing process. Their names can usually be found on the bonds themselves. These are:

Individual or Company	Activities
American Bank Note Company	Produced plates for Confederate Bonds prior to outbreak of war which were subsequently seized by a US marshal.
Archer & Daly	Firm produced stamps, banknotes and bonds for the Confederacy until 1864 when equipment seized for "alleged inefficiency".
John Douglas	One man band who produced 3 bonds and various other fiscal paper. Based in New Orleans until city captured by Union forces in 1862.
Blanton Duncan	Son of Kentucky Congressman. Formed first Kentucky regiment and was present at Bull Run. Set up printing shop
George Dunn & Company	George Dunn was a Scottish lithographer who concentrated on design and engraving leaving printing to others.
Evans & Cogswell	Firm originally formed in 1836. Evans obtained essential material from London where he used the offices of Thomas de la Rue & Co. Firm bought out by Blanton Duncan but was revived in 1862.
Fred Geese	Bavarian lithographer. Worked for Evans & Cogswell and engraved one set of bonds in 1864.
Hoyer & Ludwig	Firm involved in all kinds of printing. Printed notes and bonds for the Confederacy and the Southern States.
Dr. James T Paterson	Scottish dentist friendly with Vice President Alexander H Stephens. Became an engraver in order to avoid conscription. Lost Confederate contracts in 1864. Eventually committed suicide in 1870.
Ritchie & Dunnavant	Public printers for the Commonwealth of Virginia.
Wagner & Company	Firm bought out by Blanton Duncan.
George Wojciechowski	Polish lithographer who did work for Evans & Cogswell. Name appears on several issues but quality generally poor.

Art and Design

In the early days of photography, designs on bonds and shares were an obvious way for contemporary artists to depict exotic (and often far fetched) images of a company's trade. Not only were cherubs liberally used but often grand illustrations of factories, locomotives, mines and ships, were peppered across the certificates. Mythological designs might indeed have reflected the mythological activities of some of the companies.

Countries normally suggested their own designs, which is why Chinese and Russian foreign bonds look distinctly Chinese or Russian despite most bonds being designed and printed by western firms. The art departments of security printing companies produced designs for client approval and as well as lettering, these designs would include *vignettes* related to the country, town or organization issuing the certificates. Because designers and printers were used for several issues and issuers, there are many common designs, sometimes for consistency but more usually because it saved the printer money.

However, not all bearer material was carefully printed. There are cases, and the bonds issued by the US Confederacy, are prime examples, where fear of forgery took second place to speed of issue. Out of the 170 or so different bond types issued by the Confederacy, only the Tri-value Cotton Bonds of 1863 were engraved and these by unknown European printers.

Proofs & Specimens

Certificates were rarely accepted blindly from a printer. Seemingly minor typographical errors could potentially cause untold financial damage and for this reason, considerable attention was paid to the designs and wording on certificates. Thus, the printer usually produced "proofs"

enabling detailed checking, a process followed by the production of "specimens" which provided the issuer a last opportunity to give the 'all clear'. Specimens are easily identified by the word "specimen" stamped across the certificates or hole punched close to the signature line. In some cases a "0000" serial number is printed on the face.

Several collectors specialise in this area. Material is inevitably in mint condition and, of course, far rarer than the finally issued certificate. On the other hand, specimens lack signatures, famous or otherwise, as well as the usual array of company seals, revenue stamps and finger smudges.

The Role of the Artist

Those more interested in the work of Renoir or Rembrandt may find the relatively simple graphic art employed in scrip design somewhat lacking in depth. But is it? Commercial art has different objectives to 'works of art' and in the case of bonds and shares, the prime objectives were to persuade investors to part with their money safely and deter the forger.

This was a period that largely pre-dated photography, when it was very much up to the printer, designer or artist to portray a company or government in its most favourable light. What better place than on the bonds or shares themselves; and what better opportunity to enhance a company's reputation.

Thus the investor could gain a broad knowledge of the company's activities scattered amongst contemporary art styles. Perhaps the most collectible and outstanding of these are those associated with Art Nouveau and Art Deco; styles which originated in the latter part of the nineteenth and early twentieth centuries.

Few share certificates can match Compagnie des Maritimes de Bruges for design and colour.

Art Nouveau and Art Deco

Despite its UK beginnings primarily led by William Morris, Art Nouveau rapidly spread across Europe influencing painting, sculpture, architecture, industrial design, and fashion, to name but a few. The 1890s' saw its emergence in France, Belgium, Germany and Spain usually under different names; so in Germany it was called Jugendstil and in Spain, Modernista. Although the style spread to the USA, it was not adopted for the design of that country's stocks and bonds unlike Europe. Its use of free flowing, swirling lines and flowers typifies many of the certificates of the time. Examples abound, but perhaps two of the most well known are the bonds and shares of Paris France (Alphonse Mucha) and Hispano-Suiza (Ramon Casa I Carbo).

The Art Deco period commenced around 1900 overlapping Art Nouveau. Influenced by the designs of architect, Charles Rennie Mackintosh, its style differs markedly from its predecessor; the lines are straight rather than swirling, the designs geometric, and the images simple, resulting in a generally harsher impact in comparison. The concept was taken up by the 'Vienna Succession' in 1903 when Joseph Hoffman, Koloman Moser and Fritz Werkstatten promoted the style in the German speaking countries. Its style reflected the growth of 'new' industries such as automobiles, telecommunication and aircraft. The period culminated in 1925 when the first "International Exhibition of Modern Decorative and Industrial Arts" was held in Paris. But it was not until 1966 that the name Art Deco was adopted. The style was not applied to many bonds and shares but there are a number of classic examples issued in France (*Plavic-Film*), Belgium (*Comibel*) and Germany (*Metallwarenfabrik Wilhelmshaven*) issued during the period 1920-1940.

Other Artists and Styles

Many famous artist works decorate bonds and shares, often to provide credibility. Examples include the painting of 1659 depicting Mercury and Argus by Diego Velazquez on the shares of *Banco de Cartagena*. The original painting now sits in Madrid's Prado Museum. Shares issued 1956-1981 by the Italian Republic incorporate the art of many well known 16th and 17th artists such as Paolo Caliari, Giambattista Tiepoli and indeed, the great Michelangelo whose "David' adorns a 12 year bond issued in 1978.

Art, of course, is in the minds of the beholders and the portrayal of a naked lady on Playboy Enterprises stocks in the 1980s' may or may not meet those high standards. But nevertheless it did at least portray the company's business!

Example of a fine Art Deco style bond, issued in 1923 by Metallwarenfabrik Wilhelmshaven.

Hispano Suiza, best known for high quality cars, was favoured by European royalty and also had some of the finest 'Art Nouveau' styled share certificates of the time. This example, dated 1918 was designed by the Spanish artist Ramon Casa I Carbo and depicts the Italian actress, Teresa Mariani next to her pride and joy!

Bearer share in the Banco de Cartagena with vignette of painting by Velázquez – 'Mercury and Argos'

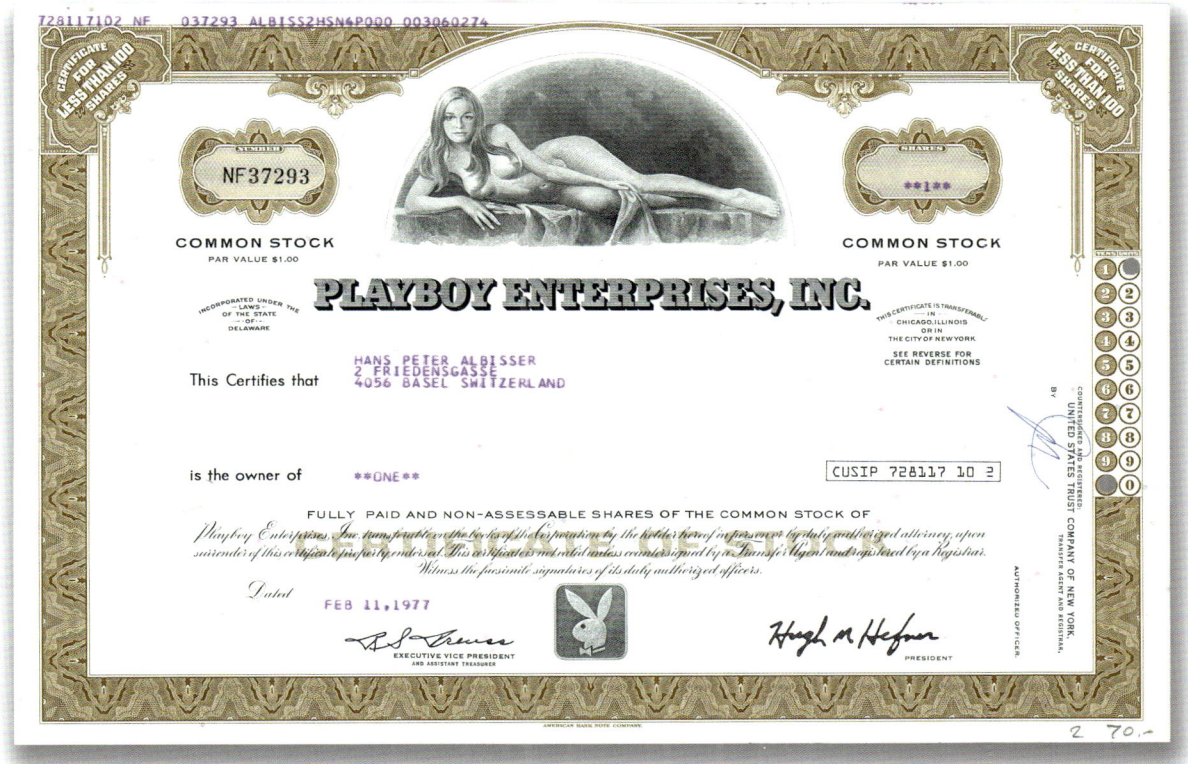

Many certificates portray a company's business, this one clearer than most! Current Playboy certificates are rather more modest.

Forgeries!

Paper, in all its guises, has always been susceptible to forgery and even its replacement by electronic media has certainly not eliminated the problem. The reason for fraud is obviously financial gain and whether the instrument concerned is a banknote or a bond, the potential rewards may well justify the risk – at least to some. Most forgeries of bonds and shares took place in the past to swindle original investors but no doubt a growing collectors market will encourage more crime. An interesting case came to light in 2012 when Italian police seized around $6 trillion worth of fake US Treasury Bonds. Such events may well be more common than we know.

The subject of Confederate Bonds has already been touched on describing their print and design but it is also worth noting that many of the bonds, because of their simple printing, have proved too tempting to the forger. The most copied bond was that depicting Stonewall Jackson (February 20, 1863 7%). Around $10-15 million of bonds are believed to have been forged, according to Ball. They can often be identified by the addition of the words "Second" or "Third" and printed on white paper. Perhaps fortuitously, many of these counterfeit bonds which came to light in the Coutts hoard (see Part 2) were printed on such brittle paper that they simply disintegrated when the eventual purchaser tried to press out the creases.

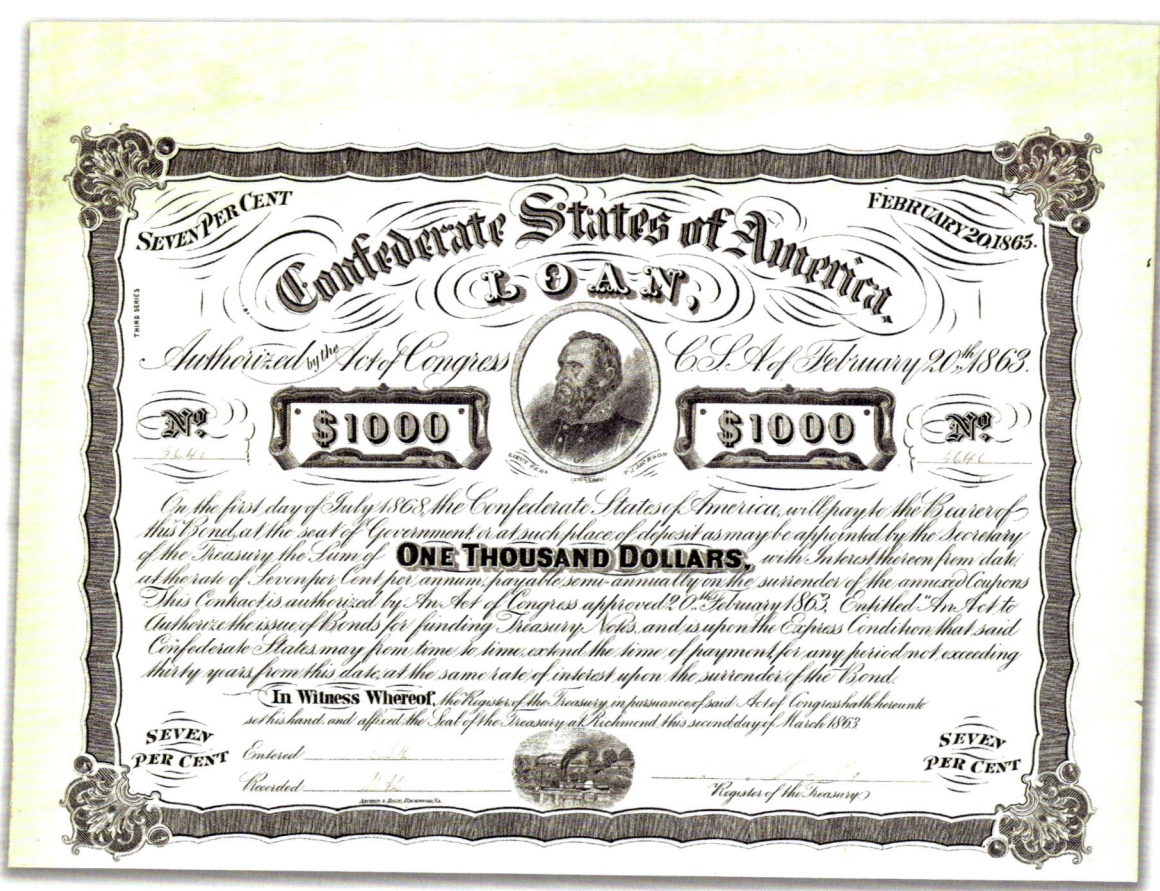

Example of the frequently forged Confederate bond depicting Stonewall Jackson

Most forgeries are relatively easy to spot and the collector should always be conscious of the possibility. Watch out for misspelled words, strange colouring or paper which simply feels wrong (too thick, too thin) or more obviously still, certificates signed in biro or felt tipped pen dating from the distant past....or not! Most genuine items are recorded somewhere and it is not difficult to establish authenticity

Part 8

BUILDING A COLLECTION

Hopefully, the preceding pages will have fired the urge to collect, and might have also suggested a theme. This section sets out some guidelines on starting and building a collection. Whether your objective is financial appreciation or simply, appreciation, the comments here are equally relevant. So, let's first look at the key elements:

- Condition;
- Rarity
- Age and historical significance;
- Ownership and signatures; and,
- Attractiveness.

Condition

It's always good to own pristine examples but very often such items simply do not exist, either because of age or more likely because the certificates themselves (as tradable instruments) have suffered from frequent changes of ownership. Thus, on each sale they will have been 'manhandled', sometimes folded and sometimes, in the case of bearer material, having their coupons clipped or new coupon sheets attached. Smaller issues and higher denomination bonds may have changed hands more frequently, it being far easier for a broker to count one £1,000 bond than fifty £20 bonds.

Handling damage is not limited to bearer material, indeed registered certificates can also suffer. Sold shares are usually returned to a company's registrar who may, if diligent, have matched the document to its original 'stub', maybe even glued them together. Others will have suffered holes or indelible cancellation marks.

It is important when considering condition to bear the above in mind and it is important to consider condition relative to the issue itself. Below average condition, should never be the sole reason to decline an item. It is more than possible, that some items will only be found in poor condition for various reasons, such as poor quality paper, small issue (and therefore more frequent handling), age, or even the physical size of the certificates. A few examples of bonds and shares usually only found in poor condition are listed below:

At the other extreme is unissued material. By their nature, such items lack the sort of accoutrements, collectors like to see, such as embossed seals, signatures and revenue stamps. But set against these is the fact that unissued items are almost invariably rarer than their issued cousins. There are 3 reasons why material may be unissued:

- Printer proofs ("specimens");
- Back up (registered) shares for future issue; and,
- Replacement certificates for lost bearer items ("duplicates").

The latter is often referred to as 'reserve stock' and usually applies to bonds rather than shares. Serial numbers are omitted so that the original number can be inserted if eventually issued. Such certificates are often overprinted, 'duplicate' and because of their greater rarity, often carry a higher value.

Issue	Reason for Condition
Chinese Marconi 1918	Poor paper, small issue.
City of Moscow 1908, £500 bond	High denomination, well traded.
City of Riga, 1913	Issue almost wholly repaid. Most of remainder well battered and probably mislaid at some point.
Russian Rothschild bonds of 1822	Soft paper, early date.
Confederate Bonds	Early date and poor quality paper.

Bearing in mind earlier comments, and as a general guide only, the following 'grades' are usually used by dealers and auction houses:

Description	Condition
Extremely Fine (EF)	Some minor folds, almost as issued.
Very Fine (VF)	Some folds and creases, slight wear.
Fine (F)	Circulated and worn but slight damage.
Poor (P)	Much used, some damage.

Rarity

'Rarity' can arise for four reasons; high demand, small issue, high level of redemption (re bonds) and age. Most better quality pieces have at least two of these attributes and a certificate which meets only one, may not necessarily have a high value. It is therefore unwise to buy solely for reasons of rarity. High demand is essential if the main objective is capital appreciation but don't forget, demand can change; for example, the Chinese Marconi loan was at one time considered one of the rarest and consequently, most sought after bonds. It is now out of favour, not helped by the soft, and poor quality paper, on which it is printed. At its height, a £1,000 bond sold for £4,000, now it rarely exceeds

£100 Chinese 'Marconi' bond. Typical example of quality directly affected by soft paper and frequent handling.

£300. Perhaps, unlike other Chinese issues, its lack of a link to gold, is the prime reason for its fall from grace.

In short, rarity must always be balanced with condition and demand, and must never be taken as a guarantee of future appreciation.

Age and Historical Significance

In the case of registered shares, age is undoubtedly a major determinant of value. Material pre-dating 1830 is rare but depending on your chosen collecting theme, age may or may not be relevant. Thus, Chinese and Confederate bonds are not particularly old but nevertheless both have other attributes, namely rarity and historical significance. Early British material (for example, shares in the Vauxhall Bridge Company dated 1826) are often printed on vellum as are the early Spanish trading companies and the American turnpike road shares of the late eighteenth century. Much early material, such as that relating to the South Sea Bubble and the East India companies derive value from their history rather than condition.

Vellum share certificate of 1814, in the Vauxhall Bridge Company

Ownership and Signatures

Value added by a famous signature cannot be overstated. Not only is it easy to miss a signature (it might be on the face or back of a certificate), it is also easy to fail to appreciate its significance. Always check, you never know what you might find. But don't assume all signatures are famous or collectable.

Attractiveness

Whilst this may be a feature denigrated by the aficionado, it nevertheless greatly contributes to overall interest and appeal. That said, unless your objective is framing, buying solely on beauty is not advisable for financial gain (a bit like getting married!).

Taking Care & Selling

Storage

Once the collection has begun, a little housekeeping is required. Firstly, insure it. The danger is not only from theft but also fire so ensure replacement value is fully covered. Secondly, it is both important and beneficial to you as a collector to house your certificates attractively.

Always keep certificates flat and dry. There are albums available with acid free sheets and you should use these whenever you can. If you live in a humid environment, allow air to circulate and avoid piling plastic album sheets on top of one another.

Repair and Cleaning

Like any kind of restoration work, 'paper conservation' is a highly skilled craft. Professional repairs can be expensive and should only be carried out if the certificate itself warrants the cost. But bear in mind it might sometimes be better not to repair.

Most bonds and shares have experienced a tough life, apart from those that have spent their time in a bank vault. A repaired item will never have the same value as an 'extremely fine' piece and it should always be described as having undergone repair when listed in dealers' or auctioneers' catalogues.

If you plan on a bit of 'DIY', take great care. If you feel it essential to use an iron, only do so with a sheet of paper between iron and certificate but under no circumstances iron vellum – it shrivels up.

Framing

Frames are not recommended for rare pieces. Light can discolour them and your local framer, using tape to affix certificates to the mount (map), can do irreparable damage. It's also a good idea to insist on acid free backing materials but whether you use normal or non-reflecting glass is a matter of choice. Whichever option you choose, do not hang in direct sunlight. The damage inflicted may well not be obvious until the certificate is removed from the frame.

Cataloguing and Research

Keep a careful log of your collection. Note prices paid and dates purchased and check prices realized of similar items at auctions. Compared with more established collectable fields such as stamps and coins, relatively little has been published. Hopefully this will change but right now there is always the opportunity to pen a piece for publication in a magazine, such as the International Bond & Share Society Journal, or even a book. Catalogues have long been promised but so far not much is available.

Selling your Collection

At some stage or other your collection will be sold. If using an auction house, choose carefully. Take account of the value of your material and its appeal to particular markets. For example, German material usually sells better in Germany. Don't forget, auctioneers have to live and their income derives from the premium, which is usually taken from both buyer and seller (c.20% each way).

THE LAST WORD

Building a collection of bonds and shares is not only unusual, it is also rewarding. In doing so you are preserving the history of finance. Its features of history, finance and art, make the subject unique. The preceding pages have covered some of the things to look for and outlined only a few of the fascinating stories behind these pieces of paper. There is more research still to be done and more to learn **before** the hobby achieves the status of stamp or coin collecting. It differs from both, most particularly in that every single item is unique – defined not only by a certificate's design but more especially by its serial number, its registered owner and original signatures.

The following pages list some of the societies, auctioneers and dealers across the world. A bibliography lists the many sources of reference used by the author and collectors are encouraged to read more and share their own experiences.

The subject has much to offer and I wish you luck and years of enjoyment doing your own research!

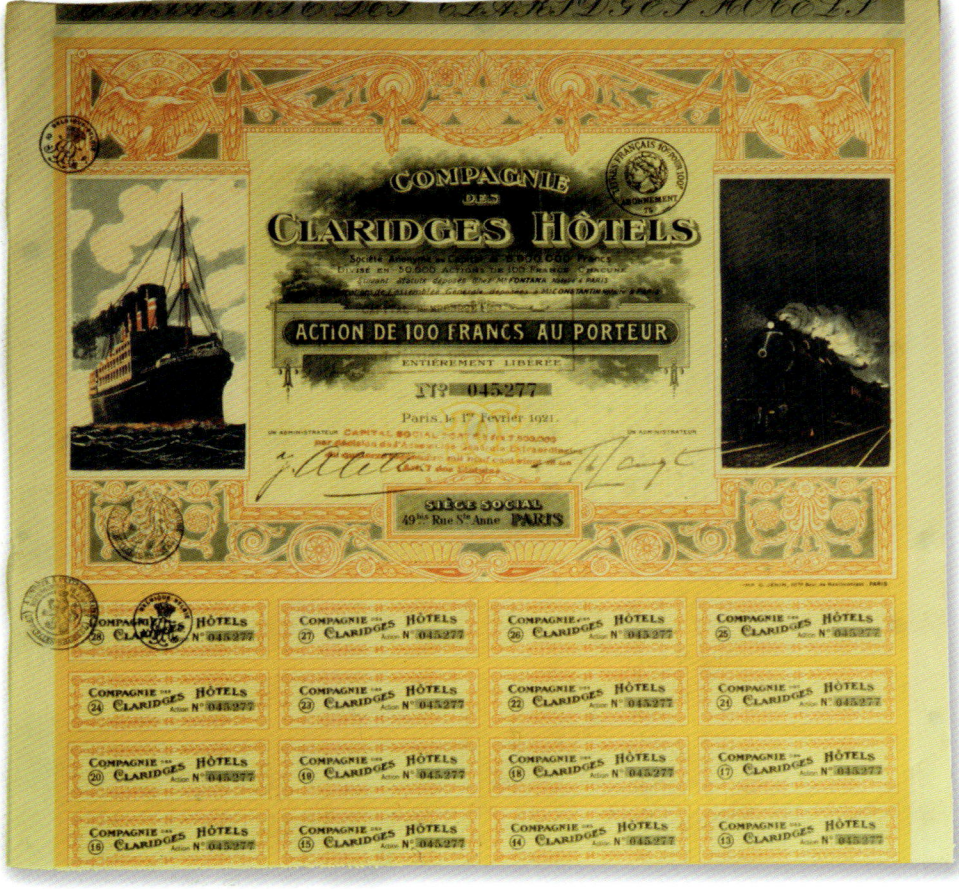

BIBLIOGRAPHY

Anderson, William G, *The Price of Liberty – the Public Debt of the American Revolution,*
    University Press of Virginia, 1983

Asimov, Isaac, *Our Federal Union – The United States from 1816-1865,* Dobson Books Limited, 1975

Australian Dictionary of Biography:
* Pat Simpson, *Arthur Wellesley Bayley,* 1979
* Bruce Mitchell, *Edward Hammond Hargraves,* 1972

Ball, Douglas B, *Comprehensive Catalogue & History of Confederate Bonds,* BNR Press

BBC Radio 4, *Alfred Loewenstein,* July 2014

Biographical Dictionary of American Business Leaders, John N Ingham, Greenwood Press, 1983
* *The Rockefeller Family*
* *Thomas Alva Edison*
* *Morgan Family*
* *Vanderbilt Family*
* *Alexander Hamilton*
* *William Bingham*
* *Nicholas Biddle*
* *Herbert Clark Hoover*

Bunbury, Turtle, *Baron Albert Grant – A Pioneer of Public Relations,* www.turtlebunbury.com

Catton, Bruce, *The Coming Fury – the American Civil War,* Victor Gollancz Limited, 1972

Clikeman, Paul M, *The Greatest Frauds of the Last Century,*
    Robins School of Business, University of Richmond, re; Kreuger & Toll, 2003

Concise Dictionary of National Biography, Oxford University Press, 1995

Davies, Norman, *A History of Europe,* Oxford University Press, 1996

Dictionary of Business Biography, Butterworths, 1986:
* *Clarence Charles Hatry, David Fanning*
* *Jabez Spencer Balfour, Esmond L Cleary*
* *Lord Rothschild of Tring*

Dictionary of National Biography 1885-1900, Volume 55, James Taylor (1753-1825),
    Edward Irving Carlyle

Dimson, Marsh and Staunton, *Triumph of the Optimists,* Princeton University Press, 2002

Edwards, Susan, *Hughesovka, A Welsh Enterprise in Imperial Russia,*
    Glamorgan Record Office, 1992

Elliot, Geoffrey, *Don't panic, we've seen this before,* Telegraph Media Group, 2007

Emden, Paul H.:
- *Money Powers of Europe,* Samson Low, Marston & Co.,1939
- *Randlords,* Hodder & Stoughton, 1935

Encyclopaedia Britannica on-line:
- Samuel Insull
- Thomas Alva Edison
- Richard Trevithic
- East India Company

Ferguson, Niall, *The Ascent of Money – A Financial History of the World,* Penguin Books, 2009

Flight Safety Foundation, *Alfred Loewenstein,* www.flightsafety.org

Freeman, J Michael and Aldcroft H Derek, *Transport in Victorian Britain,* Manchester University Press, 1988

Gleeson, Janet, *The Moneymaker (the story of John Law),* Bantam Press, 1999

Grace's Guide, British Industrial History, *John Taylor (1779-1863),* 2013

Grant, Geoffrey L, *The South Sea Company,* Scripophily Magazine June and September 2000

Grant, Kay, *Samuel Cunard Pioneer of the Atlantic Steamship,* Abelard-Schuman, 1967

Gregg, Richard T, *Gregor MacGregor Cazique of Poyais 1786-1845,* International Bond & Share Society

Grossman, Peter Z, *American Express – the unofficial History of the People who Built the Great Financial Empire,* Crown Publishers Inc., 1987

Hartley, Richard, *Bewick Moreing in Western Australian Gold Mining 1897-1904: Management policies & Goldfields responses,* Australian Society for the Study of Labour History, 1993

Harvard Business School (website), *South Sea Bubble Short History,* 2010

Hatch, Alden, *American Express - A Century of Service,* Doubleday & Company, Inc., 1950

History.co.uk, :
- *Cornelius Vanderbilt*
- *William Durrant*
- *Paris-Bordeaux-Paris Race*

Holbrook, Stewart H, *The Age of the Moguls,* Doubleday & Co., 1953

Ingham, John N, *Biographical Dictionary of American Business Leaders,* Greenwood Press, 1983

International Bond & Share Society Journal:
- *A Great British Birthday – 300 Years of Union,* **Brian Mills,** 2007/1
- *26 Million Old German Bonds & Shares in Berlin,* **Rudiger K Weng,** 1995/4
- *Alfred Lowenstein,* **Howard Shakespeare,** 2000/3
- *The Spanish Royal Trading Companies,* **Howard Shakespeare,** Spring and Autumn 1989
- *The World's First East Indies Company,* **Brian Mills,** 2000/4

Investopedia, *Ponzi Schemes*, website

Jackson, Stanley, *J. P. Morgan, A Biography*, Heinemann, 1984

Jewish Virtual Library, T*he Jewish Colonial Trust*, www.jewishvirtuallibrary.org

J P Morgan (website), *Three generations of Bankers*

Kann, E, *The History of China's Internal Loan Issues, Finance & Commerce*, Shanghai, 1934

Kindleburger, Charles P, *A Financial History of Western Europe*, George Allen & Unwin, 1984

Kwarteng, Kwasi, *War and Gold*, Bloomsbury 2014

Kynaston, David, *The City of London*, Chatto & Windus, 1994:
  - *Volume 1 - A world of its Own 1815-1890;*
  - *Volume II – Golden Years 1890-1914;*

Lewis, Elizabeth Wittenmyer, *Queen of the Confederacy – The Innocent Deceits of Lucy Holcombe Pickens*, University of North Texas Press, 2002

Michie, R C, *Money, Mania and Markets*, John Donald Publishers Ltd., 1981

Mining Practices at Mary Tavy, www.crying-fox.com

Moore, Tim, *Gironimo, The Giro d'Italia*, Yellow jersey press, 2014

Moscow, Alvin, *The Rockefeller Inheritance*, Doubleday & Co., 1977

National park Service, US Department of the Interior (nps.gov), *Dutch Colonies*

New Netherland Institute, *Cornelius Vanderbilt*, website

New York Times, *Kylsant now Leads in World Shipping*, 29th November 1926

Oxford Dictionary of National Biography, Barney Barnato, diamond merchant and financier, Colin Newbury, 2004-14

Penn University Archives & Records Centre,
  - *Charles Willing 1710-175*
  - *William Bingham 1752-1804*

Pitcher, Harvey, *The Smiths of Moscow, A Story of Britons Abroad*, Swallow House Books 1984

Raafat, Samir, *Heliopolis Palace Hotel*, Cairo Times 19th March 1998

Roberts, Andrew, *The tale of the half-billion-pound sting, Review of Jabez Spencer Balfour*, The Telegraph 9th March 2004

Rothschilds bank, Website www.rothschild.com/our_history/

Seabrook, F Paul, *German Dollar Bonds*, 2007

Shakespeare, Howard J., *France – The Royal Loans*, Squirrel Publishing 1986

Simar, Jacques, *Edourd Empain, Esprit Fécond, Entrepreneur Conquerant*, The Scripophily Centre, 2013

South African History on-line (SAHO), *Barney Barnato*

Standage, Tom, *The Victorian Internet*, Walker & Company, New York, 1998

Starley Bikes (website), *History of Starley Bikes*

Spartacus Educational (website), *Robert Bruce Lockhart*

Swanberg, W A, J*im Fisk, The Career of an Impossible Rascal*, Lowe & Brydone Ltd, 1960

The British Museum website, *An introduction to English banking history*

The Henry Ford Website, *History of the Rouge*, 2014

Thomson, David, *Europe Since Napoleon*, Pelican Books, 1966

University of Virginia, Miller center, *Life Before the Presidency, Herbert Clark Hoover*, 2014

UK Debt Management Office website, *Bank of England*, 2014

US National Archives & Records Administration (www.archives.gov),
    The Treaty of Guadalupe, **Tom Grey**

UShistory.org, *Signers of the Declaration of Independence, Robert Morris*

Westwood, J N, *The Shorter Oxford History of the Modern World, Endurance and Endeavour – Russian History 1812-1980*, OUP, 1981

Wheatcroft, Geoffrey, *The Randlords*, Weidenfield & Nicholson, 1985

Wikipedia:
- *Kreuger & Toll*
- *Clarence Hatry*
- *General Electric (Thomas Edison)*
- *SA Minerva Motors*
- *Mary Williamson Averell (wife of E H Harriman)*
- *Lucy Pickens*
- *Herbert Clark Hoover*
- *East India Company*
- *Ford Motor Company*

Wilkinson, Doug, *Golden Papers*, Perth Westralian Library Foundation, 1986

Wilson, Derek, *Rothschild – A story of Wealth and Power*, Andre Deutsch, 1988

Windsor, David Burns, *The Quaker Enterprise*, Frederick Muller Ltd., 1980

Woodland, John, *Money Pits*, Ashgate, 2014

BELGIUM

Association Bege de Scriptophilie (ASBL)/
Belgische Vereneging voor Scriptophilie VZW)

info@scripophily.be
www.scripophily.be

Vlaamse Vereniging voor Financiele Historie
(VVFH)

wfh.scriptofilie@gmail.com
www.users.telenet.be/francis.nys

FRANCE

Association des Collectionneurs de Titres
Financiers

www.actif.scriponet.com

Scripo Club de France

scripoclubdefrance@online.fr
www.scripoclubdefrance.free.fr

GERMANY

Erster Deutsches Historic-Actien-Club

webmaster@edhac-ev.de
www.edhac-ev.de

NETHERLANDS

Vereniging van Verzamelaars van Oude
Fondsen

contact@vvof.nl
www.vvof.nl

NORWAY

Norsk Selskap for Scripofili

osk-bjor@online.no
www.aksjebrev.com

PORTUGAL

Associacao Portuguesa de Coleccionadores de
Papeis de Valor

apcpv.permuta@hotmail.com
www.papeisdevalor.org

SWEDEN

Svenska Föreningen for Historiska
Värdepapper

info@aktiesamlaren.se
www.historiskavardepapper.se

SWITZERLAND

Scripophila Helvetica

infor@scripophila-helvetica.com
www.scripophila-helvetica.com

UNITED KINGDOM

International Bond & Share Society (IBSS)

secretary@scripophily.org
www.scripophily.org

USA

International Bond & Share Society
(US Chapter)

usachapter@scripophily.org
www.scripophily .org

Index

Page numbers shown in italics refer to illustrations